MOVIES AND POLITICS

GARLAND REFERENCE LIBRARY
OF SOCIAL SCIENCE
(VOL. 730)

MOVIES AND POLITICS
The Dynamic Relationship

James Combs
General Editor

GARLAND PUBLISHING, INC. • NEW YORK & LONDON
1993

© 1993 James Combs
All rights reserved

Library of Congress Cataloging-in-Publication Data

Movies and politics : the dynamic relationship / edited by James Combs.
    p.   cm. — (Garland reference library of social science ; vol. 730)
  Includes bibliographical references and indexes.
  ISBN 0-8153-0043-3 (alk. paper)
  1. Motion pictures—Political aspects. 2. Politics in motion pictures.
I. Combs, James E. II. Series: Garland reference library of social
science ; v. 730.
PN1995.9.P6M6   1993
791.43'658—dc20   92-23456
                                                                  CIP

Printed on acid-free, 250-year-life paper
Manufactured in the United States of America

Dedication

In loving appreciation

of two aunts

Bernice Combs

and

Una Mae Hicks

CONTENTS

Preface — xiii

Acknowledgments — xv

Introduction — 3

PART I

Political Ideology and Movie Narrative — 27

Chapter 1

Who's Running this Show?
Ideology, Formula and Hegemony in
American Film and Television — 31

John G. Cawelti

Chapter 2

Film, Politics, and Ideology
Toward a Multiperspectival Film Theory — 55

Douglas Kellner

PART II

Political Myth in the Movies   93

Chapter 3

The Prices of Power
Women's Depictions in Film   97

June Sochen

Chapter 4

Leatherstocking in 'Nam
Rambo, *Platoon*, and the American
Frontier Myth   115

Harold Schechter and Jonna G. Semeiks

PART III

Political History and Movie Culture   129

Chapter 5

"Grief in the Limelight"
Al Capone, Howard Hughes, the Hays Code
and the Politics of the Unstable Text   133

Richard Maltby

Contents

Chapter 6

Designing Multi-Cultural America
Modern Movie Theatres and the Politics
of Public Space 1920-1945   183

Lary May

PART IV

Political Communication and the Movies   236

Chapter 7

Politics and Auteurs
From Chaplin to Wajda   239

Charles Maland

Chapter 8

Political Propaganda in the Movies
A Typology   271

Dan Nimmo

Afterword	295
Contributors	297
Index	299
Film Index	303

PREFACE

This is a book that collects in one volume some of the best contemporary thinking about the relationship between movies and politics. The editor has included the word "dynamic" in the title because he wants to communicate the sense that the relationship under study is fluid, charged, and transactional. To that end, he attempted to recruit the best talent available to illuminate the plural dynamics of movies and politics. Too, an effort has been made to give some organization and direction to this area of inquiry, in the hope that both academic scholars who study film and those in the film industry, including reviewers, will be more acutely aware of the political dimension of film. A previous effort by the editor for Garland, *American Political Movies*, was a brief filmography of feature films of political significance. The scope and perspective of this volume is obviously much more eclectic, giving the reader an idea of the various ways that movies and politics may be usefully viewed. After this, it will then remain for future scholars and other students of the movies to expand the horizons of theory and research into a fascinating if mercurial political relationship. The nature of the transaction between art and society has bedeviled inquirers for a long time, and hopefully the present effort will help in some small way to demystify a specific form of that relationship, the world of power and the world of motion-picture art. The interested reader is not only the final judge of whether we have succeeded, but also is the one who is charged with sustaining in the future the intellectual curiosity about studying the relationship between what is going on up on the screen and what is going on out in the world.

ACKNOWLEDGMENTS

Acknowledgments often sound suspiciously like Academy Awards acceptance speeches, a seemingly endless series of "thank-yous" to people the reader hasn't a clue about. Yet both in the production of films and books about films, there are people who need to be acknowledged for their help in bringing both movies and books to light. I am most appreciative of the help of stalwart Garland editor Marie Ellen Larcada, whose urban and publishing survival skills are considerable and functional. Indeed, the author's experience with Garland has been such that it has been a pleasure to work with a company that seems to know what it's doing, a not universal organizational attribute in the publishing business. Thanks are also due Chuck Bartelt, whose computer skills helped alleviate the hysterical moments of a computer novice. Also, very special thanks to Paul Musick, Dianne Chapman and the rest of the computer lab staff at Virginia Highlands Community College for their patient assistance and helpfulness in printing the manuscript. I would also like to thank the authors of the articles in this volume, who were cooperative and punctual in the process of editing, again a not altogether universal academic trait. Finally, I would like to acknowledge the help of Sara Trowbridge Combs, whose computer and wifeing skills were indispensable to the successful completion of both the book and the marriage.

Movies and Politics

INTRODUCTION
Understanding the Politics of Movies

What about the movies is political? For those interested in either politics or the movies, this is an important question. Since the motion picture is a powerful mass medium that literally spans the twentieth century, it seems fair to say that the toy that became an industry likely has had some relationship with the political life of that passing century. But just how? It is not enough to simply reflect that surely a mass medium that has been such a pervasive part of American leisure that it rivals baseball as the national pastime has played a major role in the development of American life. We speak of "movie-made America," and witness a former "matinee idol" of old Hollywood become President, complete with an awesome array of phrases, stories, and even expectations derived from his immersion in the national medium of the movies. In the wake of the cinematic Presidency, serious writers, such as David Thomson in *Suspects*, Robert Coover in *A Night at the Movies*, and Christopher Durang in *A History of American Film*, have examined the interplay between the "fictions" of the movies and the "facts" of the way we live, with the clear suggestion that, like the notion of the movie-made Reagan, movies are mentors and metaphors for all our lives and maybe even for our politics. At this most exalted and macrocosmic level of inquiry, it is difficult to specify exactly the nature of the relationship between our cumulative movie experience and political life. We are here dealing with terms such as "consciousness," "the national mind," and mentalités, all of which suggest the development and propagation of socially coalescing ideas and images over time, some of which might have been derived from and reinforced by several generations' experience with the movies. In this general view, the movies become a contributing source in the ongoing conduct of national social and political discourse. [1]

Even if we readily agree with this attractive idea, we still need to explore both the unobservable and observable ways in which movies and politics intersect. In the former case, we will need to make inferences about the movies as part of the dynamic flow of expression that emerges in history, and the political context of motion picture expression as it emerges in time. That in itself is a daunting task, since it involves the exercise of what we might call political aesthetics, the interpretation of movies in the historical context in which they emerged and also how in ways we do not fully understand, they "participated." A political aesthetic would examine aesthetic objects-feature films, for example-not just for their cinematic beauty, but also for the "truth" that they might reveal, often quite unwittingly, about the political time in which they appeared. Just like any art form, film cannot be expected to exhibit isomorphic correspondence and temporal direction with the politics of an era. American movies are usually not controlled by nor often even cognizant of politics, but even those many films which are not official propaganda nor about a political subject can offer us clues about the political ethos, or "character," of a period, especially the films the careful inquirer deems "representative" of that age. This requires both an informed understanding of the political history in question and a sense of how the movie process, not to mention the art process, works. We may assert, however, that movies are a part of history as valid evidence of the developing sensibilities of people, and may be studied as observable aesthetic artifacts of the unobservable processes of attitude formation and change among populations, constituting the "climate of opinion" or "structure of feeling" characteristic of an age.[2]

In the latter case, there is a great deal of evidence connecting the movie world and the political world that is quite observable.[3] Careful researchers have discovered a myriad of legal, and not-so-legal, relationships between movies and politics, some of which have affected the content of motion pictures. The movies were born in economic controversy, and even the film industry's move from New York to Hollywood seems to have involved escape from one kind of urban politics in the East to another in the West. From its inception, the movie industry was embroiled in politics, suffering and surviving through episodes of censorship, regulation, legal battles, union struggles, underworld influence, blacklists, inquisitions and persecutions, activism, and both cooperation and conflict with government. Of particular interest again is how the political and legal environment affects the making of movies, and what degree of freedom moviemakers have to make movies about politically charged subjects. It is patently untrue to say that movies have always avoided politics, or for that matter always toed the party line by reproducing on film the current political orthodoxies. Like other popular art forms, moviemakers have found ways to incorporate contemporary political themes and controversies in clever and oblique ways. And they have occasionally found politically relevant subjects to be worthy of audience interest. In 1907, for example, a movie called *The Candidate* appeared, depicting a pompous politician getting his well-deserved "comeuppance" from workers and his wife. In 1909, the young D.W. Griffith was making *The Voice of the Violin*, wherein a young man is lured by, but finally rejects, Marxist ideas. In the same year his famous *Corner in Wheat* emerged, with a story line involving a wealthy grain speculator hoarding wheat to drive up the price. *Corner in Wheat* was perhaps the first movie portrait of one of the hated plutocrats of the populist and progressive era, giving substantial flesh to the imagined lavish lifestyle and unjust exploitation of such an economic "trust" tycoon who comes to a bad, ironic end.

Since then the interplay between Hollywood and Washington has been ongoing and complex. Very early on, politicians courted the studios and the stars, seeing that the medium was a powerful and useful means of communication that could be turned to political uses under the right circumstances (as it was during such episodes as the concerted effort to defeat Upton Sinclair's bid for Governor of California in 1934, and of course, during World Wars I and II). The stars were sought to do such political chores as endorse war bonds, make appearances for and endorse candidates, and even during the infamous "inquisition of Hollywood" in the post-World War II Red Scare, assure us of their basic, if more glamourous, Americanism. By the late 1960s, we began to speak of "political Hollywood," with politicized stars such as Jane Fonda and Robert Redford among the liberals, and John Wayne, Jimmy Stewart, and Charlton Heston among the conservatives. With the election of Ronald Reagan, the interplay became a strange union, one that could have only happened in a movie-made land, now with highly observable and astonishing political consequences. At this point in the history of Hollywood, it has become hard to believe that our political life has not been profoundly affected by the movies and the industry and culture that surrounds them. If there had not been a Hollywood, nor the by now several generations of Americans familiar with the movie world, it is likely that our social and political life would have been different.

In one of his last writings before his untimely death, Gerald Mast noted that students of the American cinema must deal with both the "sociological" and "narratological" aspects of movies-in-history, including the observable dimensions of the movie world as it relates to politics and society, and the "way in which traditional narrative motifs (as old as narrative itself) acquire unique and particular inflections."[4] This volume includes work by scholars who are interested in both political dimensions of the movies, attempting to make sense of the sociological and narratological aspects of the movies. More specifically, they understand that these dimensions are not mutually exclusive, and attempt to delve into the complex interplay of the sociological and the narratological. The people united in this collection all have in common a conviction that in one way or another the movies are political, and that it is possible to use some systematic way of studying the movies to find out exactly what about them is political. Readers will discern that for all of the disparity of approach of our collected authors, they all implicitly regard the relationship between the movies and politics as dynamic, as an interplay of influence that occurs in the temporal crucible of political history and the concomitant process of political aesthetics, specifically here the making of movies in political and social contexts.

Thus the general perspective taken here might be called the political process, the ways in which the conduct of politics-in-time is related to other social activities that transact with the political. Movies have to be understood in the context of the political process, indeed as one important way of understanding what is happening politically. If by process we mean the configuration of events that give unfolding political meaning to a time and place, then movies become one of the aesthetic responses that "punctuate" that temporal configuration. This is not to say that politics is everywhere, on the mind of moviemakers in every movie, and in every movie equally. It is to say, however, that one cannot fully understand the movie process—the ways in which movies are made, and what they express about a society—if you exclude their place in the political process. Not all movies are about politics, but then again not all movies are not about politics. The job of the inquirer is to specify those ways in which we can make valid inferences about movies as part of the political process.

For that reason, we want to offer an inclusionary view of what constitutes the political by including investigation of all those social messages that might have some overt or covert political meaning, even if they are not understood as such. Moviemakers, for example, may not have the slightest intention or interest in communicating a political message, but they might do so simply by virtue of the inclusion of social messages which resonate with audiences, and offer inferentially valid statements of use to the political inquirer. When, for example, a particular "cluster" of films appear at a particular time, it may be the case that such a phenomenon is a response that conjoins moviemakers and moviewatchers in ritual play that has possible political meanings attached. The "invasion-annihilation or dehumanization" theme in the vast cluster of science-fiction films of the early 1950s was not there by any identifiable design, but it nevertheless had more than an accidental relationship with the underlying mass tensions created by the rhetorical threats and "imagination of disaster" of the contemporary Cold War. These often crude but highly popular vehicles quite unwittingly "displaced" Cold War anxieties into a palatable science-fiction setting that spoke in an indirect and safer way to latent but very real popular fears. On the other hand, other political manifestations, such as the "anti-communist" films of the late 1940s and the "military preparedness" movies of the 1950s appear to be quite by design, with political intentions and government cooperation that are subject to documentary and biographical analysis. Indeed, such inquiries are not mutually exclusive: the political relationship between, for example, the Pentagon and Hollywood in making war films is quite observable, allowing scholars to establish the motives and meanings that sustained the government-studio relationship during a period of Cold War consensus among bipartisan elites and elites who controlled the studios and thus the nature of the movies that were made. Too, the confluence of political interests that did converge at that time produced movies that were viewed by audiences living in a political time and place. Audiences derive many meanings from movies, including the unobservable process of political learning, the acquisition of ideas and images which in diffuse, long-term, and often unconscious ways affect people's attitude toward politics.

We may surmise that those among the mass who expose themselves to popular fare such as the movies are engaged in a learning process, even if they are unaware or dimly aware of that fact. Watching movies therefore takes on a decidedly pragmatic function, allowing audiences to engage their imaginations in such a way that they learn from doing so. The unobservable process of political learning through movies is no less real because it cannot be seen or likely wholly measured. Indeed, it is such subtle effect on the creation, maintenance, or change in political attitudes that is likely the most important process at work, but the most difficult to understand. In any case, since it is virtually impossible to understand fully movie audience experience, we may have to make inferences from small samples of contemporary movie watchers as to what may well be going on with the universe of moviewatchers. We will have to make larger leaps of inferential faith when we surmise the political meanings derived from movies witnessed by millions of people in the past. Such leaps are necessary if limited in reliability, but omitting such educated surmises does not let us reason from movie to audience to social consequences. A movie may be understood as a work of art separate from its historical circumstances, but if we are interested in its political significance, we have to be able to say that movies expressed something of political meaning for a particular time and place, and for at least some people who lived then. We must also remember that movies are also vehicles of learning for those involved in making them, especially those creative talents who attempt to infuse meanings into movies. Although much of what they do is observable—shooting scripts, memos, memoirs, and so on—they are also part of the unobservable process of "attituding" about the political present. It is they, after all, who create movies in the context of a present, the "symbolic realities" that attract audiences who then play with them in the process of learning. So learning is going on among both those who make and those who attend movies, helping both understand what's happening through the creative force of the movies.

In this volume we will see the major ways in which contemporary scholars attempt to understand the political process as it is both manifest and latent in the movies. Although their approaches may be quite different, they all share the conviction that the movies are important to understand, and can be understood, whether they are dealing with the observable political environment surrounding the movies or the unobservable social attitudes that the movies express. Let us briefly introduce the reader to these modes of political inquiry into the movies.

WAYS OF POLITICAL SEEING

Over the past several decades, modes of political inquiry have developed which have furthered our knowledge of the dynamic relationships between the movies and politics. It is the objective of this volume to expose the interested reader to these modes of inquiry through the work of leading exponents of these multiple, although not mutually exclusive, perspectives. The work here included represents the "leading edge" of inquiry stemming from these academic traditions, and hopefully will inspire other scholars to build upon these traditions. We identify these modes as political ideology, political myth, political culture, and political communication. Each perspective is a way of political seeing, looking at and finding both observable and unobservable relationships that advance our knowledge of movies and politics.

Political ideology is a perspective that stems from academic roots running deep and strong in European scholarship, particularly those that are neo-Marxist. This mode of inquiry looks at the world and sees it dominated by power relations, particularly those relations which are economic in nature. The capitalist system and the ruling class that dominates that system sustain themselves through a variety of means, not the least of which is the control of the so-called "superstructure" of society, the system of laws, mores, roles, and so forth—in other words, the system of ideas that undergird the power relations of rulers and the ruled that is at the actual base, or "substructure" of society. The hegemony of the powerful is thus not restricted to the control of economic assets such as modes of production, financial institutions, and the allied State that protects their interests. Rather hegemonic power extends to the realm of culture, pervading the law, school curricula, religion, and popular culture, indeed all those areas of social life which communicate ideas. The law consists of a body of ideas which defend property interests; the school transmits the official ideology of the ruling class to new generations of schoolchildren, transforming school into an agency of indoctrination; religion serves as a narcotizing drug, offering solace and resignation rather than social criticism, and enlisting God on the side of the existing social structure; popular culture—such as the movies—serves the function of offering social dramas which justify ruling ideas and actions.

Warfare, for example, is justified as a politically valid policy that is worth the sacrifice of ordinary Americans. It is presented both in patriotic and male bonding and adventure terms in war movies, comic books, television shows, novels, and so on. Political ideology, then, is not a marginal afterthought of capitalist rule but rather a central feature of the system, helping to perpetuate those ideas which cloak the true nature of things in palatable terms. Ideology is thus the ideational superstructure of an economic substructure, resulting in a condition of "false consciousness" that hides not only our dependent material class position from us but also teaches us that the system is benevolent, wise, and just, urging us toward obedience and deference.

The critical study of the functioning of political ideology in capitalist society has led some scholars to focus on what is called "the culture industry." Many of the radical critics of American society were European emigrés (Adorno, Horkheimer, Lowenthal, and Marcuse) who were impressed by the awesome power of the highly centralized industries that controlled the means of mass communication. They began to argue that elite control in America was not restricted to the control of Wall Street, the Federal Reserve Board, the key committees of Congress, and the like, but also through the ideological "good offices" of cultural industries such as the newspapers, radio and television networks, and of course Hollywood. These scholars thought that the American culture industry gave overwhelming ideological legitimation to the extant system, so much so that individuals no longer had any critical abilities that might free them from false consciousness or attract them toward alternative cultural discourses. The movies, for instance, were viewed as a major source of bourgeois discourse that perpetuated the hegemony of social values and practices that support the system. The movie discourses of classical Hollywood—the triumph of good over evil, the responsibility of authority figures, the celebration of middle-class home life, the personal wickedness of social enemies, the efficacy of violence, and so forth—gave vivid and entertaining life to didactic messages that in other forms might have been too obvious or downright boring.

The first generation of ideologically oriented scholars tended to see the culture industry as a monolithic source of officially sanctioned propaganda. But this was a view that increasingly had to be modified. Even though culture industries are still in large part highly centralized and controlled by elite powers, they were never merely an instrument of propaganda nor a source of monolithic messages. The movies were often as likely a medium of ideological subversion as ideological indoctrination. It began to become clear that the mass public, and movie audiences, were not fools, and got a polysemic variety of messages from movies that were not necessarily those approved by the authorities. Too, it became obvious that moviemakers, like other mass communicators, were in the business of entertaining people, and if that involved ideological subversion, so be it. The popular aesthetic of the movies was not dictated by political ideology as much as the complex interplay of industry and audience. Even though the powerful had an interest in influencing what went up on the screen, oftentimes they were overruled by the desire to make a buck, or socially critical messages were too subtle for them to notice (as with film noir). As we approach the end of the twentieth century, it seems clear that the mass media, including the movies, are more an arena of ideological conflict and confusion than a mere conduit of agreed-upon values. In that sense, they probably accurately represent the ideological condition of the country, since the pluralism of audiences with different demands and interests, the multiplicity of media outlets, and the persistence of norms of free expression all mitigate against ideological conformity and support.

Ideological analysis has been much criticized for overly relying on deterministic and materialistic arguments that seem at once to say that ideology is both determinative and derivative. In order to avoid "idealist" formulations, ideology is said to be an epiphenomenon of a material social system of power and wealth; yet at the same time, ideology is claimed to be an integral force of social power, which comes dangerously close to saying that ideas shape society and history, rather than the opposite. The logic of ideas in the movies would be of secondary interest, since what is really important is the primary force of concentrated material power. In more recent Marxist studies, this difficulty has been faced and amended through the use of the work of Gramsci and others. It has been realized that popular culture, including the movies, includes ideological conflicts and even oppositional stances. Further, it is now clear that hegemonic power is never complete, is often at war with itself or even other hegemonies, and that multiple and active audiences may not accept the ideological word as it is handed down. Popular audiences used to consuming movies and other fare are critical and selective: in a sense—in good Marxist terms—the masses are something of a hegemonic force in themselves, since they "mediate" a good bit of what is offered them for their own purposes, and dictate in some measure what movies will be made by voting with their attendance. Finally, it is now also apparent that ideologies do not operate only in an "up-and-down" fashion; rather they also operate across an ideological spectrum, "back-and-forth" in the dialectic of historical forensics as mood and circumstance change. The movies become a popular mode of expression of such tensions and conflicts, most admirably delineated for the political period of the 1950s by Peter Biskind in his book, *Seeing is Believing*.[5] Film roles and themes became a way of "locating" ideological conflicts between liberals and conservatives, generations, role conceptions, types of authority, and so on. In this way, ideology is not merely forensic debate by intellectuals nor elite-sponsored propaganda, but rather something that is a vital part of popular art and even popular life. If ideology is an integral part of popular storytelling, then we might be able to surmise the ways in which it is a part of popular thought. This is not to say that ideological interpretation of popular movies will reveal a populace that is rational, nice, or democratic, especially if we look at the "revenging Vietnam" films, vigilante movies, horror films, or even pornography. But it makes the people, traditionally an important concept in Marxism, a crucial component in the formation and direction of ideology. This may mean that at least some among the many will share the ideological hegemony that elites hope to perpetuate, but at least it is recognized that no ideology can succeed unless enough people believe in it. The movies become then a major way that we can understand what ideology is and where it is going, without ourselves necessarily being trapped inside our own ideologies, determining the way we see the movies.

The literature analyzing the functioning of ideology in contemporary society, and in popular activities such as the movies, is now vast.[6] But one discerns that there is little agreement as to what exactly ideology is and does, although it is deemed—in an almost Hegelian sense at times—to be important and determinative. The difficulty is not so much in the "reformed" materialist conception of society and history as it is in the specification of the symbolic and the "real," and the relationship between the cultural milieu that includes such potent learning as goes on with the movies and the organizational

Understanding the Politics of Movies 13

order with which it transacts. This will require further work on the functional meaning of ideology, how the "logic of ideas" in fact does operate at both the macrocosmic and microcosmic levels, specifically what ideology means for both elites and masses and how much "consensus" or "conflict" on ideological formulae they in fact do share. It might even be helpful to examine the political science literature on what people say they believe, and how much belief has been undermined by the gap between ideology and practice. With the movies, it might be useful to examine concepts such as the "ideograph," since this points to an effort to confine analysis of verbal ideas and visual imagery in an eiconic theory of the movies.[7]

More comprehensively, the ideological dimension of contemporary modern society must be correctly understood in its historical role. There is a grave danger that contemporary ideological studies, especially those that focus on cultural criticism, are becoming too precious, engrossed in a kind of aestheticism that eschews the dynamics of art and society, or feels morally superior to the popular art produced by the purveyors of popular culture (such as the movies), imbued by a version of aesthetic idealism that judges cultural artifacts by their political correctness. Such ideological sideshows miss the point of the study of ideology-in-society in the first place: that societies may well exist in the context of ideology, and that the complex interplay of art and life becomes the "cultural background" for the inherent conflicts built into ideological formulae and the society that "carries" them. The movies are one such battlefield, and it doesn't take long in observing the movies to see how those conflicts are manifest on screen, and behind the screen. Indeed, popular audiences of movies often find, and are provided, with depictions that can only be termed "vulgar Marxism" in that on screen power often follows the money. Despite their alleged anti-Marxist sentiments, popular audiences appear to believe that what we here call vulgar Marxism explains a great deal. So it may be that there are latent ideological sentiments and formulations that lurk out there in a populace that is often alienated, cynical, and "turned off" by the systematic prevarication of a political system responsive only to monied interests. In the twenty-first century, new ideological statements in a "post-Marxist" world may call such relations of power something other than Marxism, but the roots will be in the Marxist criticism of society that began in the nineteenth century, and will no doubt continue in the future in different form but with a similar vision of the world. Since the movies will no doubt continue as a major popular art form, then ideological analysis of the movie process will remain a vital and illuminating dimension of the study of politics and film if those who conduct such work remember both their roots and their promise.

Political myth is the second conceptual tradition that is an important way of politically seeing the movies. Myth is a term bandied about as much as ideology, and indeed the two terms are often confused: one often feels that sometimes writers on ideology in movies are actually talking about myth, and those discussing myth are actually talking about ideology. It is a major project of those interested in politics and the movies to clarify the respective definitions of ideology and myth. Ideology will be used, variously, in the sense of the forensic logic of ideas, belief systems, a superior (or inferior) form of consciousness, the apologetics for domination, the ideational weapons for change, the indispensable glue that holds society together, the verbal mechanisms of illusion and false consciousness, and so on. Perhaps it is helpful to remind ourselves that myth is a term rooted in story (mythos) and thus may be best understood in terms of the logic of narrative. Ideology is a term rooted in ideas, at either a forensic or popular level, and thus is a matter of either logical exposition or popular experience, "living out our ideas." Myth then is a subject of narration, while ideology is a subject of ideation. Mythologic is distinct from ideologic by being inextricably bound to narrative, while ideology is at least in principle independent from the logic of story. A myth is essentially a cultural story, while a set of ideas may belong to any culture—whether the means of production should be publicly or privately owned, what extremes of equality or inequality are proper, and so forth. On the other hand, myth and ideology in a particular political culture such as that of the United States are inextricably linked. The myth of American exceptionalism may be manifest in culturally salient stories about the founding fathers or the frontier epic; the ideology of "Americanism" translates into values and beliefs which can be expressed in either forensic or popular ideas devoid of narrative. Yet the psychologic of political learning is such that both myth and ideology are not separate, but rather part of the same psychic "schema." But even though widespread ideological sophistication and articulation is nonexistent, shared mythic experience is, in stories from children's fairy tales ("The Little Engine That Could") to folklore ("urban legends"), popular culture (Disney, Saturday morning TV, detective fiction), and other sources quite vibrant. If that is the case, then movie experience appeals more readily to myth than to ideology.

The conceptual difficulty again is that myth is used in a wide and inconsistent variety of meanings—as story, as corresponding with the rhythm of the seasons, as the actions of gods and heroes, as false belief, as the ritual dramatization of social action, as the Noble Lie of the State, any cultural fiction that is enduring, and so on. Despite uncertainty over what myth is, it is a concept that still may have some explanatory power in the study of society, and cultural artifacts such as the movies in particular. The myth of the frontier, and the West as a mythic drama, has been an integral part of the American imagination. The captivity narrative alone has inspired much storytelling, and indeed motion picture treatment. The Western became one of the enduring genres of the movies, rooted in some very basic cultural self-images. It is likely the case that the power of the Western myth has been such that it has had calculable social consequences. Simply the American penchant for violent solutions, the belief in heroes "standing tall," the creation of "new frontiers," the defense of gun ownership, all are latter-day residues of a myth drawn from an heroic time. Yet again myth is not independent of ideology, since obviously myth becomes the grounding story for ideological formulations, such as, say, the arguments of the National Rifle Association. Such myths are sometimes referred to as "master myths," since they are over-arching and defining myths for the political culture, those stories that add up to the story of us. This does not mean myths are an "ideological veil" for ideology, but it does mean that they do not necessarily translate into movies as ideology. If myth is expressed in a symbolically significant story, then it is instantiated in movies as that, and its ideological content may not be intended nor received as such. In that sense, for example, the Western—*Stagecoach, Red River, Shane, Once upon a Time in the West, Lonesome Dove, Dances with Wolves*—can be understood in mythic terms without reference to an ideological "translation." Myth and ideology may simply be two levels and kinds of knowledge, without any necessary dependence of the one upon the other. Moviemakers may be quite aware of the mythic origins and significance of a proposed movie, without any accompanying particular ideological ax to grind, simply because they are dimly aware through experience and cultural sharing that audiences respond well to stories derived from myth and laden with mythemes. If violent action leads to desirable resolutions and happy endings, a myth has been acted out on screen. Different ideologies—liberal, conservative, and radical—may find such mythic patterns good or bad, useful or harmful, but in any case those patterns are simply different types of knowledge that appear on the screen.

The effort to understand political myth through the study of the movies may then bear fruit. Perhaps mythic knowledge is a form of knowing that is more widespread and deeply rooted than ideological knowledge. If movie audiences respond to myth-laden stories, then this may be because they are familiar with the "archetypes" and narrative traditions to which the culture is heir. These can be quite manifest and recognized, as with such heroic traditions as the Westerner, the adventurer, or the private detective; or it can be more latent and often unrecognized, as with the "Christic" hero, ranging from Terry Malloy of *On the Waterfront* to *E.T.* But it is tempting to argue that mythologic in the movies is understandable because it is a popular language that is a "deeper" structure than ideology, at least ideology at the forensic level of articulate ideological communication. Narrative conventions and role conceptions translate into popularly comprehensible films, sustaining appeal through their participation in culturally sanctioned stories. This is not to say as we did with ideology that there are no conflicts and ambiguities in the movies, rather that they are just as understandable as mythic controversies (heroes, villains, and fools; stories of adventure, mystery, and romance) as ideological representations. Mythic knowledge is not necessarily a "simpler" form of knowing just because it might be more readily available or palatable to movie audiences. This can be amply illustrated by reference to one of the primary mythic experiences we have of the movies, the depiction of social roles.

Social roles involve the patterns of action that people take toward one another. Since societies develop conceptions of how roles should be played, role enactment becomes a major source of learning for the individual, what is generally termed "socialization." In the welter of human relations, role enactment is problematic for the individual, who is therefore looking for cues as to how to act. Popular fare such as the movies becomes a source of mythic enactment, not only in the visible display of fashion in talk and dress, but more subtly in modes of action. The movies become a forum for the dramatization of mythic action, both in terms of unrealizable fantasy and what we might call "ideals" of action which we incorporate into our own lives. Both male and female norms of heroism invite mythic treatment in the movies, in the inherent sense of how a man or woman is supposed to act in the world, and in the relational sense of proper and just action toward members of the same, and opposite, sex. In that way, the movies are a patently normative medium, since the depiction of roles suggests how one should act. Through the movies, we see something quite fantastic, but consider translating it into the real, since we wish the real to be more fantastic.

Although the process of role learning through the movies (and other popular media, from Barbie dolls to TV) is unobservable, we can observe what kinds of role depictions occur at different times, what kind of politics seems to be connected with role depictions, and what reactions audiences have to such depictions. There are, of course, different audiences for different mythic roles, since there are different and competing myths in American society about roles. Male roles may include both solitary and social men, men engaged in "male bonding" or in concert with women, men who are domestic or adventurers, men who are dominators or dominated, the "wrong man" or the right man, and so on. Female roles may show women in various guises of allure or ordinariness, women who are alone or social animals, women bonded to men or to other women, women who are domestic or "out in the world," women who are powerful and powerless, and so on. In a complex and pluralistic society such as the United States, one might expect competing myths involving women and men, many of which find their way into the movies. Even though there may be monistic and simplistic pressures from certain quarters to depict men and women in only one "approved" way, the movies have never cooperated, even from the very beginning.[8] And since role conceptions are always changing—traditional roles may become fashionable again, new roles may fascinate, new tensions between roles may emerge—the movies have obliged by letting us play with these multiple self-conceptions. The mythography of the movies is inclusive enough, and flexible enough, to allow for different strokes for different folks. This is not to say that there are not more dominant, or "stronger," stories in the American mythos, nor that there are forces that would prefer some stories to disappear. But it is simply the case that movies have never been altogether an agent of a singular political force, liberal, conservative, or radical. One can observe the films of any period and find a multiplicity of sex roles. For that matter, one can look at any genre and find the same. In that sense, the movies probably do accurately represent the ambiguity and ambivalence we as a nation tend to have about ourselves.

For this reason, we might speak not of American mythology but rather of American mythologies. The Western, for example, is an enduring and flexible movie genre in which a wide variety of role structures and conflicts can be included, appealing to changing audience moods and interests. Compare, if you will, *Little Big Man* with *Dances with Wolves*.

Role mythemes in the movies, then, may be studied for their political significance. The ostensibly nonpolitical depiction of any kind of social role may have long-term consequences since it involves learning. The movies may well be a powerful source of social learning, although in ways we may only infer. However, we should not deny the power of the learning simply because of the subtlety of the process. Nor should we forget that the process of learning is transactional: the movies are learning from society, and their potential and actual audiences, and society is learning from the movies. The movies are a powerful agency of mythmaking, but it is myths made in the context of the movie business and the ongoing social process of attempting to understand ourselves and the changing world. Myth is not static, but rather dynamic, a welter of stories that informs each generation of who they are and what the world is like. Myth becomes political when its stories become salient for those who attend to it, and it is the wise politician who is able to sense mythic trends in the movies. It is a short span of actual time from the myth of *Easy Rider* to the myth of *Dirty Harry*, but it is a giant chasm of political time, signifying the consequences, and it is in those consequences that mythologies become observable, letting us observe results that are not always nice.

The idea of political culture emerged as a concept in political science in an attempt to specify the conditions for different types and developments of political systems.[9] It has since taken on a wide variety of meanings. Here we take it to mean the different ways in which various peoples rule themselves, and the cultural context of politics. The United States has a distinct political culture with institutionalized habits of self-rule that persist over time. We do political things differently than, say, the Japanese or Brazilians or Gabonese. We also have a distinct culture that involves complex relationships with the political system. We may study the cultural components of American politics, and the political components of American culture. This of course includes the study of American political ideology as an expression of cultural life, and American political mythology as well. But for our purposes here, political culture as a concept is of use to us because it directs our attention to history. The distinct cultural history of twentieth century America includes the development of the movies, inducing complex interplay with the political system. The movies are an expression of political culture, and we can specify the ways in which movies have portrayed the way we do things politically, our history, and our culture. One of the reasons we are what we are as a political culture is because of our cumulative movie experience. The movies have become indispensable in our political and cultural self-conceptions.

The movies also have a history, and it is one of the daunting tasks of movie scholarship to reconstruct and interpret that history in its cultural and political context. The movies are, after all, popular culture, and must be understood as a form of entertainment with enormous cultural consequences—the rise of Hollywood as institution and symbol, the development of the star system and celebrity, the expansion of "fun morality" and leisure habits derived from Hollywood's leisure class, the contribution of the movie industry to the expansion of advertising and public relations, industry cooperation with official and private propaganda agencies, and so on. And, for our specific purposes here, there were also consequences for the political culture—movie industry involvement with the war efforts during World Wars I and II, the Pentagon-Hollywood connection, "script approval" by agencies such as the Federal Bureau of Investigation, court battles over censorship and many other topics, political activism in the movie industry, including the studio executives, the stars, and other figures (the "Hollywood Ten" were directors and screenwriters), and of course, the election of a movie star as President. The political ascendancy of Ronald Reagan suggests a cultural and political merger between Hollywood and Washington that is a significant, and virtually unprecedented, historical event. In any case, the observable data of the movies and political history are there, and the definitive political history of Hollywood has yet to be written.

The concept of political culture, then, orients the inquirer in directions that relate the movies to political history. But it is also a cultural history, realizing again that the politically significant can locate in a wide spectrum of cultural objects and processes, including, for examples, architecture and theater design, music, vernacular speech patterns, canons of professional writing and adaptation, legalities and illegalities of movie production, unionization and deunionization, changes in ownership, and so on. The movies now have a long history, one that involves the relationship of economic and political structures with the production of cultural artifacts, and the relations of institutions and industry with the mass consumption of the movies. In the history of twentieth-century America, the movies are an important part of the "flow of social discourse" that constitutes, and sustains, a political-culture-in-time. The movies have existed in a politico-cultural context of the ongoing exercise of power, with which both the industry and the artists it employed had to contend. Such a cultural perspective, informed by a keen historical sense, can help us do both "thick description" of the social and political meanings given historical and cultural experience by those who live it, and diagnosis of what those meanings are for the society, and its politics, as an historical entity.[10] Such cultural description can reveal an insightful array of symbolic and material arrangements, adding to our fund of knowledge about the movies and political culture.[11]

The final way of seeing movies and politics we term political communication. Some social observers see societies as networks of communication, and it is their task to specify the ways in which these societies communicate. This means that the key to understanding society, and politics, is through the actual processes of communication. The movies, then, can be observed as mass communication, to be sure, but also as political communication. In the former instance, the movies are a form of mass communication with its own distinctive grammar, or media language and logic, including syntax, inflection (rhythm, accent, and tempo), and vocabulary.[12] It must be understood as a medium, with its own ability to communicate certain kinds of messages, and evoke certain kinds of responses. Further, those messages take on patterns of internal arrangement, allowing us to read the semiotics, or "signs and meanings" in the movies that only that medium can communicate. Film genres, film creators (auteurs), studio "signature" films (such as MGM's musicals), and other patterns of communication can be discerned as systems of signs with internally coherent meanings peculiar to that type of film communication. Medium logic dictates their particular way of seeing the world, but within those canons of communication the movies have the potential to "reach" large and diverse audiences whose movie experience lets them understand intuitively.

Political communication scholars are especially interested in what the movies communicate about politics. Some movies are obviously about politics (*Mr. Smith Goes to Washington*, *The Candidate*) and invite analysis as to how politics and politicians are depicted. But it may also be the case that ostensibly non-political movies can be legitimately interpreted for what they tell us about the politics of a particular era. In other words, movies not only have internal dynamics peculiar to the medium that structures their messages, they also have external dynamics that structure what they say about the world. Both organizational and aesthetic constraints may structure what a movie says about politics, but it also may be the fact that external "probes" by filmmakers—testing the public mood, inferring what people might soon like to see, becoming interested in a new novel or script, responding to public events—may affect the inclusion of politically charged communication in feature films. Political communication may become part of the internal sign system of movies without the creators, producers, and distributors of the film even becoming aware of it (the people who made film noir didn't know they were making film noir). But this requires inferences from films, trends in films, "clusters" of films and so on to the larger external world of politics that requires bold inferential logic. Nevertheless, political interpretation of films, based in the idea that the corpus of films a society and a time creates have political meaning, is a project of political communication that is worthwhile and ambitious. Perhaps a fruitful line of inquiry is to see the movies as an agency of political mediation, a communication process in which the present, including the political present, is given adequate representation in popular forums of art such as the movies.[13]

If such political mediation is a part of the creative process, it might be useful to look at movie auteurs as political communicators with regard to their ability to communicate, and ours to understand, a vision or perspective that has political significance. We may include here both directors who achieve fairly clear auteur status—Ford, Hawks, Welles, Hitchcock, and so on—and also teams of people who work on movies together, depending upon how one views the creativity process. This is of interest since an auteur may represent in his or her films something about the social and political world that seems to be shared by segments of the movie audience, and by extension, the mass public. The benefit of focusing on auteurs is that it links a creative force in moviemaking with the creation of a larger, and politically relevant, vision that has social salience. This would give us evidence of how a political perspective might in fact become important in the process of moviemaking, and how such a "charged" vision develops in the often trial-and-error careers of directors, teams, screenwriters, producers, and even studios. Finally, we can examine the entire body of work of an auteur as to what kind of politics it shows and recommends, the extent to which this might have popular meaning, and indeed how much political bearing it has in "informing" the political world of both masses and elites.

It is also of interest to examine the ways in which moviemakers include different types of communication which may constitute a form of political communication. It is rare that one sees political science depicted in a film (although Jean Arthur does give James Stewart a civics lesson on "how a bill becomes a law" in *Mr. Smith Goes to Washington*), but one does see images of political rhetoric (Lincolnian speechifying in *Young Mr. Lincoln*). Most importantly, the movies have at times incorporated political propaganda, a form of communication usually included for persuasive purposes in an effort to "propagate" a message. The ways in which the movies have accepted and utilized political propaganda, initiated from a variety of sources, requires more extensive analysis. Propaganda in the movies can include government-sponsored themes and appeals (war movies during wartime, and "trailers" after films advocating the purchase of war bonds), government-studio cooperation on "preparedness" movies (such as 1950s GI-training-for-toughness films), product placement in films, messages advocating various forms of socially desirable behavior, and so on. But specifically political propaganda becomes difficult to always identify, if there is some sort of covert intention to deceive or dupe (which seems rare, even though the House Un-American Activities Committee during the post-World War II "Red Scare" combed movies written or directed by avowedly leftwingers in vain for "communist" content). If political propaganda is defined as the advocacy in forms of expression of a political position one wishes to propagate, then propaganda in the movies can include the director or some other creative force (studio "perspective," such as Warner Brothers in the 1930s) engaged in propagandizing. In that case, movies as various as Hitchcock's *Lifeboat*, Penn's *Little Big Man*, and Lee's *Do the Right Thing* are propaganda films. As a major form of political communication, propaganda then becomes an integral part of films with a political perspective and message aimed at persuasion. Since we cannot say that all movies are propaganda films, we are then faced with the task of defining and delimiting those that are, and describing the process by which a movie becomes an identifiable propaganda film.[14]

WHAT IS TO COME

In this introduction, we have identified four distinctive ways of politically seeing the movies: as political ideology, as political myth, as political culture, and as political communication. These frames of reference organize the world to be observed, and in so doing give it coherence and meaning, leading to an understanding of the dynamic relationship between movies and politics. But the reader interested in understanding this relationship cannot truly grasp the power of such organizing frames of reference until she or he sees it in action, so to speak, as a mode of inquiry. To that end, the editor has collected what he believes to be representative and superior inquiries into movies and politics, done by scholars in the forefront of each political way of seeing. In other words, if the reader wishes to read or write further using one of the four general perspectives we have identified, he or she should build upon the kind of analysis presented in this book. Each way of seeing has its own political logic, the argument that this way of seeing politics and movies makes logical sense to adhere to and to use in one's own inquiries. Once you accept the logic of political inquiry each frame of reference contains, then it leads to certain kinds of questions, hypotheses, relevant facts, analyses, and conclusions. In the introduction to each section, the editor will point to strengths and weaknesses that the reader should be aware of, and point to some directions that inquiry within that frame might take in the future. In that way, such a collection, if used properly, can be a useful map for a coming generation of students of movies and politics to find their way.

NOTES

1. David Thomson, *Suspects* (New York: Knopf, 1985); Robert Coover, *A Night at the Movies* (New York: Simon & Schuster, 1987); Christopher Durang, *A History of the American Film* (New York: Avon Bard, 1978); Rush Welter, "On Studying the National Mind," in John Higham and Paul K. Conkin (eds.), *New*

Directions in American Intellectual History (Baltimore: Johns Hopkins University Press, 1979): 64-82; Bruce E. Gronbeck, "Popular Culture, Media, and Political Communication," in David Swanson and Dan Nimmo (eds.), *New Directions in Political Communication* (Newbury Park: Sage, 1990): 179-216.

2. James E. Combs, *American Political Movies* (New York: Garland, 1990).

3. Garth Jowett, *Film: The Democratic Art* (Boston: Little, Brown, 1976).

4. Gerald Mast, review of Dana Polan, *Power and Paranoia: History, Narrative, and the American Cinema, 1940-1950*, in *Journal of American History* 74 (December 1987): 1098-1099.

5. Peter Biskind, *Seeing is Believing: How Hollywood Taught Us to Stop Worrying and Love the Fifties* (New York: Pantheon Books, 1983).

6. See Douglas Kellner, "A Bibliographical Note on Ideology and Cultural Studies," *Praxis* 5 (1981): 84-88.

7. Michael Calvin McGee, "The 'Ideograph': A Link between Rhetoric and Ideology," *Quarterly Journal of Speech* 66 (February 1980): 116.

8. Lary May, *Screening Out the Past: The Birth of Mass Culture and the Motion Picture Industry* (New York: Oxford University Press, 1980).

9. See, originally, Gabriel A. Almond and James Coleman (eds.), *The Politics of the Developing Areas* (Princeton: Princeton University Press, 1960).

10. Clifford Geertz, *The Interpretation of Cultures* (New York: Basic Books, 1973): 27.

11. For splendid examples of such analysis, see Lary May with the assistance of Stephen Lassonde, "Making the American Way: Modern Theatres, Audiences, and the Film Industry 1929-1945", *Prospects* 12 (1987): 89-124; Gary Edgerton, "Recreational Architecture as Popular Culture: The Symbolic Design of the American Movie Theater," in Ray B. Browne, Marshall W. Fishwick, and Kevin O. Browne (eds.), *Dominant Symbols in Popular Culture* (Bowling Green: Bowling Green State University Popular Press, 1990): 154-164.

12. Robert P. Snow, *Creating Media Culture* (Beverly Hills, CA: Sage, 1983).

13. Dan Nimmo and James Combs, *Mediated Political Realities*, 2nd ed. (New York: Longman, 1990).

14. See Richard Wood (ed.), *Film and Propaganda in America: A Documentary History* (New York: Greenwood Press, 1990).

PART I

Political Ideology and Movie Narrative

The two articles included in this section on political ideology in the movies represent well the complexities of contemporary thinking about the role of ideology in society. John Cawelti and Douglas Kellner are sensitive to both the power and the problems of ideological analysis. Cawelti clearly sees that the easy labeling of a film, an *auteur*, or a studio as "liberal" or "conservative" falls short of complete analysis and may actually be misleading. Further, the explanatory power of ideology often is less than persuasive, since it attempts to trace ideas, and the representation of ideas, back to economic structures and interests. In a sense, the attempt to explain things by relating the subjective and objective is a difficult task at best. But it is made easier, and more palatable, by examining the representation of ideas that express the view of an identifiable objective interest, or is shared as something valuable by a large segment of a population. In fact, a cultural artifact like the movies can be both, but it need not be. Following Gramsci, Cawelti suggests that we limit the use of "ideology" to those patterns which are demonstrably serving some hegemonic purpose. The key term here is demonstrability: for movies can be shown to further some hegemonic purpose, either one imposed or one accepted, or both. During World War II, for instance, war films clearly served a national hegemonic purpose supported by both political and motion picture elites; but it was also widely shared by large segments of the American populace. On the other hand, that popular support was enhanced through the mystification of warfare—soldiers engaged in daring adventure, wives and lovers faithful and sacrificial on the home front, the enemy stigmatized as an evil to be exterminated without remorse. The war was justified in the ideology of righteous nationalism and anti-fascism, but largely depicted as the "G.I. war" won through democratic camaraderie and individual bravery. However, war films do not always serve an elite hegemonic purpose, but actually can serve a mass hegemonic purpose, at least in the sense of catering to what it is about warfare people wish to believe. The war films of the 1920s had a very different perspective on World War I than the films made during the war. More recently, the Vietnam War movies have tried to fathom the meanings of that experience. But in neither of these two instances is it correct to say that the films served a demonstrable elite hegemonic purpose. It is likely more accurate to say that these films represented widespread desire for a retrospective on the wars that imbued them with some kind of meaning. To the extent that such war films accurately represented mass feelings about wars that seemed to have gone wrong, they can be said to be a cultural artifact with mass hegemonic overtones. The hegemony of public opinion that so impressed Tocqueville made for the creation of popular fare that did not necessarily serve certain elite interests. In some measure, the "Vietnam syndrome" was movie-made.

Cawelti is also acutely aware of the consequences of such multiple ideological sources and interests, namely that this tends to make popular culture such as the movies "ideologically anti-ideological." But it is also clear to him that this has made the movies' ideological content ambiguous, suggesting that what we must understand more fully is the continued predominance of formula in the movies and the relationship of formulaic stories to hegemonic ideologies. Formulas have their ideological uses, as movie genres such as war movies, women's movies, and so on often attest. The question before us is whether these flexible and persistent movie formulas represent different ideologies which emerge in response to social change (a woman's movie from the 1990s, such as *Thelma and Louise*, is different in some ways than, say, *Mildred Pierce* or *Way Down East*). There may be formulaic ways in which prudently anti-ideological moviemakers do after all express ideologies that are either archaic or incipient, allowing people to bask in nostalgia for a prelapsarian world of ideological consensus and rectitude, or adopt new ideologies in the making. It may be the case that simply by depicting things, the movies make an ideological difference, either relegating to the past ideological stances (e.g., Jeffersonian pastoralism) or subverting current dominant thinking through inadvertent and often unintended formulaic depictions (1920s flapper movies which became an agency of female independence). Cawelti suggests, however, that political meanings can be manipulated by those who understand the power of dominant ideological formulations without the public, or the movie audience, being aware of it. Further investigation into how such manipulation can be imported into or out of film is needed, as well as the extent to which publics and audiences are covertly manipulated, and indeed are willingly amenable to pleasurable manipulation.

Douglas Kellner makes a major effort to incorporate popular film into a "multiperspectival" cultural theory, recognizing the power of ideology but also that popular culture is "polysemic" and demands "multivalent readings." Even with this multiplicity of meanings, popular films can be usefully studied in their historical "conjuncture" with politically charged struggles and debates, including not only those events that are obviously political, such as warfare, but also processes and conflicts that are not so obvious, such as gender relations, treatment by organizational powers, and the like. Through the critique not only of economic relations, but also the representation in popular culture of all forms of social relations, the student of ideology discovers how power and the relations of power are "encoded." Reading those codes, and how "transcoding" over time works, becomes a major research task, one that will not only reveal the mystifications of power imbedded in film by the dominant ideology, but also the demystifications of power written into those movies with an "oppositional" or subversive ideology and theme. Through incorporating a multiplicity of perspectives that inform each other—Marxism, feminism, structuralism, post-structuralism, and psychoanalysis—the inquirer can use an arsenal of analytical tools in understanding ideological codes.

Kellner is also sensitive to "reading texts against the grain," observing multiple and confused meanings in movies that often make for strange interminglings of "progressive" and "reactionary" themes and actions. Examining such subtexts or plural texts in the context of historical change reveals something of the ideological confusion and yearnings of both moviemakers and movie audiences. Some movies may even express a tension between hegemonic purposes in the making of movies and mass purposes in the understanding and use of movies. It may be the case that movies often serve as an instrument of *ideological mediation*, a process of ideological learning from both "parties" to the transaction. Following the neglected work of Ernst Bloch, Kellner reminds us that ideology is "Janus-faced," with both dominative and emancipatory "moments" that characterize popular artifacts such as the movies. In often conflicting ways, movies may express both hegemonic and utopian elements, moments of human folly and potential (the classical Western, after all, included both the use of raw violence against native aborigines and outlaws, and the creation of democratic community). Movies may help mediate, or "transcode," the ideological mix of a political system undergoing great stress and likely great change. In historical retrospect, the movies may well tell us a lot about what we were learning about ourselves and the people who rule us in the process.

Following the work of scholars such as Cawelti and Kellner, students of political ideology in the movies will have such questions to investigate. Building on them, they might well ponder the question of *ideological authority*. As students of high art have long pointed out, in some measure such art has lost its authority, simply because of its easy availability and with the multiplicity of many art forms and fashions from which to choose. Thus the role of art as an ideological ally of entrenched elites, always a tenuous relationship, becomes untenable. Perhaps the movies have lost something of the ideological authority they might once have had (again, during wartime or economic crisis) with the demise of studio control, the star system, and their function for audiences. Or, conversely, perhaps they are now acquiring a new kind of ideological authority as a means of expression of alternative, and in some cases anti-social, desires and frustrations. Changes in ideological function of a popular art such as the movies may make at least some movies a bastion of emancipatory expression that hold out hopes, however utopian, of transcending the present.

WHO'S RUNNING THIS SHOW?
Ideology, Formula, and Hegemony in American Film and Television

John G. Cawelti
University of Kentucky

Some movies are obviously political.* Films like *Z, Missing, Country,* or *Advise and Consent* are explicitly concerned with historical or imagined political events. In these movies, the story itself is about politics to the extent that any discussion of plot, character, or theme must deal, in some way, with social and political issues. Another group of movies is implicitly political: the story itself may be about romance or adventure, but the setting is political or there are political issues in the background. This tends to be the case with most war and spy movies. *Casablanca,* for example, centers around the romance of Ilsa and Rick, but the fate of that romance and of its protagonists is shaped by the wartime setting of their love. Still another class of films—*Murphy's Romance, Fatal Attraction, In the Heat of the Night,* and *Guess Who's Coming to Dinner* are instances—don't seem at first to be political at all, but if we extend the conception of politics to include "sexual" or "racial" politics, these films, too, assume a political aspect. Though there are political events in *Snow White and the Seven Dwarfs, Indiana Jones and the Temple of Doom,* or *Star Wars,* it seems a bit much to say that these films are primarily about politics. Certainly *Snow White* can be said to have an implicit sexual politics as some feminists have argued, but does it have a sexual politics in the same sense as *Murphy's Romance*?

Yet many critics would insist that, even in this last instance, politics, in the form of ideologies, is a vital element and must be analyzed or deconstructed or otherwise ferreted out.[1] Still, though it can and has been done, it seems to me problematic to talk about the ideologies of Walt Disney and Steven Spielberg as if the most important things about their delightful romances, comedies, or adventures are the way in which they reflect the ideologies of capitalism. Many otherwise excellent studies of individual films and genres are marred by an oversimplified and reductive explanation of their supposed political implications. Will Wright's *Sixguns and Society*, for example, sets out a persuasive analysis of the changes in plot, character, and theme which have occurred in the western film since World War II, but when he attempts to show that these changes are direct reflections of structural changes in American capitalism in the same period, his discussion seems unfortunately arbitrary. One could easily come up with many kinds of changes in American society and culture that could be implied or reflected by the story patterns Wright defines.

It is this arbitrary quality of so much ideological analysis that makes it so often unsatisfying as if any one of a hundred other interpretations might do as well. *High Noon*, for example, has been often interpreted as a statement about Hollywood redbaiting (liberal) as it has been described as a reassertion of the old American ideal of rugged individualism (conservative). The plot of the movie easily accommodates either interpretation (which may be one reason why it was so successful). However, if it can be either liberal or conservative or possibly both, it would not seem to be making a clear ideological statement. Much the same thing might be said about Howard Hawks' "answer" to *High Noon*, the John Wayne film *Rio Bravo*. This film could be interpreted as liberal in the degree to which it stresses the significance and cooperation of women and Chicanos and attacks the ruthless land baron's attempt to substitute his own power for the town's law. On the other hand, the film could be described as conservative in its portrayal of the heroic sheriff whose rugged individualism saves the day.

It seems to me that the problem lies in confusion and ambiguity about the way the concept of ideology is used in the analysis of popular culture. In this essay, I would like to explore a way of thinking about the ideological analysis of works of popular culture like films and television programs that I find clearer and more flexible in its application both to individual films and genres and to their larger cultural context.

Some critics, especially those in the Marxian tradition, think that all patterns of communication and thought are ideological, and even that we are imprisoned in our ideologies, like the men in Plato's cave, with little hope of ever breaking out.[2] But if this is so, the very idea of ideology must itself be ideological, a notion which seems self-contradictory, or, at least, paradoxical. For, if the idea of ideology means anything at all, it must imply that we can recognize and analyze the limitations and self-deceptions involved in such structures of thought and communication, that there is a "true consciousness" against which the "false consciousness" of ideology can be measured. If ideology is really everywhere and inescapable, then we might as well give up the attempt to understand it.

Fortunately, I think there is a way out of these difficulties if we follow a brilliant suggestion about ideology by the Italian Marxist thinker, Antonio Gramsci.[3] Gramsci perceived that ideology was invariably related to hegemony. Ideologies, in other words, are patterns of thought connected with the establishment and maintenance of power and status in society by a particular combination of social groups. Ideological patterns thus consist of such things as stories, myths, beliefs, symbolic patterns and other mental structures which function to unify a grouping of social power and to establish, justify and otherwise maintain its hegemony over other groups in the society. I would suggest that we limit the use of the term ideology to patterns which are demonstrably serving some hegemonic purpose. This is, I believe, a very important consideration, because it implies that the same patterns of thought and communication may be ideological in some contexts, but not in others, and also that some patterns such as stories may be partly ideological, partly not.

Of course, this threatens to confuse the issue again, but I think we can begin to clarify the fog by going at this problem from the other end: by defining kinds of structure which are not ideological. One such kind is the archetypal or transcultural pattern. Presumably archetypal structures exist because they embody some fundamental aspects of human life or consciousness. We use them because they are widely understood to appear to generate similar responses among many different people at different times. Indeed, the concept of archetypes which apparently began to develop out of the traditional typological interpretation of the Bible sometime during the Renaissance, has become one of twentieth century modernism's ruling ideas. It appears in many different forms, from Freud's psychoanalytic symbolism through Jung's collective unconscious, Frazer's conception of archaic vegetation rituals, and Northrop Frye's universal mythology based on life cycles, down to the structuralist theory of basic intellectual processes based on binary oppositions. While none of these theories of archetypal structure has been generally accepted, their complex usefulness in the analysis of many different human phenomena by disciplines ranging from literature and folklore to psychology and cultural anthropology seems convincing that significant non-ideological patterns do exist. Even though I probably don't understand Sophocles' *Oedipus Rex* in exactly the same way a fifth century citizen of Athens or even a contemporary feminist would, I still find the play deeply fascinating and moving and I doubt that this is simply a result of my peculiar class bias or of the influence on me of the hegemonic ideologies of a capitalistic ruling class. Feminists have argued that Oedipus is a story of male rivalries over the possession of a woman and therefore an instance of gender ideology and this may be to some extent. However, it still seems to me that whatever its theme, the play embodies the archetype of tragedy which has been a particularly powerful structure for most Western cultures.

Certainly, archetypal patterns can be used ideologically. For instance, some conception of gender differences has always been one of the most fundamental human archetypes. Yet, for centuries, putative differences between men and women have been used to justify male hegemony. However, the fact that archetypes can be used ideologically doesn't mean that they always are or must be. The force behind ideology is the thrust toward hegemony. The persistence of archetypes depends on the way in which people find them understandable, meaningful, and even pleasurable. While it may not be easy to differentiate between ideologies and archetypes, and it may not be impossible to determine the precise degree to which a particular archetypal pattern is functioning ideologically, the distinction is, as we shall see, extremely useful in understanding certain political aspects of American popular culture.

Most archetypal theories assume that the patterns in question are universal because they embody basic human characteristics or concerns. I don't think, however, that the archetype concept necessitates total universality. There are probably some patterns that are universally human, others that are characteristic of groups of cultures, such as the differences between Eastern and Western civilizations, and still others shared by different cultures in the same time period. For our present purposes, we need only acknowledge that there exist patterns of thought which persist not by furthering one group's power over another, but because they are pleasurable or meaningful to more than one social group, or subculture, or culture.

Formulas are the ways in which a particular culture repeatedly expresses archetypal patterns.[4] One hopes there are cultures without the archetype of machismo or male heroism, but many seem to have it in one form or another. However, the cowboy, the private detective, and the rebellious policeman are major American formulas for heroic adventure. There are such formulas for many different kinds of stories and for most other kinds of communications such as news reports, letters, jokes, sermons, personal encounters, etc.[5] The purpose of formulas seems to be to enable communications of all sorts to take place with a minimum of ambiguity and misunderstanding. While it is doubtless true that highly formulaic exchanges do not convey much real information, they do seem to be very important to people, perhaps because they represent aspects of communication beyond the conveying of information.[6] When people watch still another episode of *Miami Vice* they may not learn much of anything about either Miami or vice, but they do have the experience of sharing with others a vicarious excitement and a comforting sense that even in a totally corrupt milieu, decency, heroism, and independent individual action can prevail, at least temporarily. The same might be said of Clint Eastwood's *Dirty Harry* series or the Charles Bronson *Death Wish* movies.

It has been argued that crime and detective stories are highly ideological because they reinforce a particular conception of morality and law, which justifies the existing social order and condemns those who oppose it.[7] But there are surely many other equally compelling reasons for the ubiquity of popular formulas. A well-established popular genre, like the detective story or the romance, enables screenwriters and directors to create more films with some chance of attracting an audience through widespread recognition of a certain story type. It works for producers because they can better calculate the audience demand for a certain kind of story and thereby minimize their risks. And audiences feel comfortable with formulas because established patterns make stories more readily accessible and easily understood.[8] Such considerations do not seem necessarily ideological.

However, it would also be excessive to claim that such popular genres as the detective story have no ideological implications whatever. While detective stories were originally developed in England and America, they have become increasingly popular in other European countries, including Poland, Bulgaria, the USSR, and even China. There are decided differences, doubtless partly ideological, in the development of the detective story genre in these different countries.[9] The problem is how to distinguish between the formulaic and the ideological. For this I believe we need both external and internal evidence. Most ideological interpretations, especially those offered by scholars from the disciplines of literature and history, depend on a structural analysis of texts, informed by a set of assumptions about the kind of structures which are inherently ideological. Among these are moralistic oversimplifications, such as sharp distinctions between good and evil, or between heroism and villainy; the presence of plot structures with social or political analogies, such as characters and events representing social groups; the use of positive and negative stereotypes for characters who symbolize social groups, such as racist and sexist characterizations; and the presentation of dominance and submission in social relationships, such as the reaffirmation of feminine dependence on men in traditional popular romances. While such structures may well have ideological implications, it is important to note that oversimplification, moralistic differentiation, and stereotyping are also characteristic of formulas. In the British spy story, villains are frequently portrayed as racially inferior to the hero. When John Buchan and Sax Rohmer do this it seems distinctly racist and therefore ideological. However, as Umberto Eco suggests, Ian Fleming presents his villains of mixed race like Dr. No and Goldfinger with such an air of burlesque exaggeration that they don't seem to have much ideological significance.[10] In general, I doubt that internal characteristics are ever sufficient to determine that a particular text is ideological.

Two sorts of evidence seem particularly relevant to determining the degree to which particular texts are ideological: the purpose of those who create and distribute them and the response of audiences. Neither of these is particularly easy to discover. The problem is further complicated by the question of whether we are dealing with conscious or unconscious intention. Audience response has always been a very slippery thing. However, methods of analysis have been recently developed which should prove extremely helpful along these lines.

In addition to the problems associated with the determination of intent and response, we must also recognize that audiences often use communications in ways very different from that intended by their producers. There are many instances where a film or television program was intended by its producer to have a distinct ideological impact, but clearly does not. A much-studied example is the television series *All in the Family* which sought to ridicule the racist and sexist biases of Archie Bunker. The original story structure carried the message that bigotry was bad and tolerance good. It was produced by Norman Lear, a man of strong liberal convictions. Nonetheless, a significant proportion of the audience completely misinterpreted the show's intended meaning. This audience response, in turn, inspired a transformation in the original conception of the Archie Bunker character, making him much more complex and sympathetic in his attitudes. A different example of a similar phenomenon is illustrated by the audience use of the popular romance, as defined by Janice Radway. Most popular romances, at least the traditional ones of the Harlequin type, are clearly very sexist in their internal structures, stressing feminine dependence on men, stereotyping gender differences (e.g. women are emotional while men are strong), and emphasizing the importance of monogamous marriage. Yet, Radway has shown how at least one group of readers had used romances to foster a partial resistance to male domination.[11]

Such examples of audience resistance and reinterpretation make it clear that ideological analysis cannot depend entirely on internal structures, but must also examine texts in their social and cultural contexts. In particular, a much more complex and thorough study of reader and audience responses needs to be carried out. The last decade has been particularly rich in new theory concerning audience and reader response. The few studies that have been carried out of actual groups and their responses to particular sorts of communications have been richly surprising and suggestive.[12] Students of literature and culture should no longer leave such studies to the oversimplified methodologies of traditional audience surveys.

II

It may be characteristic of American popular culture that formula is often more important than ideology. Todd Gitlin describes the interesting case of the typical roles assigned to businessmen on American television programs. It seems that businessmen are much more likely to be portrayed in a negative fashion, as greedy and inhumane, than most other kinds of characters such as policemen or doctors. (One survey showed that " 'good' business characters in prime time outnumber the 'bad' two to one, whereas the ratio for police was twelve to one and for doctors, sixteen to one.")[13] This seems odd in light of the pro-business ideology of most of television's producers and much of its audience. Gitlin goes on to explain that the reason for this frequent use of businessman villains is not ideological but a consequence of "TV conventions." He thinks that it is conventional that "white-hats fight black-hats." Therefore, shows need "obligatory villains" who are "naturally going to be individuals who have the power to hurt their victims." Gitlin goes on from this point to an elaborate and rather unconvincing explanation of how this use of businessmen as villains relates to another American ideology, that of individualism. It seems simpler to conclude that this casting of businessmen is simply a matter of convention or formula. When we look at movie genres like the western or the hardboiled detective film, the graspy railroad tycoon or the corrupt and greedy financier is a similarly stereotypical "black-hat." Indeed, this formula is related to a very old popular archetype in which villains are portrayed as men of great power in order to make them effective antagonists for the hero. Since, in our society, businessmen represent the most common form of power, it is not surprising that they should be disproportionately chosen for a negative role, even though prevailing ideologies may be in conflict with such a characterization.

Thus, from the outset, formulas play a major role in the creation of popular stories and dramas. In addition, there seems to be a tendency for popular genres to become less and less ideological as time goes by. Even when popular narrative types originate with a strong ideological impetus, as they often do, this original thrust is usually watered down as the genre undergoes the transformations necessary to maintain its popularity over a substantial period of time. A good example of this can be seen in the history of the spy story.

The spy story originated as a popular genre in England in the late nineteenth and early twentieth centuries and was, in the first phase of development, strongly racist and nationalist. Its struggle of hero and villain, its symbolic actions, and its central themes reaffirmed the

English class order and its gentry. In the espionage adventures of writers like John Buchan, Sax Rohmer, E. Phillips Oppenheim, William LeQueux, and Dornford Yates, "clubland heroes" showed themselves competent to defeat the various evil and barbaric enemies whose attacks and conspiracies threatened to overthrow the good society of the homeland.[14] The villains in these stories were usually either representative of political enemies, such as Germany, or coming from "inferior" or "mixed" races. This racial villain either symbolized the threat of a third world colonial revolt as in the "yellow peril" of Fu Manchu or of internal subversion by anarchists or communists. Thus, in its first phase, the spy story was a unified expression of class, political, and racist ideologies justifying the social and cultural hegemony of the British upper classes and showing them to be fully able to defeat the nefarious plots of national enemies, rebellious colonials, and radical subversives.

In the 1930s, when younger writers like Eric Ambler and Graham Greene took over the narrative formulas of Buchan and Rohmer, they transformed the ideological significance of these patterns. In their works, the heroes, rather than being members of the gentry, are usually from the middle classes; the conspiracies they become involved with are not the works of foreign enemies but of greedy businessmen who seek to foment wars and revolutions in order to profit from them. Ambler and Greene replaced the conservative ideological content of the spy story with a much more leftist view of the world, an anxious concern about the rise of fascism, and a rising fear about the coming of another world war.

The espionage thrillers of Ambler and Greene were just as popular, if not more so, as the earlier spy sagas of Buchan and Rohmer, and the breadth of their appeal suggests that even the more conservative members of the public found such leftist gestures as Ambler's making a Soviet agent one of his most sympathetic characters an acceptable gambit. In fact, Ambler's and Greene's novels were just as popular in America, and it was largely through these writers and the highly successful movies based on their novels that the spy story was imported to America.[15]

Another important development in the 1930s was the creation of spy thrillers in which the ideological content receded into the background. This is particularly evident in Alfred Hitchcock's two masterful thrillers from this period, *The Lady Vanishes* and *The Thirty-Nine Steps*. The latter movie is particularly indicative of this trend since it was based on Buchan's most popular thriller in which gallant gentleman Richard Hannay, with the assistance of a couple of aristocratic friends, defeats a vicious German conspiracy to destroy the British fleet. In Hitchcock's film the espionage element is pushed into the background and a romantic comedy wonderfully enacted by Robert Donat and Madeleine Carroll is foregrounded. It is as if international politics has been usurped by sexual politics, though it might be more accurate to say simply that the spy story in this film has been largely deideologized.

There seem to be several explanations for these phenomena of re- and deideologizing. First, it is evident that a narrative formula can be refurbished for a different audience by infusing it with a new ideological content. This is particularly important when a formula is being carried over into a different culture or into a later time period. It is also likely that as it undergoes such transformations, a formula loses many of its ideological associations and becomes simply a convenience for the creation and reception of stories. This process clearly took place in the next phase of the history of the spy story with the development of the highly popular James Bond series. The Bond saga began as a light-hearted revival of the heroic British spy story typified by Buchan. Despite his mild air of amorality, the original Bond was really a British gentleman with all the appropriate tastes and values of an updated clubland hero. His enemies were also political and racial, evil minions of the Russian secret service plotting to further the Cold War by various devious conspiracies. However, Fleming soon dropped the Cold War symbolism and created a new deideologized enemy, the apolitical international criminal conspiracy S.P.E.C.T.R.E., a sort of United Nations of crime. Along with this new kind of enemy, the hero's characteristics became more those of an international professional and playboy than of a distinctly British gentleman. Significantly, when Sean Connery retired from the part, producers Salzman and Broccoli chose Roger Moore, known for his portrayal of the nonideological adventurer, the Saint, as the new James Bond.

I believe that we can trace similar processes of ideological watering down in the history of most popular genres and in the case of many particular movie and television series. The western has come so far from its original ideological conflict between pioneers and Indians that it has lost most of its power as a popular genre. The television series *M*A*S*H* began as a protest against war, but as the series developed and remained popular it lost much of its anti-war focus and became, as Gitlin puts it, a comedy about "the joy of muddling through" with a capacity for "reinforcing all manner of human motives." The popular romance originally reinforced the ideologies of monogamous marriage and male domination, but more recent romances with a feminist bias are attempting to reideologize the genre, though the end result will probably be, as in the spy story, a tendency toward deideologization. In general, popular story forms begin with a definite ideological thrust, but, as they come to accommodate a wider range of meanings and attitudes, they lose much of their original ideological import.

This tendency for popular cultural formulas to become more susceptible to a wide range of interpretations and hence less ideological is also related to the commercial nature of American mass communications and its control by entrepreneurs. Because commercial success in mass communications is largely dependent on an organization's ability to make the largest possible audience want to read, see or hear its wares, there is a great concern with what is thought of as "balance" or "objectivity" in media presentations. This means, in effect, discovering those formulas which will be most understandable and least offensive to the widest possible audience. Though, in recent years, entrepreneurs have discovered that there are large profits to be made by creating books, magazines, films, and even television programs aimed at distinctive segments of the mass public, this has not led to a notable increase in ideological programming, except in the area of religious broadcasting, a phenomenon which has flourished with the coming of cable television. Even in the area of selective production entrepreneurs are more likely to look for narrative formulas with minimal ideological content, at least on the surface. Three of the great recent successes in selective production—horror films for teenagers, romances for women, and pornography for men—are low in ideological content, except in the areas of gender and sexuality, which are actually at the center of these types. These developments may imply that sexual politics have become the major arena of ideological conflict, but that is material for another investigation. The entrepreneurs who control mass communications are constantly subjected to pressures which involve attempts at ideological control. These pressures come from three major directions. First of all, federal, state, and local governments have, at various times, attempted both to manipulate and to censor the content of mass communications. The same thing can be said of candidates for office as the Bush-Dukakis campaign so depressingly demonstrated. While the controllers of the media usually try to resist the most obvious and blatant forms of political control, those involved in broadcasting are very careful to avoid any content that might be construed as blasphemy or obscenity.[16] They do this both to avoid expensive legal battles and the loss of any significant segment of their audience. Organized religious, moral, and political interest groups constantly wield another sort of pressure on the controllers of mass communications through the threat of audience boycotts and the withdrawal of advertising dollars. Finally, the content of mass communications is also very strongly influenced by those groups the entrepreneurs hire to produce movies, programs, etc. Many studies have shown that the creators and "gatekeepers" of mass communications are much more liberal in their outlooks than their employers. However, these "gatekeepers" are usually very careful not to push their own ideological preferences for fear that they will lose their reputations for "objectivity" and, along with it, their jobs. Thus, in spite of continual ideological pressures from various points on the political, social, and cultural spectrum, the system of American mass communications tends to filter out and gloss over overt ideological conflicts both by avoiding clear ideological statements and by separating effective communications formulas from their ideological implications.

Of course, the avoiding of ideological statements is itself a sort of ideological stance and to understand this is essential to our understanding of the dominant cultural hegemonies of American mass culture. Indeed, this attitude has seeped over into politics, where "merchandising" a candidate has become far more important than programs or social issues.[17] In twentieth-century America, the control of the public's attention has fallen increasingly into the hands of groups who are much more interested in selling products than in communicating ideas and political programs. Certainly, this is from one point of view an aspect of the ideology of capitalism, but the very tendency to downplay ideological conflict and to make noncontroversial and political formulas the chief content of mass culture probably has a decided influence on the kinds of formulas these groups seek out and foster. Because of this, popular formulas often have a latent ideological content which may be in some ways more powerful because it is less obvious.

III

American popular formulas usually dramatize social problems in such a way that organizational, governmental, or community solutions seem inadequate. Instead, only heroic actions by individuals can lead to what are usually, at best, temporary allocations of justice. This pattern is so obvious and has been so often noted that it hardly needs demonstration.[18] Whether the social context is the old West or the modern city and the hero a cowboy, a police detective, or a spy, the effective protagonist finds that he must operate outside of usual organizational channels or constraints in order to succeed in defending the innocent, convicting the criminal, and bringing justice to the most powerful criminals, usually represented as those who are capable of hiding behind the law and manipulating it for their own benefit.

On the face of it, one might attribute this pattern to the lasting influence of the American ideology of individualism and, to some extent, one would probably be quite correct. Certainly American formulas of the hero originated in and were parallel to the "rugged individualism" which played such an important role in nineteenth-century American life. However, it seems doubtful that contemporary Americans, who must act every day in a society that is dominated by large organizations and bureaucracies, still believe in this simplistic version of individualism, however attractive it may be. In fact the most recent extensive study of American values, *Habits of the Heart* (1985) by Robert Bellah and others, provides compelling evidence of the profound and widespread dissatisfaction with which middle-class Americans regard the central ideological elements of traditional individualism.

Without more analysis of audience responses, we cannot be sure how and why Americans respond to the heroic individualism of so many popular formulas. Obviously they enjoy them greatly and will probably continue to do so, as the success of recent films like the *Rambo* and *Rocky* series, the Chuck Norris *Missing in Action* series and the Charles Bronson *Death Wish* series indicates. However, it is less easy to say that these films have a clear ideological significance. *Rambo*, in particular, sets the heroic individual not only against Russians and North Vietnamese, but even more angrily against traitors in the American government. If anything, the message of *Rambo* and films like it is a universal suspicion and distrust of all organizations and governments. While this may be in part a statement of the ideology of individualism, it seems just as true that the portrayal of the hero as outlaw is a traditional dramatic archetype that has been present in many different cultures.[19] In this sense, Rambo, with his little band of escaped prisoners fighting their way through the Vietnamese jungle to wreak vengeance on the usurpers who have betrayed them, is simply another avatar of the same archetype that produced Robin Hood and his band of heroic outlaws roaming Sherwood Forest to avenge the wrongdoings of the villainous Sheriff of Nottingham and the usurping King John.

If we try to say that these legends persist because they embody the same ideological content, we run into the problem that we are dealing with one legend created for a medieval English audience and one for a twentieth-century American public. These very different audiences can surely not be imagined to understand and respond to the same ideology. Yet it is demonstrably true that they did respond to the same basic story patterns. We could perhaps argue that the Hollywood version of Robin Hood in the highly popular 1938 film starring Errol Flynn bears a greater ideological resemblance to *Rambo* than the original legend. That would probably be true since different versions of an archetype created by the same culture in more or less the same time period will probably have ideological as well as archetypal resemblances. But again, this is not always the case, for the version of Robin Hood in the film *Robin and Marion* and in the recent British television series clearly have different ideological implications than the prewar Robin Hood. Actually, the careful comparison of different versions of the same legends and the same archetypes is a method that might teach us a lot about the relationship between archetypes, formulas, and ideologies.

It would be my speculation that such story patterns as that of the heroic outlaw have persisted and continue to be infused with new life because they are primarily dramatically effective archetypes and only secondarily bearers of ideological meaning. If this is the case then the negative portrayal of organizations both foreign and domestic may be as much a way of evading ideological meaning as it is of asserting it. Other aspects of American popular culture seem to bear this out. The treatment of problematic issues such as racism, sexism and war have often revealed a similar pattern. The mass media tend to employ what producers believe to be conventional stereotypes, until these stereotypes are challenged by social and political actions to the point that evasion is no longer possible. In the case of racism, for example, the controllers and gatekeepers of film, radio, television and the press were probably much less racist in their attitudes toward blacks than the white American public as a whole, yet little was done in the mass media to portray the situation of black Americans. Then the Civil Rights movement enforced recognition of the racial issue by taking collective public actions which the media could not fail to cover. The same thing happened in the case of the Vietnam war and in the struggle for women's rights. While television coverage of the war may have had some influence on the public's growing opposition to it, there is little doubt that it was the anti-war movement with its collective demonstrations which made the war an issue. After that, television coverage of the war became more ideological.

Once a social or political issue has arisen in such a way that it can no longer be evaded through the use of traditional formulas and stereotypes, the media generally continue to soften the ideological implications of their presentations. First of all, the treatment of subjects which might be ideologically problematic are concentrated into "specials" which acknowledge the existence of a potential political or social conflict, but seek to restrict or confine its presentation to a single program or a special series. In the late forties, for example, when the controversy over racist segregation was beginning to come to the public's attention, Hollywood gradually recognized the need to treat black Americans in something other than the traditional racist stereotypes. One of the first such attempts was the film *Pinky*, which was advertised as a film of a special, controversial nature, but which, ironically, starred a white actress as the film's black heroine and dealt with the problem of whether a mulatto who looked to be white should attempt to "pass." In the 1950s, the CBS television network produced the brilliant and controversial series *See It Now* as a means of acknowledging the existence of political and social problems in America, and as sort of a safety valve to release the ideological energy of such brilliant newsmen as Edward R. Murrow. The practice continues down to the present day with series like *60 Minutes* and occasional documentaries such as those on the Pentagon Papers.[20] In addition, the creation of special problem films as a means of carefully controlling the expression of ideological controversy remains a major network and studio practice. Currently, violence and sexual abuse against women and children is a major topic of these special films, and, while the television dramatization of these problems undoubtedly does much good, the issue is notably absent from most of the standard dramatic and comic series which make up the major part of television broadcasting.

The other major deideologizing practice of the mass media is to assimilate new political and social issues into existing popular formulas, thereby transforming character types from ideological symbols into new versions of traditional stereotypes. Thus, in the last two decades we have seen a large number of women and blacks becoming parental authority figures in situation comedies, doctors and lawyers in soap operas, and heroic individuals in stories of crime and espionage. While there is doubtless some ideological significance in seeing women and blacks in social-dramatic roles hitherto largely restricted to white males, such transformations are also a way of avoiding basic social problems by helping us imagine that similar changes have taken place in society and politics. Assimilations like this into existing formulaic patterns also no doubt help reinforce existing ideologies, though perhaps in a somewhat attenuated fashion. In fact, I think we can find many cases in which the mass media have backed away from what their controllers thought to be overly ideological messages over the whole range of the political spectrum. That the media tend to resist anything that appears to be radical or leftist is no news. What has become more obvious recently in such cases as that of Jerry Falwell and his supposed moral majority is that the media would also rather avoid obviously conservative ideological content, again with the exception of specials such as the talk shows of William F. Buckley, Jr., who probably succeeds not because he is a conservative, but because he is such a dramatic and interesting personality. The media's general reluctance to address ideological issues from both ends of the political spectrum is probably one reason why both liberals and conservatives find themselves frustrated and dissatisfied with the political evasiveness of mass communications, which adds insult to injury by masquerading, as we have seen, as "objectivity and balance."

The reason for this seems fairly obvious. Those who control the institutions of mass communications and popular culture firmly believe, with certain key exceptions, that they will make more money by appealing to the largest possible audience. They think this means making every effort to avoid offending any substantial segment of the public which has buying power. All of the major media, shaped as they have been throughout their history by the ideologies of advertising and marketing, have methods for the evasion of social and political controversy built into their systems of production and distribution. Thus, the cultural hegemony of entrepreneurs, producers and distributors which controls American popular culture is, above all, ideologically anti-ideological. They would prefer to ignore social conflicts between different groups of Americans as much as possible, but they are immensely alert to the slightest changes in the constitution of the buying public.

The controllers of television found it necessary to begin presenting black characters in a new way when the Civil Rights movement made racism an inescapable issue. It is probably also fair to say that it was equally significant that the Civil Rights movement showed that black Americans and their sympathizers were a potentially important group of consumers.

The cultural hegemony that controls American popular culture exists in a fashion curiously askew to those groups which struggle for power and seek to create a political hegemony in American society. The manipulation of mass communications is vitally important to the creation and maintenance of power in American society as it is in any modern nation. Yet the predominance of formula and its relationship to the anti-ideological ideology of those who control the mass media makes such manipulations difficult and ambiguous, a situation that seems to become more difficult with each major presidential campaign. That few twentieth-century political or social groups have been able to use the mass media to their ideological advantage over a long period of time is one reason why politicians and conservative businessmen as well as labor leaders and radical intellectuals share a deep suspicion and distrust of "the media" in America. This ambiguous relationship is probably one important factor in preventing a total concentration of power in America. Yet there is an ominous lesson in Ronald Reagan's remarkable success at using mass communications to help make Americans accept political initiatives which seemed to be leading to a concentration of economic and political power which the public would neither have accepted nor believed possible twenty years ago. Reagan's secret, which he doubtless learned through his lifelong involvement in the hegemony which controls American popular culture, was an understanding of how to reinvest such basic formulas as those of the heroic individual and government corruption with new ideological energy. By identifying himself and his political-economic program with the formula of heroic individualism at war with the incompetent and corrupt bureaucracies, Reagan created an image for himself which resembled *Rambo* in some ways and *Mr. Smith Goes to Washington* in others. After eight years in office, Reagan still knew how to portray himself as a political outsider, the honest man from the west, and to blame the failures of his policies on others. This is a good indication of how, in skillful and unscrupulous hands, the formulas of popular culture can be given new ideological meanings without the public being aware of it. This, in America, is where I believe the chief danger of hegemonic manipulation of popular culture for ideological purposes lies. To forestall the further concentration of such power, we need to study more carefully the complex dialectic between formula and ideology in American movies and television.

NOTES

*I'd like to thank Ellen Rosenman and James Combs for reading and commenting on a draft of this essay.

1. Some examples are Terry Eagleton, Frederic Jameson, and Dominick LaCapra. The distinguished British critic Raymond Williams in *Marxism and Literature* (1977) develops a much more flexible and complex conception of ideology. Though I use different terms, I hope that I am thinking about these things in somewhat the same way as Williams whose socio-cultural analyses of literature and popular culture I greatly admire. Bernard Bergonzi has a good comparison of Eagleton and Williams on ideology in *The Myth of Modernism* (1986).

2. The problem with the concept of ideology is summed up in the *International Encyclopedia of the Social Sciences* which has two articles on ideology by Edward Shils and Harry M. Johnson which use almost diametrically opposed definitions of the concept. In its current usage the term has become so diffuse that it's difficult to know just what it means. Bergonzi quotes Kevin Ryan on Eagleton's use of the term: "continually invoked but never clearly enough defined to be very meaningful, the term begins to sweat blood from all the duty it has to do." (1986, p. 198) For a

sampling of the diverse meanings that can be ascribed to "ideology" cf. the collection of essays *Ideology and Classic American Literature* edited by Sacvan Bercovitch and Myra Jehlen (1986). An interesting way of looking at ideology which I don't pursue in this paper is as a concept characteristic of a certain class at a particular phase of history. In this way the statement that ideology is itself ideological makes some sense. For some insightful comments along these lines as well as a useful short history of the concept of ideology cf. George Lichtheim, "The Concept of Ideology" (1967, pp. 3-46).

3. Gramsci's prison notebooks are the chief text for his observations on hegemony. Cf. *Selections from the Prison Notebooks* (1971). See also Gramsci, *Selections from Political Writings, 1910-1920* (1977); Robert Bocock, *Hegemony* (1968); Roger Simon, *Gramsci's Political Thought: An Introduction* (1982); and James Joll, *Antonio Gramsci* (1977).

4. I take the discussion of archetypes and formulas largely from Cawelti, *Adventure, Mystery and Romance* (1976) esp. chapter one. One can of course talk about ideological formulas, but, in general, the context will clarify the usage of the term.

5. On news formulas, cf. John Fiske and John Hartley, *Reading Television* (1978); on sermons, Bruce Rosenberg, *The Art of the American Folk Preacher* (1970); on personal encounters, the work of Erving Goffman, esp. *The Presentation of Self in Everyday Life* (1959).

6. Information theory with its emphasis on the large amount of redundancy which characterizes most communications may offer insight into another aspect of thought patterning different from either the ideological or the archetypal. A recent book by William R. Paulson, *The Noise of Culture: Literary Texts in a World of Information* (1988) offers some striking suggestions along these lines.

7. Two examples of ideological analysis of crime and detective genres are Jerry Palmer, *Thrillers* (1979) and Stephen Knight,

Form and Ideology in Crime Fiction (1980). Knight's work, though very well done, moves in almost the opposite direction from that I propose, in that he tries to reduce form to ideology. I am trying to suggest that at least some aspects of form exist independent of ideology.

8. An interesting discussion of the market forces underlying the proliferation of formulas in twentieth-century popular culture is M.J. Birch, "The Popular Fiction Industry: Market, Formula, Ideology" in *The Journal of Popular Culture* (1987).

9. An unpublished paper by John Neuses discusses the dialectic between ideology and formula in Soviet and Eastern European detective stories.

10. Umberto Eco and Oreste del Buono, *The Bond Affair* (1966, pp. 59-60).

11. Janice Radway, *Reading the Romance* (1984, pp. 86-118). The complexity of the interplay between formula and ideology is suggested in the case by Radway's feeling that her women's use of romances to create a space of their own apart from their husbands also made male domination more acceptable and thus functioned ideologically to perpetuate male hegemony. New kinds of romances with a more feminist orientation are beginning to appear and it will be interesting to see how they make use of or transform the traditional formulas of popular romance.

12. In addition to Radway, Cathy Davidson's *Revolution and the Word* (1986) and Michael Denning's *Mechanic Accents* (1987) make highly suggestive uses of some of the new methods of response analysis. Cf. my review of Denning and some other recent books on popular culture in *American Literature* (1988). A very interesting book by Thomas Roberts, *An Aesthetics of Junk Fiction* deals in a very complex way with the relationship between audiences and popular formulas.

13. Todd Gitlin, *Inside Prime Time* (1983, p. 268).

14. Cf. Cawelti and Bruce A. Rosenberg, *The Spy Story* (1987).

15. I refer to such films as *The Mask of Dimitrios* (Ambler 1944), *This Gun for Hire* (Greene 1942), *The Ministry of Fear* (Greene 1944) and *Background to Danger* (Ambler 1943). These films involved major directors and stars such as Fritz Lang, Orson Welles, Alan Ladd, Veronica Lake, Peter Lorre and many others. In addition, successful films were made of Greene's *Orient Express*, *The Confidential Agent*, and *The Third Man* and Ambler's *Epitaph for a Spy*. See Cawelti and Rosenberg (1987) and Leonard Rubenstein, *The Great Spy Films* (1979).

16. The immense public outcry over Martin Scorsese's film *The Last Temptation of Christ* (the *Lexington Herald-Leader* published more letters to the editor on this topic than on any other since I have subscribed to the paper) indicates how infrequently producers release films which challenge widespread religious ideologies. Most religious movies, such as the enormously successful *Ben-Hur*, are either carefully deideologized or made to avoid any significant doctrinal disputes.

17. Michael J. Arlen, *The Camera Age* (1981), deals extensively with this tendency and with the techniques that have been developed to "fine-tune" a candidate's image.

18. Two different, but basically similar, analyses of the "American monomyth" are Robert Jewett and John Shelton Lawrence, *The American Monomyth* (1977), and Cynthia Hamilton, *Western and Hard-Boiled Fiction in America* (1987).

19. On the age-old myth of the heroic bandit see Eric Hobsbawn's brilliant study, *Bandits* (1969).

20. *60 Minutes* is perennially the top-rated nonfiction program on television, but significantly enough, the few attempts that have been made to duplicate its success have not worked out. *60 Minutes* remains a highly popular ghetto of political and social issues, perhaps because its major format is the relatively non-ideological one of the individual exposé. Similarly, the other main

forum for the airing of political and social issues, the late-night talk show, is both personalized and at an hour when its audience is necessarily restricted. One recent development is an exception—the emergence of social and political issues on daytime talk shows such as Oprah Winfrey's. These shows, however, resemble in many ways the newspaper advice columnists who have long dealt with issues disguised as "lifestyle" problems.

Works Cited

Arlen, Michael J. *The Camera Age: Essays on Television*. New York: Farrar, Straus, Giroux, 1981.

Bellah, Robert et al. *Habits of the Heart*. Berkeley: University of California Press, 1985.

Bercovitch, Sacvan and Myra Jehlen. *Ideology and Classic American Literature*. Cambridge: Cambridge University Press, 1986.

Bergonzi, Bernard. *The Myth of Modernism and Twentieth Century Literature*. New York: St. Martin's Press, 1986.

Birch, M.J. "The Popular Fiction Industry: Market, Formula, Ideology." *Journal of Popular Culture*. Vol. 21 no. 3 (Winter 1987): 79-102.

Bocock, Robert. *Hegemony*. New York: Tavistock Press, 1986.

Cawelti, John G. *Adventure, Mystery and Romance*. Chicago: University of Chicago Press, 1976.

_____, and Bruce A. Rosenberg. *The Spy Story*. Chicago: University of Chicago Press, 1987.

Davidson, Cathy. *Revolution and the Word*. New York: Oxford University Press, 1986.

Denning, Michael. *Mechanic Accents: Dime Novels and Working-Class Culture*. New York: Methuen, 1987.

Eco, Umberto and Oreste del Buone. *The Bond Affair*. London: MacDonald, 1978.

Fiske, John and John Hartley. *Reading Television*. London: Methuen, 1978.

Gitlin, Todd. *Inside Prime Time*. New York: Pantheon, 1983.

Goffman, Erving. *The Presentation of Self in Everyday Life*. Garden City, N.Y.: Doubleday, 1959.

Gramsci, Antonio. *Selections from Political Writing, 1910-1920*. New York: International Publishers, 1977.

_____. *Selections from the Prison Notebooks*. New York: International Publishers, 1971.

Hamilton, Cynthia. *Western and Hard-Boiled Fiction in America*. Iowa City: University of Iowa Press, 1987.

Hobsbawn, Eric J. *Bandits*. New York: Delacorte Press, 1969.

Jewett, Robert and John Shelton Lawrence. *The American Monomyth*. Garden City, N.Y.: Doubleday, 1977.

Joll, James. *Antonio Gramsci*. New York: Viking, 1977.

Knight, Stephen. *Form and Ideology in Crime Fiction*. Bloomington: Indiana University Press, 1980.

Lichtheim, George. *The Concept of Ideology and Other Essays*. New York: Random House, 1967.

Palmer, Jerry. *Thrillers: Genesis and Structure of a Popular Genre*. New York: St. Martin's Press, 1979.

Radway, Janice. *Reading the Romance: Women, Patriarchy and Popular Literature*. Chapel Hill, N.C.: University of North Carolina Press, 1984.

Roberts, Thomas J. *An Aesthetics of Junk Fiction*. Athens, Ga.: University of Georgia Press, 1990.

Rosenberg, Bruce A. *The Art of the American Folk Preacher*. New York: Oxford University Press, 1970.

Rubenstein, Leonard. *The Great Spy Films*. Secaucus, N.J.: Citadel Press, 1979.

Simon, Roger. *Gramsci's Political Thought: An Introduction*. London: Lawrence and Wishart, 1982.

Williams, Raymond. *Keywords*. New York: Oxford University Press, 1976.

_____. *The Long Revolution*. London: Chatto and Windus, 1961.

_____. *Marxism and Literature*. New York: Oxford University Press, 1977.

_____. *Society and Culture, 1780-1950*. New York: Harper and Row, 1958.

Wright, Will. *Six Guns and Society: A Structural Study of the Western*. Berkeley: University of California Press, 1975.

FILM, POLITICS, AND IDEOLOGY
Toward a Multiperspectival Film Theory*

Douglas Kellner
University of Texas, Austin

Film is intensely political and ideological, and thus the viewer who wishes to discern how films embody political positions and have political effects should learn to read films politically. This means not only reading film in a socio-political context, but seeing how the internal constituents of a film also either encode relations of power and domination, serving to advance the interests of dominant groups at the expense of others, or oppose hegemonic ideologies, institutions, and practices. Thus reading film politically involves situating film in its historical conjuncture and analyzing how its generic and cinematic codes, its subject positions, its dominant images, its discourses, and its formal-aesthetic elements all embody certain political and ideological positions.

In *Camera Politica: The Politics and Ideology of Contemporary Hollywood Film*, Michael Ryan and I (1988) demonstrate how the most popular Hollywood films and genres from the 1960s to the late 1980s transcode social and political discourses and represent specific political positions within debates over the Vietnam war and the 1960s, gender and the family, the corporation and the state, U.S. foreign and domestic policy, and other issues which preoccupied U.S. society over the past decades. Building on this work, I discuss in this paper some theoretical perspectives on ideology and radical cultural criticism which I'll illustrate with some examples drawn from Hollywood film in the age of Reagan and Bush. In these remarks, I'll specify some problems with the classical Marxian conceptions of ideology and ideology critique, and will propose some perspectives that will help contemporary criticism overcome these limitations. Here, I shall draw on critical work done over the last two decades and will focus my comments on the need to develop methods that I call a multiperspectival cultural theory.

Ideology and Film: Critical Methods

Within the Marxian tradition, Marx and Engels initially characterized ideology as the ideas of the ruling class. The concept of ideology set out in *The German Ideology* (Marx-Engels 1975, pp. 59ff.) was primarily denunciatory, and attacked ideas which legitimated ruling class hegemony, which disguised particular interests as general ones, which mystified or covered over class rule, and which thus served the interests of class domination. In this view, ideology critique consisted of the analysis and demystification of ruling class ideas, and the critic of ideology was to ferret out and attack all those ideas which furthered class domination.[1] This tradition of ideology critique—which has continued within the Marxist-Leninist tradition and other neo-Marxian circles as well— assumes that there is a dominant ideology which is the ideology of the ruling class. The problems with this concept are, to begin, that it presupposes both a monolithic concept of ideology and of the ruling class which unambiguously and without contradiction articulates its class interests in ideology. Since its class interests are predominantly economic, on this model, ideology refers primarily, and in some cases solely, to those ideas that legitimate the class rule of the capitalist ruling class, and "ideology" thus constitutes those sets of ideas which promote the capitalist class's economic interests.

In the last two decades, however, this model has been contested by a variety of individuals and tendencies who have argued that such a concept of ideology is reductionist because it equates ideology merely with those ideas which serve class, or economic interests, and thus leaves out such significant phenomena as gender and race. Reducing ideology to class interests makes it appear that the only significant domination going on in society is class, or economic, domination, whereas many theorists argue that gender and race oppression are also of fundamental importance and indeed, some would argue, are entwined in fundamental ways with class and economic oppression (see Cox 1948; Rowbotham 1972; Robinson 1978; Said 1978; Marable 1982;

Nicholson 1985; Spivak 1988; and Fraser 1989). Thus many people have proposed that ideology be extended to cover theories, ideas, texts, and representations that legitimate interests of ruling gender and race as well as class powers.

From this perspective, doing ideology critique involves criticizing sexist and racist ideology as well as bourgeois-capitalist class ideology. Moreover, doing ideology critique involves analyzing images, symbols, myths, and narrative as well as propositions and systems of belief (Kellner 1978, 1979, 1982). While some contemporary theories of ideology explore the complex ways that images, myths, social practices, and narratives are bound together in the production of ideology (Barthes 1956; Jameson 1981; and Kellner and Ryan 1988), others restrict ideology to propositions stated discursively in texts.[2] Against this restrictive notion, I would argue that ideology contains discourses and figures, concepts and images, theoretical positions and symbolic narrative forms. Such an expansion of the concept of ideology obviously opens the way to the exploration of how images, figures, and symbolic forms constitute part of the ideological representations of sex, race, and class in film and popular culture.

To carry out an ideology critique of *Rambo*, for instance, it wouldn't be enough simply to attack its militarist or imperialist ideology, and the ways that the militarism and imperialism of the film serves capitalist/imperialist interests by legitimating intervention in such places as Southeast Asia, the Middle East, Central America, or wherever. One would also have to criticize a cultural text's sexism and racism to carry out a full ideology critique, showing how representations of women, men, the Vietnamese, the Russians, and so on are a fundamental part of the ideological text of *Rambo* (see Kellner 1991). Consequently, reading the ideological text of *Rambo* requires interrogation of its images and figures as well as its discourse and meanings. The figure of Rambo represents a specific set of images of male power, American innocence and strength, and warrior heroism which serve as vehicles of masculist and patriotic ideologies which were resurrected during the Reagan era.

Indeed, it is often the ideological images and figures of popular cultural texts which constitute the political imaginary through which individuals view the world and interpret political processes, events, and personalities. In a mass-mediated image culture, it is images that help constitute an individual's view of the world, sense of personal identity and gender, playing out of style and life style, and socio-political thought and action. Ideology is thus as much a process of representation, figure, image, and rhetoric as it is of discourse and ideas. To illustrate the need and desirability of expanding the concept of ideology critique, let us now undertake a reading of *Top Gun* which emphasizes the ways that it transcodes a certain Reaganite ideology and which analyzes the various dimensions and ideological strategies of the film.

Top Gun: Reaganite Fantasy

Top Gun (1986) was one of a series of films during the 1980s that encoded the Reaganite ethos of militarism, advocating a strong military while celebrating conservative and military values. Like *Rambo* and the other "return to Vietnam" films, *Iron Eagle*, *Red Dawn*, and others, *Top Gun* celebrates individualistic heroism, military valor, and conservative American values. Like these other films, it operates in a binary universe where there is a struggle between good and evil in which the enemy is absolutely evil and Americans represent the embodiment of "goodness." Coming at the end of the Cold War with the Soviet Union, *Top Gun* is not as fiercely anti-communist as some of the films just mentioned, but its "enemy" seems to be Soviet communists, though the Foreign Other to the good Americans is indeterminate enough to encompass Soviet allies like Libya or Iraq (i.e. the "enemy" flies MIGs, Soviet planes, but is not identified as Russian, though the MIG fighter pilots have red stars on their helmets; yet, since this was the epoch in which the U.S. bombed Libya, the film's enemy could be read as Arab nations using Soviet MIGs and no specific anti-Soviet ideology is articulated in the film).

In many ways, *Top Gun* embodies the social attitudes of Reaganism more thoroughly than other popular films of the epoch. Appearing in 1986, before the Iran-Contra crisis, the stock market crash and revelations of market manipulations, and exposés of the savings and loan scandals, *Top Gun* represents the ascendancy of a triumphant Reaganism at its last moment of supremacy before its fall from uncontested hegemony. The film was the most popular box office draw of the year, suggesting that it tuned into the social ethos of the epoch, and put on display the central values of Reaganite conservativism.

Top Gun is primarily about competition and winning—women, military honor, sports, and social success. It unabashedly celebrates the value of being *top* gun, the elite, the best, the winner. The story features the exploits of Pete Mitchell, code-named Maverick, and winningly played by Tom Cruise. Cruise's Maverick embodies the values celebrated during the 1980s of winning at all costs, of putting competition at the center of life, and going all out to win in every domain of social existence from dating, to sports, to career.

The film opens with titles indicating that in 1969 the Navy Air Corps set up a school to train elite aerial fighters, and in a later training session, it is announced that the U.S. needs to maintain its ratio of expert aerial fighter pilots in the contemporary world. The message is that even in a high tech, computerized society, individual initiative and skill are crucial, indeed essential to military survival. At one point, Maverick valorizes individual intuitive ability rather than cognitive abilities: "You don't have time to think up there. If you think, you're dead." The same anti-intellectual ethos pervaded the *Star Wars* films and inadvertently put on display the anti-intellectualism and thoughtlessness that was an essential part of Reaganism, promoted daily by President Reagan and by the commercial media which shared his values and anti-intellectualism. Advertising, for instance, works by addressing and manipulating fears and fantasies, and not by utilizing rational discourse; Reaganism and popular culture work, I suggest, in a similar fashion.

The opening title sequence, through its montage of sound and images, establishes the ethos of the film. As the titles cross the screen, eerie music provides a background to silhouetted images slowly moving through a misty early morning dawn. The images of men are coupled with images of airplanes and the music shifts to more upbeat rhythms and the sounds of airplane motors and staccato radio messages produce a rich sound collage. A V-sign is flashed and a plane takes off from an aircraft carrier "somewhere in the Indian Ocean." The modernist image construction and collage of image and sound codes the fighter pilots with a mystical aura, drawing on the cultural codes of *Triumph of the Will* which opened with a picture of an airplane magically moving through clouds to the accompaniment of martial music in a fusion of images of nature and technology. *Top Gun* opens with a similar fusion and the project of the film will be to fuse high-tech imagery, mythical heroism, and masculinity into a figure of the "top gun" who succeeds in every walk of life and who will produce a proper role model for Reaganite youth.

The music track cuts to a rock background and two fighter planes and their crews take off for their daily mission. The fighter pilots and their planes have mythical names (Ghostrider, Merlin, Cougar, Maverick, etc.) and the image construction utilizes off-center framing, quick cutting, and high-tech sound montage to infuse the fighter pilots with awesome power and glory. Enemy MIGS suddenly appear and after ritualistic dogfighting with the MIGs, one of the fighter pilots, Cougar, loses control and Maverick must risk his life to escort his dazed comrade back to the destroyer where the planes are based. Cougar decides to quit and loses his status as "top gun" fighter, eligible to go to the elite training school. Instead Maverick and his co-pilot Goose get their chance to prove themselves and enter the competition for the best of the best. In the Reaganite universe, only the elite succeed and the faint-hearted must fall by the wayside, deprived of the success and honor reserved for the top guns and top dogs in the deadly competition for wealth and power in which only the winners succeed and everyone else is a loser.

The clouds, fog, shiny planes, high tech control centers, and handsome and heroic young pilots in the opening sequence code the naval aviators as modern heroes, as quasi-mythical embodiments of the mystery and power of modern technology. Here high tech image construction with the best cameras, editing equipment, and personnel invest the figures with aestheticized glory and the dazzling fight scenes and gee-whiz sound effects likewise encode the flight and fighting scenes with the awe and power of aestheticized technology. As with fascism as a political movement (see Benjamin 1968), military films like *Top Gun* aestheticize war and thus provide soft-core propaganda for the military. Indeed, the credits at the end provide "special thanks" to the pilots of the U.S. Navy F-16 aircraft and credit a large number of military officials and pilots who participated in the film, thus certifying its credentials as official, U.S. government-approved propaganda.

One wonders how many pilots and soldiers who fought in the Gulf war were influenced by such cinematic propaganda. Hollywood films are not innocent entertainment, but lethal weapons in the service of dominant socio-economic forces. *Top Gun*'s ideological project is to invest desire in the figure of heroic fighter pilots and high-tech war, which it does with attractive star figures, cinematic high-tech wizardry and special effects, rock music and the sounds of speed and power, and, of course, the high-tech planes and gadgets. During an initial *Top Gun* training session, one pilot whispers to another, when watching a video of a high tech explosion/kill, "this gives me a hard-on." Indeed, this is the project of the film itself which turns on the spectator to the thrill of technological death, fusing eros and thanatos, libidinal energy and destruction, in images of technowar, thus helping to produce the psychological disposition to thrill to images of technodeath in events like the Persian Gulf war.

The scene cuts to Miramar, California, home of "Fightertown U.S.A," where the "top gun" school is found. Here, Maverick begins his competition with "Iceman," who is viewed as the top fighter pilot, the one to beat. Iceman and his partner "Slider" are your perfect all-American fraternity boy jocks who reek with self-confidence, privilege, and the conviction that they are the best and deserve whatever they get. Maverick and Goose, by contrast, are more marginal characters and vaguely working class; they are the underdogs who will fiercely compete to become top dogs, celebrating the values and life style of the dominant elite by their single-minded pursuit of the same values and goals.

It is soon clear that success with women is part of what it means to be "top gun." After their initial orientation session, the pilots go into a local bar, filled with attractive women coming on to the largely military male clientele. As the spectator voyeuristically enters the bar, one sees images of female flesh and flashing smiles, projecting images of erotic paradise for the technowarriors of the Top Gun school. Film in general produces images that mobilize audience desire and ideological films channel desire into certain modes of thought, behavior, and role models that serve the interest of maintaining and reproducing the status quo. Thus, showing the pilots with beautiful woman helps to invest the images of the military with erotic energy and turns on female spectators as well to equate sexual excitement with the military and uniforms, thus helping to supply the actual would-be warriors with the sexual prizes that serve as part of the stimulant for military service and heroism.

The message of the bar scene is thus that if you join the military, wear the uniform, and exhibit the marks of rank and honor, you'll score with the women, that, in short, military guys get the girls. As he enters the bar, Maverick quickly spots an attractive woman and makes his move, singing to her, clowning, and coming on. She rejects him for an older man, but he follows her into the women's room where he continues his pursuit; competition and entrepreneurship demand innovation and courage to score the big bucks, glory, and girls promised by conservative ideology of the era.

The next day as he enters his flight class, Maverick sees that the woman is his flight instructor and he cowers down beneath his dark glasses. The woman, Charlie (Kelly McGillis), is the perfect Reaganite female: competitive, out for promotion, and proper in her behavior. She incarnates a conservative appropriation of feminism in which women compete as equals with men while retaining their "femininity." "Charlie" has a man's name, but thoroughly feminine looks, sensibility, and behavior. She also represents the new woman in the military, and during a period in which the volunteer army depended on women recruits, her image of a successful and attractive military woman provides free recruitment advertisements for the volunteer army; many women probably found themselves in the deserts of Saudi Arabia during 1990, awaiting a violent war, as a result of appropriating positive images of women in military life promoted by films like *Top Gun*.

Top Gun also replicates conservative Hollywood cinematic and ideological codes. It utilizes the conventions of romance to validate Maverick as the prototype of the successful male. In subtle ways, the film also reinscribes the domination of women by men and the conventions of male-dominated romance. At first, Maverick finds himself subordinate to Charlie: she is his teacher, who has a Ph.D. in astrophysics, and is a figure of the new woman authority figure who is a threat to male power and domination. As their relationship evolves, it is she who initiates the romantic connection after his initial overtures. As the moment of their sexual involvement approaches, she states: "This is going to be complicated." By the end of the film, however, Charlie is rendered subordinate to Maverick. As he returns to the *Top Gun* flight school, a hero and now an instructor, the audience sees the return of Charlie who bestows upon Maverick an adoring glance; their eyes meet and this time it is Maverick who says, "This is going to be complicated," establishing himself as the initiator and the master of the relation. This narrative ploy not only utilizes the traditional Hollywood trope of the happy ending to mobilize audience pleasure in Maverick's total triumph, but also invests pleasure in his mastery of the strong woman.

The film also provides strong images of family, father/son male bonding, and the continuity of generations—familiar conservative themes during an era in which such values had been strongly contested in the 1960s and 1970s. Maverick is the son of Duke Mitchell, a fighter pilot who had died under mysterious circumstances. In a key scene, Maverick visits Viper (Tom Skerritt) who tells him of his father's heroism and how his military record was stained when he, Viper, and others had strayed across the border to pursue the enemy (presumably in Laos or Cambodia) and thus had broken rules. Maverick talks of his family to Viper—presented himself as a good family man—and Viper comes to assume a surrogate father role to Maverick.

The images of Maverick's partner Goose also reinforce the family ideology. In one café scene, soon before Goose's death, Goose, his wife, and his children enjoy themselves with Maverick and Charlie. Goose plays the piano and sings "Great Balls of Fire," with eventually the whole group joining in. The singing of popular rock 'n' roll songs, and the ever-present rock soundtrack background, also invest the characters with positive energy, for their association with rock music associates them with the cultural signs of pleasure and sociality, aspects which are fused with images of family in this scene. The cafe scene ends with Goose's wife saying to him, "Goose, you great stud; take me to bed or lose me forever." For the top guns, therefore, marriage, good times, and intense sexuality come together in one convenient package and that package is marriage and family: the ultimate destination of Maverick and Charlie, with Charlie repeating the "take to me bed" phrase to Maverick soon after as they kiss in a moon-lit night beside the bay as the scene cuts to black.

As in all good fantasies, the hero is tested and this happens when Maverick and Goose are engaged in a training exercise and their plane spins out of control; they are forced to evacuate and Goose is killed. Maverick feels guilty and resigns the top gun school, though his father figure Viper talks him into returning to graduate. At the graduation ceremonies, there is a call for the top candidates to go immediately to a crisis assignment: Iceman, his partner Merlin, and Maverick are selected. The scene cuts to the "Indian Ocean, 24 hours later," where a communications ship is missing and must be rescued; MIGs are all around the area and there is a fear that the enemy will reach the ship first. Iceman and a partner and Maverick and the Iceman's former partner Merlin are sent out on patrol and encounter the enemy MIGs.

Maverick saves Iceman and manages to knock out a series of MIGs, thus becoming the hero of his military peer group. These final battle scenes celebrate the vital role of the military and military heroism: the Top Gun shows that he has All the Right Moves and in Risky Business with the enemy he triumphs, blowing away MIG after MIG to the delight of the audience.

Top Gun's take on race is nowhere near the virulent racism that infected *Rambo*, *Iron Eagle*, and many other political films of the era. The enemy is faceless and though it is dangerous and must be destroyed it is indeterminate. Indeed, only one significant scene involves race in the whole film and it is a mark of the subtle racism practiced by conservative politicians and filmmakers when they couldn't get away with more blatant racism. After his partner Goose's death, a guilt-ridden Maverick finds it impossible to fly at his usual heroic level and when his new black partner chides him for failing to adequately perform during a flight exercise, Maverick grabs the black and rather nastily tells him: "I'll fire when I'm ready to fire. Have you got that?" This singular eruption of violence, the only time that Maverick loses his cool, functions to put an uppity and too-ambitious black in his place and puts on display white fears of blacks taking their positions or out-performing them.

Previously, the black pilot was a silent figure, frequently on the edges of the frames picturing the top guns; in these images, he is an icon of the integrated military which provides equal opportunity for whites and blacks and which provides blacks the possibility of advancement. Only in this one scene is the black given narrative prominence and here, he is coded negatively. Indeed, there is no narrative reason why Maverick should have to remonstrate with a black partner, a white would have done just as well, except that the ideology machine *Top Gun* wants to exploit lingering hostilities toward people of color to gratuitously drive the audience to pity and sympathize with the temporarily limp hero.

Even more revealing, the black fighter pilot is the only main Top Gun trainee whose name is never mentioned or highlighted: his code name Sundown is faintly visible on the bottom of his helmet as he flies with Maverick, but his helmet is suddenly blank when he confronts Maverick on the ground, as if he has no personal identity and is merely a figure of the uppity black. Thus, while all the white pilots have their code names prominently displayed, the black is without significant identity. This omission (perhaps inadvertent) points to the inferior position of blacks who manage to become integrated into the white power structure and points to the complicity of popular Hollywood cinema in keeping blacks and people of color in a subordinate position. Indeed, *Top Gun* presents a primarily white elite, without the ethnicity that characterized the classical Hollywood war film or the multiculturalism that characterized many contemporary war films (i.e. *The Boys in Company C*, *Platoon*, or *Heartbreak Ridge*).

Thus, through image and narrative construction, the Reaganism of the 1980s is ideologically infused with Tom Cruise's winning smile and military heroism is celebrated as the way to gain social acceptance and prestige. The military adventures of the Reagan and Bush regimes require willing accomplices and films like *Top Gun* help with recruitment and the production of proper attitudes. The society also needs highly competitive young people to spur the economy to new entrepreneurial heights and the film's celebration of competition and winning as the supreme value helps promote properly capitalistic social values as well. Furthermore, it provides appropriate gender models too. Not surprisingly, Charlie appears back at the Top Gun school where the triumphant Maverick asked to be assigned after his heroic feats. They are obviously coupled at the end, so the narrative machine of the film satisfies all desire for closure: the hero wins his glory, gets the girl, and satisfies all of his goals. The traditional Hollywood happy ending thus serves to validate specific socio-political values—as it always did. Conservative film form and conservative political values march together toward the American utopia that it was Reagan's political genius to sell to a public ideologically nurtured on Hollywood fantasies. Reaganite political discourse and Hollywood film thus provide complementary visions of a very specific ideological fantasy.

Thus *Top Gun*'s conservativism is seamless and total: the film perfectly reproduces the conservative discourses of the period on winning and individual competition, the military, gender and heterosexual coupling, the family, patriotism, and race. The year's number one film thus allows analysis of the dominant ideology of the period which it serves to reproduce and strengthen. One of a series of popular conservative films, it anticipated the bombing of Libya and the Gulf war, while replicating the heroic fantasies of military success exposed in the Iran/Contra scandal: the revenge of the real which punctuated the military fantasies of the Hollywood White House. "It'll make a good movie someday," Reagan wistfully informed Oliver North.

To the Gulf War!

Top Gun, however, is only one of a series of conservative military films of the era (see Kellner and Ryan 1988). Together, these films prepared the country for the Gulf war by celebrating the virtues of high-tech weaponry and military heroism, creating an Arab enemy to replace the Soviet nemesis, and promoting the specific foreign policy agendas of Reagan and Bush. Thus just as late 1970s Hollywood films prepared the country for the conservative hegemony of the 1980s and early 1990s, so too did films of the Reagan and Bush era produce attitudes that would support the conservative and militarist policies of the hegemonic Republicans.

Iron Eagle (1985) presciently anticipated the turn from a communist enemy to Arab nemeses. Together, the two *Iron Eagle* films portray the move toward détente with the Soviet Union and the production of a new super enemy which has found its incarnation in Saddam Hussein and Iraq, uncannily anticipated in *Iron Eagle* I and II. It is not by accident, I maintain, that Hollywood films follow the trajectory of U.S. foreign policy: films are highly capital-intensive and the producers of the culture industries closely follow political and social trends. They are especially sensitive to winds of change, so when détente with the Soviet Union appears as an important political development Hollywood shifts its focus accordingly (leading to a box-office disaster for Sylvester Stallone's *Rambo III* which picked the Soviets as enemies in his Afghan epic at the very moment of détente). Yet Hollywood adventure films must have an Enemy, an absolutely evil Foreign Other, and both Hollywood and Reagan and Bush turned to Arab heavies for the political demonization necessary for the narratives of Hollywood film and U.S. politics at the moment when the Soviet Union was turning to Big Macs, pornography, and capitalism.

The first *Iron Eagle* is more of a teen fantasy film than a full-blown military propaganda film à la *Top Gun* or an exercise in conservative ideological masturbation à la *Rambo*. The film opens with a high-tech air war between MIGs and U.S. fighter planes with a U.S. pilot shot down. An unnamed Arab country claims that the U.S. planes violated their air space, recalling the dogfighting between U.S. and Libyan fighter planes when Libya claimed air space for itself that the U.S. claimed went beyond that allowed by international law. But in this version of the incident, the U.S. government covers over the capture and trial of the U.S. pilot, allowing him to languish in an Arab prison.

The son of the pilot is a would-be fighter pilot himself, deeply disappointed that he did not get admitted into the Air Force Academy because he failed a high school course during the time that he spent in Air Force flight simulators. The boy, Doug McMasters, his teen age friends, and a black retired pilot, Chappy Sinclair (Lou Gossett, Jr.), conspire to save him. They use their air base connections to get intelligence on the prison where the father is being held, appropriate two planes, and the son and Chappy undertake the father's rescue. In an incredibly hokey and implausible scenario, they do just that knocking out half of the Arab army in the process.

Iron Eagle is extremely racist, portraying Arabs as subhuman sadists and villains. The Arab leader, who looks a lot like Saddam Hussein, is vicious and dictatorial. Arabs torture the captured U.S. pilot and sentence him to death arbitrarily and without any due process. In the final duel scene, the Arab leader himself commandeers a plane to fight the Americans after they liberate the captured pilot and the audience is positioned to cheer when the young teenager blows the Arab leader away, replicating a disturbing trope, dominant in Hollywood adventure films from *Star Wars* to the present, in which audience pleasure is mobilized by images of total destruction. Such an audience is being preconditioned to crave the total obliteration of enemy countries like Iraq and such scenes thus produce pleasure in mass destruction—pleasure that would be mobilized by the computer videos of high-tech bombing in the Gulf war.

Iron Eagle II (1988) is more serious and more politically interesting. It enacts détente with the Soviet Union and the turn toward the Arab enemy. While the villain in *Iron Eagle* I looked like Saddam Hussein, the Arab enemy is obviously Iraq in the sequel. The plot involves a joint U.S./Soviet project to knock out an Arab secret nuclear bomb installation, fictively replaying the Israeli bombing of the Iraqi nuclear installation of 1981. Indeed, the film's credits end by giving "special thanks" to "the Ministry of Defense in the State of Israel" and thanks the Israeli Defence Forces and the Israeli Air Force. The film is an Israel-Canada co-production and if *Top Gun* can be legitimately seen as U.S. military propaganda, *Iron Eagle* II can be seen as Israeli propaganda.

The dramatic tension in the film is built around the conflicts between the U.S. and Soviet fighters, their surmounting of their former hostilities, and their pulling together to defeat the common enemy (a fantasy that Bush and his war team realized, with some success, in the present epoch). The successful conclusion is delayed by the machinations of a paranoid U.S. general who still hates and distrusts the Russians and who does everything possible to sabotage the mission (he attempted to assure that the mission would fail by initially picking the worst possible misfits for the U.S. team). This general represents the lingering obstacle to détente and his defeat and humiliation represents the need for new military thinking, new enemies, and new strategies in the post-Cold War world.

Not surprisingly, the Iron Eagle team triumphs, totally obliterating the Arab (i.e. Iraqi) nuclear installation, ending the threat of a sneak nuclear attack or nuclear blackmail. While the white and black Americans and Russians learn to work and cooperate together, they turn their hostility on villainous Arabs who are blown away with the body counts that Hollywood used to reserve for commies. In *Iron Eagle* II, however, the Arab enemies are voiceless and for the most part faceless, thus dehumanizing Arabs as ciphers who threaten but are less than human. Once again, Hollywood followed the trajectory of U.S. foreign policy, uncannily anticipating the crisis with Iraq.

Other anti-Arab films of the present era include *The Delta Force* (1986) which uses the format of the disaster film to vilify Arabs in a fictional account of a Palestinian hijacking of a passenger jet: the "terrorists" are thoroughly villainous and the film uses comic-book exaggeration to sketch out pictures of "good" Jews, Israelis, and Americans, menaced by the "evil" Palestinians. *Navy Seals* (1990) celebrates the high-tech commando forces which, according to one report, played a key role in the Gulf war (see *Newsweek* "Secret Warriors," June 17, 1991). Once again Arabs are dehumanized as fanatic terrorists, possessing deadly Stinger missiles which threaten innocent civilians. The SEAL team (named for their operations on SEa, Air, and Land) embody all virtues of courage and efficiency and obliterate literally hundreds of Arabs, previewing the slaughter of the Iraqis by the high-tech military in the Gulf war.

Film, Politics, and Ideology

In general, representations of Arabs in post-1970s Hollywood cinema are extremely racist and are disturbingly similar to perceptions of Jews in fascist films. In a variety of political thrillers, Arabs are portrayed as fanatic "terrorists" who coldly murder innocent victims (*Black Sunday, Nighthawks*) and lack human feeling. In corporate conspiracy films, they are presented, or are alluded to, as greedy capitalists (*Rollover, Network, The Formula, Wrong is Right*, etc.). Thus Arabs are serving as new villain stereotypes in Hollywood films and by the end of the 1980s were the privileged target of Hollywood manicheanism (see Shaheen 1984).

The anti-Arab films of the past years combine racist and chauvinist ideologies that present Arabs as the incarnation of evil and Americans as the embodiment of good. This manichean vision replays what Edward Said (1978) described as "Orientalism," which establishes the virtues of the West by virtue of delineation of differences between the civilized West and the savage Orient. Arabs were thus the villain of choice for Hollywood adventure films and the conservative administrations. Hollywood Orientalism thus helped produce negative images of Arabs that Bush could mobilize in demonizing the Iraqis in the Persian Gulf war.

In these same adventure film scenarios, women tended to be decentered and a pornographic erotics of violence replaced sexual eroticism, much as the cool killers of the Persian Gulf war were shown pornography films before going out on their "turkey shoots" against the literally defenseless Iraqis, showering their bombs on military and civilian targets in spasms of ejaculatory violence lit up by flashing infrared photos of anti-aircraft fire exploding in orgasmic splendor. This erotics of violence, visible daily in the Gulf war, was anticipated in the video games and war films of the preceding years and will probably help produce a pornographic military culture that may produce even more monstrous films and foreign policy adventures in the years to come.

Toward Contextual Film Criticism

Films are thus not innocent entertainment but are thoroughly political artifacts bound up with political rhetoric, ideology, agendas, and policies. Given their political importance and effects, it is thus important to learn to read films politically to decode their ideological messages and effects. As I have argued so far, reading film politically requires expansion of ideological criticism to include the intersection of gender, race, and class, and to see that ideology is presented in popular culture in the forms of images, figures, generic codes, myth, and the cinematic apparatus, as well as in ideas or theoretical positions.

Another limitation with the classical Marxian theory of ideology, sometimes referred to as the Dominant Ideology thesis (Abercrombie, et al. 1980), is the presupposition of a rather monolithic concept of ideology as class domination in a model which projects a completely monolithic ruling class and dominant ideology, without contradictions or fissures. This model, however, fails to take account of competing sectors and groups within contemporary capitalist societies, and thus fails to account for conflicts and contradictions within and between these groups and thus within ideology itself. Here one needs to see how competing class sectors and groups advance different ideologies to serve their interests. Such an expansion of the concept of ideology requires paying more attention to traditional liberal and conservative ideologies, as well as to the various neo-liberal, neo-conservative, and New Right variants that have been appearing in recent years.

This more plural and contextualist view of film, politics, and ideology draws on Antonio Gramsci's theory of hegemony (1971) which presents culture, society, and politics as terrains of contestation between various groups and class blocs. From this perspective, cultural critique should specify which contests are going on, between which groups, and which positions, with the cultural analyst intervening on what is determined to be the more progressive side (see Boggs 1984 and Kellner 1990). Expanding on Gramsci, a variety of individuals have attempted to develop a more differentiated concept of ideology which pays more attention to emergent, residual, and hegemonic ideologies within contemporary neo-capitalist (or state socialist) societies (see Williams 1977; Hall 1987; Kellner 1978 and 1979). This expansion of the concept of ideology anchors ideology critique more securely in concrete and historically specific socio-political analysis and thus grounds ideology-critique in the context within which ideological conflict actually occurs.

From this perspective, film and the other domains of popular culture should be conceptualized as a contested terrain reproducing on the cultural level the fundamental conflicts within society rather than

Film, Politics, and Ideology

just seeing popular culture as an instrument of domination. Examination of Hollywood film from 1967 to the present (Kellner and Ryan 1988) reveals that U.S. society and culture were riven by a series of debates over the heritage of the 1960s, over gender and sexuality, over war, militarism, and interventionism, and over a great variety of other issues that have confronted American society in the last decade. On one hand, *Rambo, Red Dawn, Missing in Action, Top Gun*, and the like represent aggressively rightwing positions on war, militarism, and communism that served as soft- and hard-core propaganda for Reaganism and a distinctly rightwing interventionist and militarist agenda. On the other hand, *Missing, Under Fire, Salvador, Latino*, and other left or liberal films sharply contested the rightist vision of Central America and U.S. interventionism in that area by representing the U.S. and ruling bourgeois cliques as "bad guys" in generic scenarios that are primarily sympathetic to rebels and those struggling against U.S. imperialism. Against *Rambo* and other "return to Vietnam" films, *Platoon* and *Full Metal Jacket* subvert the rightwing version of Vietnam, as films like *M*A*S*H*, Catch-22, Soldier Blue*, and others previously attacked rightwing versions of militarism and U.S. foreign policy in earlier debates over Vietnam. And in the domain of sexual politics, antifeminist films like *Ordinary People, Kramer versus Kramer, An Officer and a Gentleman*, and *Terms of Endearment* can be contrasted with more feminist films like *Girlfriends, Desperately Seeking Susan*, and *Desert Hearts*. It should be noted, however, that mainstream Hollywood is severely limited in the extent to which it will advance socially critical and radical positions; thus it is the independent film movement to which one must look for the most progressive political interventions within the terrain of American film culture (Kellner and Ryan 1988).

In any case, Hollywood films should be analyzed as ideological texts contextually and relationally, seeing some films as more progressive radical or liberal responses to rightist films and ideological positions, rather than, say, just dismissing all popular culture as reactionary and merely ideological as certain monolithic theories of the "dominant ideology" are wont to do, such as the classical critical theory of Horkheimer and Adorno (1972), many Althusserians, Baudrillard and some postmodernists, or some feminists. A contextualist film criticism reads cinematic texts in terms of actual struggles within contemporary U.S. culture and situates ideological analysis within existing socio-political debates and conflicts rather than just in relation to some supposedly monolithic dominant ideology, or some model of popular culture simply as ideological manipulation or domination. Reading films relationally involves situating films within their genres or cycles and seeing how they relate to other films within the set, and how the genres transcode ideological positions. This would involve reading *Rambo* in terms of the "return to Vietnam" cycle which can be situated within the whole genre of Vietnam films and debates over the U.S. intervention in Vietnam and its aftermath. It would involve reading *Top Gun* in the context of the series of films dealing with military life in the period (i.e. *An Officer and a Gentleman*, *Iron Eagle*, *Heartbreak Ridge*, and so on), in which some of the films treat military life in a celebratory fashion, while others present more critical visions.

For example, while *Top Gun* and *Iron Eagle* present a utopia of military life, more realistic war films like *Platoon*, *Full Metal Jacket*, or *Casualties of War* show the actual consequences of military life when actual war breaks out. Likewise, while *Heartbreak Ridge* has a generally positive view of military life, with some criticism of elite officers, it shows the dangers and anxieties involved in even a minor military excursion like the Grenada invasion, though ultimately it transcodes Reaganite triumphalism, presenting the Grenada invasion as a U.S. victory. *Taps*, *Lords of Discipline*, *Brainstorm*, *War Games*, *The Dogs of War*, *Blue Thunder*, and others present a more critical vision of the U.S. military, while *Up the Academy*, *Tank*, *Deal of the Century*, *Spies Like Us* and the like present more satirical visions.

By relating specific films to other generic examples and to the range of current debates which the genres address, rightwing films can be read, for instance, as responses to actual threats to conservative hegemony, and thus as testimonies to actual social conflicts and contradictions. Or liberal films can be read as contestations of conservative hegemony, rather than as just wimpish variations of the same dominant ideology. From this contextualist perspective, ideology critique thus involves doing ideological analysis within the context of social theory and social history. Reading films politically, therefore, can provide insight not only into the ways that film reproduces existing social struggles within contemporary U.S. society but can also provide insight into social and political dynamics (see Kellner and Ryan 1988). Even highly ideological films like *Rambo* point to social conflicts and to forces that threaten conservative hegemony, such as the liberal anti-war, anti-military position which *Rambo* so violently opposes. Thus ideology can be analyzed in terms of the forces and tensions to which it responds while projects of ideological domination can be conceptualized in terms of reactionary resistance to popular struggles against traditional conservative or liberal values and institutions.

Thus, rather than just conceptualizing ideology as a force of domination in the hands of an all-powerful ruling class, ideology can be analyzed contextually and relationally as a response to resistance and as a sign of threats to the hegemony of dominant group, sex, and race powers. Consequently, 1960s films can be read as a resistance to the social conformity and conventional cinema of the earlier era, while *Dirty Harry* can be interpreted as a response to the radicalism of the 1960s and the recent triumphs of liberalism within criminal law. Sexist and reactionary films like *Straw Dogs* or *The Exorcist* can be read as responses to feminism and the resistance of women to male domination. Blaxploitation films like *Shaft* or *Superfly* can be read as signs of resistance to black subservience to whites and as a reaction against black stereotypes in Hollywood films. And the racism of films like *Rocky* can be read as articulations of white working class fears of blacks and as testimonies to increased cultural and political power of blacks in U.S. society, while the relative absence of dramatic Hollywood narrative films about blacks in the Reagan era can be interpreted as the resistance of conservatives to black demands for racial equality and increased power. Or, *Top Gun*, *Rambo*, and the return to Vietnam films can be read as responses to U.S. defeat in Vietnam, to challenges to imperialism, and to those who would curtail the military and limit U.S. military power.

Consequently, ideologies should be analyzed within the context of social struggle and political debate rather than simply as purveyors of false consciousness whose falsity is exposed and denounced by ideology critique. Although demystification is part of ideology critique, simply exposing mystification and domination isn't enough; we need to look behind ideology to see the social and historical forces and struggles which require it and to examine the cinematic apparatus and strategies which make ideologies attractive. Furthermore, on this model, ideology criticism is not solely denunciatory and should seek socially critical and oppositional moments within all ideological texts—including conservative ones. As feminists and others have argued, one should learn to read texts "against the grain," yielding progressive insights even from reactionary texts. One can also attend to the possibility of using more liberal or progressive moments or aspects of a film against less progressive moments as when Jameson (1976 and 1979) extracts the socially critical elements from films like *Dog Day Afternoon* or *Jaws* which are contrasted with more conservative elements and used to criticize aspects of the existing society.

Ideology and Utopia

Furthermore, radical cultural criticism should seek out those utopian moments, those projections of a better world, that are found in a wide range of texts (Bloch 1986). Extending this argument a bit, one could claim that since ideologies are rhetorical constructs that attempt to persuade and to convince, they must have a relatively rational and attractive core and thus often contain emancipatory promises or moments. Specification of utopian moments within the most seemingly ideological artifacts was the project of Ernst Bloch whose great work *The Principle of Hope* was translated into English in 1986. Bloch provides a systematic examination of the ways that daydreams, popular culture, great literature, political and social utopias, philosophy and religion—often dismissed *tout court* as ideology by some Marxist ideological critique—contain emancipatory moments which project visions of a better life that put in question the organization and structure of life under capitalism (or state socialism).

Throughout his life, Bloch argued that Marxism was vitiated by a one-sided, inadequate, and merely negative approach to ideology. For Bloch, ideology is "Janus-faced," two-sided: it contains errors, mystifications, and techniques of manipulation and domination, but it also contains a utopian residue or surplus that can be used for social critique and to advance political emancipation. Bloch believed that even ideological artifacts contain expressions of desire and articulations of needs that socialist theory and politics should heed to provide programs and discourses which appeal to the deep-seated desires for a better life within everyone. Ideologies thus provide clues to possibilities for future development and contain a "surplus" or "excess" that is not exhausted in mystification or legitimation. And ideologies may contain normative ideals whereby the existing society can be criticized, as well as models of an alternative society.

Film, Politics, and Ideology

Drawing on Bloch, Marcuse, and other neo-Marxian theories, Jameson has suggested that mass cultural texts often have utopian moments and proposes that radical cultural criticism should analyze both the social hopes and fantasies in the film as well as the ideological ways in which fantasies are presented, conflicts are resolved, and potentially disruptive hopes and anxieties are managed (Jameson 1979, 1981, 1990). In his reading of *Jaws*, for instance, the shark stands in for a variety of fears (uncontrolled organic nature threatening the artificial society, big business corrupting and endangering community, disruptive sexuality threatening the disintegration of the family and traditional values, and so on) which the film tries to contain through the reassuring defeat of evil by representatives of the current class structure. Yet the film also contains utopian images of family, male bonding, and adventure, as well as socially critical visions of capitalism which articulate fears that unrestrained big business would inexorably destroy the environment and community.

In Jameson's view, mass culture thus articulates social conflicts, contemporary fears and utopian hopes, and attempts at ideological containment and reassurance. In his view, "works of mass culture cannot be ideological without at one and the same time being implicitly or explicitly Utopian as well: they cannot manipulate unless they offer some genuine shred of content as a fantasy bribe to the public about to be so manipulated. Even the 'false consciousness' of so monstrous a phenomenon of Nazism was nourished by collective fantasies of a Utopian type, in 'socialist' as well as in nationalist guises. Our proposition about the drawing power of the works of mass culture has implied that such works cannot manage anxieties about the social order unless they have first revived them and given them some rudimentary expression; we will now suggest that anxiety and hope are two faces of the same collective consciousness, so that the works of mass culture, even if their function lies in the legitimation of the existing order— or some worse one— cannot do their job without deflecting in the latter's service the deepest and most fundamental hopes and fantasies of the collectivity, to which they can therefore, no matter in how distorted a fashion, be found to have given voice" (Jameson 1979, p. 144).

Top Gun is, of course, a conservative utopia that uses the military as a scene for utopian images of community, romance, male heroism, and self-affirmation. Films like *Jaws*, by contrast, might use utopian images to provide a critique of the loss of community, and its destruction by commercial interests. Popular texts may thus also contain social criticism in their ideological scenarios and one of the tasks of radical cultural criticism is to specify utopian, critical, subversive, or oppositional meanings, even within the texts of popular culture (see Kellner 1979). Even in ideological productions of popular culture, there may be sharp critiques of capitalism, sexism, or racism, or visions of freedom and happiness which can provide critical perspectives on the unhappiness and unfreedom in the existing society. *The Deer Hunter*, for instance, though an arguably reactionary text (Kellner and Ryan 1988), contains utopian images of community, working class and ethnic solidarity, and personal friendship which provides critical perspectives on the atomism, alienation, and loss of community in everyday life under contemporary capitalism. The utopian images of getting high and horsing around in the drug hootch in *Platoon* provide visions of racial harmony and individual and social happiness which provide a critical perspective on the harrowing war scenes and which code war as a disgusting and destructive human activity. The images of racial solidarity and transcendence in the dance numbers of *Zoot Suit* provide a utopian and critical contrast to the oppression of people of color found in the scenes of everyday and prison life in the film. And the transformation of life in the musical numbers of *Pennies From Heaven* provide critical perspectives on the degradation of everyday life due to the constraints of an unjust and irrational economic system which informs the realist sections of the film.

In addition, Hollywood films, even conservative ones, put on display hopes and fears that contest dominant hegemonic and hierarchal relations of power (Ryan 1989, pp. 111ff). Ideological texts thus put on display both the significant hopes and fears of a culture and the ways that the culture is attempting to channel them to maintain its present relations of power and domination. *Top Gun*, for example, puts on display the need for individual achievement, recognition, community, and love. It presents the dubious argument that these needs can be satisfied by military life. Other films show that the present society cannot satisfy existing needs or assuage existing fears as when *Thelma and Louise* (1991) suggests that women must take radical action to maintain their autonomy in existing patriarchal society, or when a documentary like *Roger and Me* (1990) shows what is really happening to the working class.

From this perspective, radical cultural (and political) criticism should not only critique dominant ideologies but should also specify any utopian, oppositional, counter-ideological, subversive, and even, if possible, emancipatory moments within ideological constructs which are then turned against existing forms of domination. This procedure draws on the sort of immanent critique practiced by the Frankfurt school in the 1930s when they turned earlier forms of democratic bourgeois ideology against current, more reactionary, forms in fascist society. An immanent critique of bourgeois society thus turns its own values against contemporary social forms and practices that deny or contradict widely recognized values such as freedom or individualism (see Kellner 1984 and 1989). Thus while bourgeois ideologies of freedom, individualism, rights, and so on are to some extent ideologies which cover over class rule and domination, they also contain critical and emancipatory moments which can be used to criticize the suppression or curtailment of rights and freedom under capitalist society. The practice of what the Frankfurt school called "immanent critique" thus turns ideology against ideology, using more rational and progressive ideologies against more repressive and reactionary ones (i.e. turning liberalism against fascism or new right conservativism). The Critical Theorists, however, never engaged in such an immanent critique of popular culture and I am proposing here that such a project could be of use to radical cultural criticism today.

Hegemony, Counterhegemony, and Deconstruction

Developments of new ways of reading and criticizing texts by so-called New French Theory also has some important implications for the project of ideology critique. Various French poststructuralists have contested the somewhat simplistic Marxian belief that ideology resides in and constitutes the center of texts, and that ideology critique simply involves refutation and demolition of the central ideological proposition of the text. Against this procedure, theorists like Roland Barthes, Pierre Macheray, Jacques Derrida, and other post-structuralists propose new ways of reading texts and engaging in ideology critique. Texts, in the post-structuralist view, should be read as the expression of a multiplicity of voices rather than as the enunciation of one single ideological voice which is then to be specified and attacked. Texts thus require multivalent readings, and a set of critical or textual strategies that will unfold the contradictions, contestatory marginal elements, and structured silences of the texts. These strategies include analyzing how, for example, the margins of texts might be as significant as the center in conveying certain ideological positions, or how the margins of a text might undercut or deconstruct other ideological positions affirmed in the text by contradicting or undercutting them.

Such a strategy involves paying attention to the margins, to seemingly insignificant elements of a text, as well as to the specific ideological positions affirmed. *An Unmarried Woman*, for example, presents the ideology of liberal feminism whereby Erika (Jill Clayburgh) is able to develop herself more fully both in terms of relations and career after her husband leaves her for a younger woman. At the end of the film, she prances merrily down a Manhattan street with a giant painting just given to her by her lover (Alan Bates), whose offer to go with him immediately to New Hampshire she rejected so that she could also pursue a career. As Erika crosses the street, three black and Latino working women stop to look at her and the frame freezes on their faces, undercutting the film's ideological affirmation of liberal feminism by showing that most women cannot afford the luxury or have the privilege of making choices available to upper class women like Erika.

Marginal elements might be important in other ways, however. In the opening title sequence of *Beverly Hills Cop* we get rather realistic pictures of the black Detroit ghetto—precisely the world that the ideological project of the film attempts to erase as the action shifts to the upper-class world of Beverly Hills. Other texts are, as Robin Wood argues, inherently incoherent and contradictory (Wood 1986). In these cases, ideology critique would put on display the central ideological contradictions, or would attempt to show how what appears to be the central ideological position or argument is itself put into question and undermined by contradictory or marginal elements within the text. This procedure would thus show how ideologies may come into contradiction with themselves or fail, and thus demonstrates the cracks and fissures, vulnerabilities and weak points, and gaps within hegemonic ideology itself.

One should also pay attention to what is left out of ideological texts, for it is often the exclusions and silences that reveal the ideological project of the text. For instance, the "return to Vietnam" films leave out U.S. atrocities against the Vietnamese (portrayed in films like

Platoon and *Casualities of War*) and present U.S. soldiers as innocent victims of evil Vietnamese and communists. Hegemony thus works by exclusion and marginalization, as much as by affirming specific ideological positions. And, as Ryan argues (1989, p. 111), what is suppressed or marginalized often points "things that must be silenced" and that are thus "sites of positive political possibilities," indexes of forces of resistance and need.

Such methods of ideology critique therefore encourage the critic to be as much interested in how ideology fails as in how it succeeds, in how ideological texts are sites of tensions and dissonance even when they seem most harmonious and ideologically successful. Although the first *Dirty Harry* film, for example, is obviously a rightwing call to law and order, it displays a conflict between liberal and conservative views of law enforcement. While it attempts to privilege the conservative version, it depicts a society so ridden with crime, corruption, and hopeless inertia that a critical reading could demonstrate that both liberal and conservative solutions to crime are inadequate and that only radical social restructuring can address the problems that the film presents. Inadvertently, perhaps, the conclusion of the first *Dirty Harry* film, where Harry throws his badge away, points to a society so corrupt that even the rightwing solution to crime must inevitably fail. The conservative individualist hero walks away alone into (pure) nature in the film but conservative commercial and economic forces are themselves destroying the nature yearned for by conservative fantasists, thus showing the classical conservative solution to be increasingly untenable in the modern world.[3]

Iron Eagle, for instance, is constantly deconstructing its conservative ideology. When the teenage son learns that his father is being held prisoner in the Middle East, his black teen friend tells him not to worry, because "President Peanut" is out and the new President, "Ronald Raygun," will take decisive action and rescue his father. Well, the government does nothing, requiring the teen heros to carry out the rescue mission themselves (the real Reagan would, of course, realize the fantasy of attacking Arab enemies in his Libya bombing of 1986), thus putting out the message that the government is incompetent and uncaring. Indeed, this conservative fantasy portrays the military as a bunch of bunglers, who are constantly being manipulated by the teenagers who are able to steal crucial intelligence and two fighter planes for their mission.

The film's scenario also is so hyperbolic, so ridiculous, that it reveals itself as sheer nonsense, as a totally implausible teen fantasy picture that allows teenagers to be heroes, to identify with characters who carry out heroic actions that complacent adults are unable to do. This specific fantasy structure, though, limits its identity positions to teenagers and perhaps black men silly enough to identify with Cappy. No self-respecting adult, however, could identify with the fantasy or accept its narrative terms as plausible. *Iron Eagle* thus presents itself as an extremely limited teen fantasy, of limited ideological use.

Such is the "genius" of *Top Gun*, however, that it provides a relatively seamless narrative with few, if any, subversive moments, polysemic meanings, discordant voices, or critical, marginal elements. The film rigorously privileges the position of Maverick, with whom the audience is invited to identify, and affirms without question his values and goals. Tom Cruise, of course, infuses his character with a winning smile and he is invested with romantic charm and attractiveness as he pursues and wins the flight instructor Charlie. Images of him playing volley-ball, or undressing in the locker room or bedroom, present his body as hard, well-sculptured, and athletic, precisely the dominant figure of male virility and attractiveness.

Top Gun draws on cultural imagery from the last several decades to encode its hero with glory and positivity, and works to decenter and marginalize all oppositional readings. For instance, Maverick wears a black jacket and drives a motor-cycle, the image of 1950s rebellion; his name replays a popular television hero who was something of an oppositional, non-conformist—but safe—figure on 1950s TV (i.e. the cowboy gamblers Bart and Brett Maverick). With the Tom Cruise Maverick, however, these symbols of rebellion become icons of male fashion and virility. The sound-track plays 1950s and 1960s rock music, which the characters sing at key junctures in the film. Here too symbols of non-conformity and individuality become symbols of group identity and cohesiveness. In fact, Maverick's "individuality" is thoroughly consistent with military group cohesiveness and is even functional for military purposes.

Thus *Top Gun* utilizes dominant cultural imagery of the past decades to present a cultural synthesis of the present as the embodiment of everything that was best in the past: all oppositional meanings to potent cultural symbols are shorn away and they serve to celebrate the conservative present as the best of all possible worlds. Consequently, while a postmodern film like *Blue Velvet* uses an "implosion" of generic forms and cultural imagery of the past decades to produce a complex text that problematizes our relation to dominant cultural forms, *Top Gun* exploits the images, symbols, and forms of the past to privileged certain ideological positions in the present.

I am aware that this reading goes against the current emphasis on the active audience, constructing their own (oppositional) meanings from cultural texts, but I see blockbuster films like *Top Gun* as ideological machines that attempt to celebrate and reproduce dominant political positions and attitudes. *Top Gun* produces subject positions that it does everything possible to induce the audience to identify or sympathize with; while many of us may resist these positions and may not buy into these ideologies we must actively resist the text itself. Sure, we can produce any number of "oppositional" or "aberrant" readings, but we should also distinguish between texts that invite or facilitate oppositional readings and those that resist them.

Thus, films like *Red Dawn* may be of sufficient complexity and internal conflicts to produce oppositional readings (Kellner 1991) and more modernist films like *Nashville, Blade Runner, Do the Right Thing* or *Zelig* may require multivalent readings to do justice to their complexity. A film like *Top Gun*, by contrast, is an ideology machine that mobilizes desire into certain ideological positions and utilizes narrative to privilege some positions (i.e. success, winning, being top gun), while negatively presenting other positions (i.e. quitting, losing, not being a team player, etc.). The narrative attempts to position the audience to identify with certain characters' subject positions and then produces obstacles to their attaining the goal that the audience is positioned to want them to obtain (i.e. getting the girl, becoming top gun). When the narrative allows the audience desire to be satisfied by producing the romantic couple and military heroism at the end, the audience is positioned to experience these victories as good and to identify with the values and behavior celebrated.

Yet some qualifications should be made. The audience may resist the attempt at manipulation and the text may fail to obtain its ideological ends. A film like *Top Gun* is relatively successful as attested to by its box office reception and positive reception by audiences. Some films, however, may fail to find their audience and be more conflicted and contradictory than a successful ideology machine like *Top Gun*. Indeed, many Hollywood films are neither "conservative" or "liberal" because they want to play it both ways, to gain the maximum possible audience by offending nobody. Predominantly conservative texts may contain liberal features or deconstructively undermine their own conservativism, and liberal films during the 1970s were constantly reproducing conservative discourses (see the discussion of corporate and political conspiracy films and the Jane Fonda films in Kellner and Ryan 1988). Because of the sometimes complex nature of political Hollywood and the polysemic nature of popular culture texts one must adopt a multiperspectival cultural theory.

Toward Multiperspectival Cultural Theory

Cinematic texts are thus not intrinsically "conservative" or "liberal." Rather, many cinematic texts advance specific ideological positions, but they are often undercut by other aspects of the text. The texts of popular culture, like literary texts, are polysemic and require multivalent readings. They incorporate a variety of discourses, ideological positions, narrative strategies, image construction, and cinematic effects which rarely coalesce into a pure and harmonious ideological position. Yet, as I have argued, certain films advance specific ideological positions which can be ascertained by relating the films to the political discourses and debates of its era, to other films concerned with similar themes or sharing certain generic codes, and to ideological elements in the culture that are active in the film.

Such an approach to film requires a multiperspectival optic that reads film in relation to the constitutive elements of its era. Nietzsche argued that all interpretation was constituted by the interpreter's perspectives and was thus inevitably laden with presuppositions, values, biases, and limitations. To avoid one-sidedness and partial vision one should learn "how to employ a variety of perspectives and interpretations in the service of knowledge" (Nietzsche 1969: 119). For Nietzsche: "There is only a perspective seeing, only a perspective 'knowing'; and the more affects we allow to speak about one thing, the more complete will our 'concept' of this thing, our 'objectivity,' be" (ibid). Expanding this call for multiperspectival interpretation in later aphorisms collected in *The Will to Power*, Nietzsche argues: "every elevation of man brings with it the overcoming of narrower interpretations; that every strengthening and increase of power opens up new perspectives and means believing in new horizons" (1968: 330).

Applying these notions to cultural interpretation, one could argue that the more interpretive perspectives one can bring to a cultural artifact, the more comprehensive and stronger one's reading may be.[4] I argued earlier that to capture the full political and ideological dimensions of a cinematic text, one needed to view it from the perspectives of gender, race, and class, and am now suggesting that combining Marxist, feminist, structuralist, post-structuralist, psychoanalytic and other critical perspectives will provide fuller, more complete, and potentially stronger readings. Combining, for instance, ideology critique and genre criticism with semiotic analysis allows one to discern how the forms of genres, or semiotic codes, are permeated with ideology. The conflict/resolution code of most television entertainment, for example, provides an ideological notion that all problems can be resolved within the existing society by following conventional behavior and norms; the "return to Vietnam" film genre and Middle East war genre analyzed earlier in this paper provides ideological legitimation for military build-up and intervention (as well as compensation for U.S. defeat in Vietnam).

A perspective, in this analysis, is thus an optic, a way of seeing, and critical methods can be interpreted as perspectives. Each critical method focuses on specific features of an object from a specific perspective: the perspective spotlights, or illuminates, some features of a text while ignoring others. The more perspectives one focuses on a text to do ideological analysis and critique—generic, structural, formal, feminist, psychoanalytic, and so on—the better one can grasp the full range of ideological dimensions and ramifications of a text. It therefore follows that a multiperspectival method will provide an arsenal of weapons of critique, a full range of perspectives to focus on cultural artifacts.

Some qualifications to this position should be made, however. Obviously, a single reading—Marxist, feminist, psychoanalytic, or whatever—may yield more brilliant insights than combining various perspectival readings; more is not necessarily better. Yet a variety of critical perspectives utilized in a proficient and hermeneutically revelatory fashion provides the potential for stronger (i.e. more many-sided, illuminating, and critical) readings. Secondly, a multiperspectival approach may not be particularly illuminating unless it adequately situates its text in its historical context. A text is constituted by its internal relations and its relations to its socio-historical context and the more relations articulated in a critical reading, the better grasp of a text one may have. A multiperspectival method must necessarily be historical and should read its text in terms of its history and may also choose to read history in the light of the text.

Certain methodological strategies are, of course, incompatible and a multiperspectival approach must choose between competing perspectives in terms of what specific task is at hand and what specific goals one has. For some purposes it may be useful to engage in a focused feminist reading, while for other purposes one might carry through multivalent readings, getting at a text from a variety of perspectives. A multiperspectival position, however, that is not a mere liberal eclecticism, or merely a hodge-podge of different points of view, must allow its various perspectives to inform and modify each other. For instance, Marxism that is informed by feminism will be different from a one-dimensional Marxism innocent of feminism (and vice versa). A Marxist-feminist position that is informed by poststructuralism will be different from a dogmatic Marxist-feminist perspective that reduces a film to this perspective. By contrast, poststructuralism, as noted, eschews methodological dogmatism, champions a multiplicity of perspectives, and focuses attention on features ignored by some Marxist or feminist perspectives. Yet a poststructuralist perspective like deconstruction can itself become predictable and one-sided if it does not utilize other perspectives such as Marxism and feminism (see Ryan 1982 and Spivak 1988).

Each critical method has its own strengths and limitations, its optics and blindspots. Marxian ideology critiques have traditionally been strong on class and historical contextualization and weak on formal analysis; feminism excels in gender analysis; structuralism is useful for narrative analysis; poststructuralism calls attention to elements ignored by other methods and undermines naive beliefs that one specific interpretation is certain and true; psychoanalysis calls for depth hermeneutics and the articulation of unconscious contents and meaning. The more of these critical methods one has at one's disposal, the better chance one has of producing reflexive and many-sided critical readings.

Of course, a reading of a text is only a reading from a critic's subject position, no matter how multiperspectival. Any critic's specific reading is only his or her own reading and may or may not be the reading preferred by audiences (which themselves will be significantly different according to class, race, gender, ethnicity, ideologies, and so on). There is also a split between textual encoding and audience decoding and always the possibility of a multiplicity of readings. The only way to discover how audiences read texts is to engage in ethnographic surveys (see the Appendix to Kellner/Ryan 1988) and even then one is not sure how texts affect audiences and shape their beliefs and behavior. All texts are polysemic and subject to multivalent readings depending on the perspectives of the reader.

Nonetheless, one way to read texts is to situate them into their historical context, to see how they fit into specific genres and promote certain ideological positions. This form of contextualization, carried out in this article, reads texts historically and politically, as ideological arguments produced in specific contexts. The more perspectives one brings to bear in this reading, the more complete one's reading will be and the better grasp one will have on the text's ideological problematics. This contextual approach uses history to read texts and texts to read history. Such a dual optic allows insight into the multiple relations between texts and contexts, between films and history.

Yet while reading films contextually, the more theoretical tools and methods one has at one's disposal, the more complex and multi-layered one's reading will be. Applying psychoanalytical methods to reading *Top Gun*, for instance, makes it clear that the film is about phallic power and the threats to masculist values in the 1960s and 1970s and their reassertion during the 1980s. Being "top gun" obviously means being top stud as well as top fighter pilot and the two competencies are related throughout the film. When Maverick is triumphant in his military exploits he gets the girl and when he fails she leaves him; when he triumphs at the end, she is there to validate his victory.

Top Gun is full of phallic symbols and power, images of male potency, from the first images of the phallic airplanes to the closing battle scenes. Read diagnostically, it articulates fears that male power is being threatened by women and in the current society and enacts its re-privileging. Thus the psychoanalytic perspective strengthens the feminist one and not by accident have many feminists adopted psychoanalytic perspectives.

Finally, and to conclude, the theoretical perspectives on film, politics, and ideology proposed in this paper suggest that ideological hegemony in contemporary U.S. society is complex, contested, and constantly being put into question. Hegemony is negotiated and renegotiated, and is vulnerable to attack and subversion. These proposals thus contain certain political implications in the present situation where the New Right political hegemony of the Reagan years passed over to a more centrist conservatism of the Bush regime that in turn became increasingly militarist in the wake of the Panama invasion and Persian Gulf war; yet, despite the popularity of the Gulf war, Bush's hegemony is in turn vulnerable, shaky, and subject to overthrow and reversal. Reading film and popular culture diagnostically presents insights into the current political situation, into the strengths and vulnerabilities of the contending political forces, into the hopes and fears of the population. Film thus provides important insights into the psychological, socio-political, and ideological make-up of a specific society at a given point in history.

Reading film diagnostically also allows one to detect what ideological solutions to various problems are being offered, and thus to anticipate certain trends, to gain insights into social problems and conflicts, and to appraise the dominant ideologies and emergent oppositional forces. Consequently, diagnostic political critique enables one to perceive the limitations of mainstream conservative and liberal political ideologies, as well as helping to decipher their continuing appeal. It enables one to grasp the utopian yearnings in a given society and challenges progressives to develop cultural representations, political alternatives, and practices and movements which address these predispositions. Such diagnostic reading thus helps with the formulation of progressive political practices which address salient hopes, fears, and desires, and the construction of social alternatives that are grounded in existing psychological, social, and cultural matrixes. Consequently, diagnostic film critique does not merely offer another clever method of reading films but provides weapons of critique for those interested in producing a better society.

NOTES

*For critical comments on earlier versions of this text, thanks to Steve Best and Janet Staiger; I am also indebted to the audience of a December 1990 presentation of the paper at the APA for ideas incorporated into this version.

1. In *Studies in the Theories of Ideology* and *Ideology and Modern Culture*, John Thompson (1984 and 1990) examines classical and recent theories of ideology and finds that many of them sever the link between ideology and domination, and therefore rob ideology of the critical edge that it had in Marx and other neo-Marxists. I would therefore agree with Thompson on the need to link the concept of ideology with theories of hegemony and domination, and thus to delimit its application to ideas and positions which serve functions of legitimation, mystification, and class domination that assure the domination of the ruling class over other classes and groups within society, rather than equating all ideas or political positions with ideology (see Kellner 1978 for an earlier presentation of this position).

2. Thompson (1984) examines a large number of contemporary theories of ideology which want to fundamentally define ideology in terms of language and a discourse theory. Against this position, which Thompson himself abandons in his next book on ideology (1990), I would want to include image, symbol, myth, and narrative in the repertoire of ideological instruments, and would thus want to combine within ideological analysis discourse theory with myth-symbol criticism and narrative analysis in order to note the ways that images, scenes, and narratives attempt to convey ideology.

3. For another presentation of a deconstructive concept of ideology and method of reading films politically, see Ryan 1989, pp. 111ff. For a deconstructive reading of *Red Dawn*, see Kellner 1991.

4. For more on the metatheory of a multiperspectival theory, see Best and Kellner 1991 and on the concept of a political reading, posed against a variant of postmodern theory, see Best and Kellner 1987.

WORKS CITED

Abercrombie, N. et al. *The Dominant Ideology Thesis*. London: Routledge & Kegan Paul, 1980.

Althusser, Louis. *Lenin and Philosophy*. London: New Left Books, 1971.

Barthes, Roland. *Mythologies*. New York: Hill and Wang, 1956.

Baudrillard, Jean. *Simulations*. New York: Semiotext(e), 1983.

Benjamin, Walter. *Illuminations*. New York: Harcourt, Brace & World, 1968.

Best, Steven and Douglas Kellner. "(Re)Watching Television: The Limitations of Post-Modernism," *Diacritics*. (Summer 1987): 97-113.

Best, Steven and Douglas Kellner. *Postmodern Theory: Critical Interrogations*. London and New York: Macmillan and Guilford, 1991.

Bloch, Ernst. *The Principle of Hope*. Cambridge: MIT Press, 1986.

Boggs, Carl. The Two Revolutions: Gramsci and the Dilemmas of Western Marxism. Boston: South End Press, 1984.

Canadian Journal of Political and Social Theory, Special Issue on Ideology, Vol. 7, Nos. 1-2 (Winter-Spring 1983).

Centre for Contemporary Cultural Studies. *On Ideology*. London: Hutchinson, 1979.

Centre for Contemporary Cultural Studies. *Culture, Media, Language*. London: Hutchinson, 1980.

Chodorow, Nancy. *The Reproduction of Mothering*. Berkeley: University of California Press, 1978.

Cox, Oliver. *Caste, Class & Race*. New York: Doubleday, 1948; Reprinted 1970, Monthly Review paperback.

Coward, Rosalind and John Ellis. *Language and Materialism*. London: Routledge & Kegan Paul, 1977.

Crawford, Alan. *Thunder on the Right*. New York: Pantheon, 1980.

Davis, Mike. *Prisoners of the American Dream*. New York: Verso, 1986.

Derrida, Jacques. *Of Grammatology*. Baltimore: John Hopkins University Press, 1976.

_____. *Writing and Difference*. Chicago: University of Chicago Press, 1978.

Deleuze, Gilles and Felix Guattari. *Anti-Oedipus*. New York: Viking, 1977.

Exoo, Fred, editor. *Democracy Upside Down*. New York: Praeger, 1987.

Fraser, Nancy. *Unruly Practices*. Minneapolis: University of Minnesota Press, 1989.

Gouldner, Alvin W. *The Dialectic of Ideology and Technology*. New York: Seabury, 1976.

Gramsci, Antonio. *Selections from the Prison Notebooks*. New York: International Publishers, 1971.

Hall, Stuart. "The Problem of Ideology—Marxism without Guarantees," *Journal of Communication Inquiry*, Vol. 10, No. 2 (Summer): 28-44.

Horkheimer, Max and T.W. Adorno. *Dialectic of Enlightenment*. New York: Seabury, 1972.

Jameson, Fredric. "Reification and Utopia in Mass Culture," *Social Text* 1 (Winter 1979): 130-148.

_____. *The Political Unconscious*. Ithaca: Cornell University Press, 1981.

_____. *Signatures of the Visible*. New York and London: Routledge, 1990.

Jewett, Robert and John Lawrence. *The American Monomyth*. Lanham, MD: University Press of America, 1988, second edition.

Johnson, Richard. "What is Cultural Studies Anyway?" *Stencilled Occasional Paper* #74, Centre for Contemporary Cultural Studies, Birmingham, 1983.

Kellner, Douglas. "Ideology, Marxism, and Advanced Capitalism," *Socialist Review*, No. 42. (Nov-Dec 1978): 37-65.

_____. "TV, Ideology, and Emancipatory Popular Culture," *Socialist Review* 45 (May-June 1979): 13-53.

_____. *Television Images, Codes, and Messages, Televisions*, Vol. 7, No. 4 (1980): 2-19.

_____. "Television Myth and Ritual," *Praxis* 6 (1982): 133-155.

_____. *Herbert Marcuse and the Crisis of Marxism*. London and Berkeley: Macmillan and University of California Press, 1984.

_____. *Critical Theory, Marxism, and Modernity*. Cambridge and Baltimore: Polity and John Hopkins University Press, 1989.

_____. *Television and the Crisis of Democracy*. Boulder, Col: Westview, 1990.

_____. "Reading Film Politically: Reflections on Hollywood Film in the Age of Reagan," The Velvet Light Trap, 1991.

Kellner, Douglas and Michael Ryan. *Camera Politica: The Politics and Ideology of Contemporary Hollywood Film*. Bloomington, Ind: Indiana University Press, 1988.

Macherey, Pierre. *A Theory of Literary Production*. London: Routledge & Kegan Paul, 1978.

Marable, Manning. *How Capitalism Underdeveloped Black America*. Boston: South End Press, 1982.

Marcuse, Herbert. *One-Dimensional Man*. Boston: Beacon Press, 1964.

_____. *Eros and Civilization*. Boston: Beacon Press, 1955.

Marx, Karl and Friedrich Engels. *The Marx-Engels Reader*, edited by Robert C. Tucker. New York: Norton, 1978, second edition.

_____. *The German Ideology*. New York: International Publishers, 1977.

Nicholson, Linda. *Gender and History*. New York: Columbia University Press, 1985.

Nietzsche, Friedrich. *The Will to Power*. New York: Random House, 1968.

_____. *The Genealogy of Morals*. New York: Random House, 1969.

Pecheux, Michel. *Language, Semantics, and Ideology*. New York: Saint Martin's, 1982.

Robinson, Lillian. *Sex, Class, and Culture*. Bloomington: Indiana University Press, 1978.

Rowbotham, Shelia. *Women, Resistance, & Revolution*. New York: Vintage, 1972.

Michael Ryan, *Marxism and Deconstruction*. Baltimore: Johns Hopkins University Press, 1982.

Ryan, Michael *Culture and Politics*. London: Macmillan and Johns Hopkins University Press.

Said, Edward. *Orientalism*. New York: Random House, 1978.

Shaheen, Jack. *The TV Arab*. Bowling Green Ohio, The Popular Press, 1984.

Showalter, Elaine. *The New Feminist Criticism*. New York: Pantheon, 1985.

Spivak, Gayatri. *In Other Worlds*. New York: Routledge, 1988.

Thompson, John. *Studies in the Theory of Ideology*. Cambridge: Polity Press, 1984.

_____. *Ideology and Modern Culture*. Cambridge and Stanford, Cal: Polity and Stanford University Press, 1990.

Waxman, Chaim. *The End of Ideology Debate*. New York: Simon and Schuster, 1968.

Williams, Raymond. *Marxism and Literature*. New York: Oxford University Press, 1977.

Wood, Robin. *Hollywood from Vietnam to Reagan*. New York: Columbia University Press, 1986.

PART II

Political Myth in the Movies

Political myth is evident in the movies in a variety of ways, perhaps most notably in the depiction of social roles and in certain kinds of stories of enduring cultural interest and significance. In her searching inquiry into the depiction of women's social roles in the movies, June Sochen is quite aware that the popular enactment of such roles is not apolitical. For the dynamics of power relations is not confined to usual politics. Rather power is a concept that helps us understand the conduct of social roles, and the complementary and conflicting aspects of those roles. In that sense, gender politics is not something separate from the other ways in which a political system exercises power, since it involves basic questions of who tells other people what to do. Patterns of power take many social forms—intellectual, financial, cultural, and of course personal—but in all cases such power is justified in terms of myth. On the other hand, patterns of power are also unjustified, or challenged, in terms of alternative myths. But in all cases, popular media such as the movies utilize mythic resources in order to depict social roles, and degrees of power and powerlessness associated with them.

The movies have used these American mythic resources in order to depict gender relations, and with certain persistent depictions of women's roles. As Sochen points out, oftentimes filmic depictions of women involves them in paying the often high "price of power," forcing them into roles with dilemmas and constraints. For one thing, a persistent myth in the movies was the notion that women who did seek power became unattractive or desexualized by venturing into a "man's world" (one thinks of the many depictions in the 1950s of women in big business, often suggesting that such a choice had separated them from their "natural" condition). The dilemma such movies portrayed was that to the extent women sought and gained social power outside of the home, they were thereby excluded from access to the joys of the bedroom or the kitchen. Such a role division in some sense parallels the male exclusion from the domestic home if he becomes a warrior, demanding sexual renunciation and asocial loneliness (as with the John Wayne character in *The Searchers*). But often male warriors could come home (after the war was won, for instance) and reassert social power on the domestic front (the James Stewart character in *It's a Wonderful Life* never gets to go to war, but rather must stay in order to hold family and community together). But very often with female depictions the exercise of some form of social power by a woman seems to suggest the necessary sacrifice of private happiness, as if there was an invisible barrier between the public and the private. There is a strong mythic tradition of feminine one-dimensionality that persists in American culture, favoring the domestic role of wife and mother to the exclusion of other role choices, although allowing for a modicum of "power behind the throne" influence as with, say, Nancy Reagan.

Sochen goes further, however, to note that there is in the movies, and the culture, a strong "counter-tradition" in the mythic depiction of women, one that allows for representations of "strong women" who do in fact act outside the home. In some sense, the tradition has always been there, at least in the sense of depictions of women with some form of social competence. For example, Mary Pickford early on experiments with multiple roles on screen; independent characteristics such as "spunk" as exhibited by Lillian Gish in *True Heart Suzie*; or the sexuality of the early vamps such as Theda Bara, or the prototypical flapper, Clara Bow. Such women, however, almost invariably wound up in marital bliss. But it does seem fair to say that the *mythos* of woman in the movies has expanded and complicated over the years. Actresses such as Katherine Hepburn and Bette Davis often portrayed independent women, making pioneering forays into formerly male bastions, including law, sports, and murder. Even with what we might call mythic expansion of female roles in the movies, some traditions remain: women as icons of sexual allure, as "black widows," beautiful prostitutes, erotic innocents, and so on; women as defenders of the home, or as someone whose happiness depends upon her man or children; and, as noted, women who were more like a man, in androgynous or masculine guise. Sochen notes that Sigourney Weaver in *Aliens* displays a complex of traits. Although mythic roles for women in the movies may lack widespread verisimilitude, they may be important in shaping our expectations and focusing our fears and hopes in fantastic settings. The furor over *Thelma and Louise* in 1991 raised again the specter of female aggressiveness in defense of mental and physical integrity, of rebellion against male, and social, violence, and the extent to which women "buddies" forming a female bond can defend themselves in a savage world. In any case, such films indicate that role mythifying about women is an ongoing process in the movies, one with clear political implications.

Movie myth is also expressed in the types of movies which are made. Moviemakers quickly fell into the habit of making films that fit the general conventions of storytelling—adventure, mystery, romance, comedy, epic, and so on. But they also created their own genres with conventions that developed, gave new twists to, spoofed, revived, and nostalgically treasured—the swashbuckler, the Western, the horror film, *film noir*, the musical, the war movie, and so on. These genres have proven to be mythically flexible, being used and reused in response to events, moods, historical changes, foreign or domestic political threats, and the like, but in all cases demonstrating that mythmaking involves using the conventions of myth to continually remake myth. As Harold Schechter and Jonna G. Semeiks point out in their study of "Leatherstocking in 'Nam," Vietnam war movies have participated in mythmaking, indeed with a variety of myths, including the captivity narrative, the myth of the frontier hero, the mytheme of "regeneration through violence," and sentimental care for helpers and women. Some mythmaking about Vietnam may seem to us to be simple-minded and vicariously vengeful, as with the *Rambo* films, but as the authors note, such mythic depictions have roots in popular myth such as the nineteenth-century dime novels. Other depictions, such as *Platoon*, are more complex, yet they too are related to "archetypical narratives" that are understandable as part of our national mythic heritage. Vietnam in the movies became symbolically resolvable at different levels of sophistication and for different perspectives on the meaning of the war. When political tensions over an event like Vietnam are released, we have mythic resources on which we can draw to "frame" the event in a story with mythic resonance. Those tensions that history could not erase nor politics solve then become displaced onto the collective representations we see on screen. What we see with John J. Rambo or the soldiers in the platoon, may be both dream and nightmare, but they are not mere apparitions. The Vietnam movies demonstrate the power of myth and the myth of power. They let us play with an historical experience over which we were unable in fact to affect the outcome, so we translated it into mythic experience. But the movie experience also gave life to our feelings of power or powerlessness about that historical experience. *Rambo* could make us feel momentarily powerful again, but movies like *Platoon* could reinforce our sense of powerlessness to intervene in an historical nightmare. The authors see in movies the interplay of mythic power and powerlessness, and it is no small question to discover to which political condition we as a people feel ourselves drawn when we choose movies. As with deep psychic conflicts over social roles, we seek and find in movie stories myths that tell us who we are, both individually and politically.

THE PRICES OF POWER
Women's Depictions in Film

June Sochen
Northeast Illinois State University

Movies that deal strictly with political themes can safely and legitimately ignore women. After all, in reality, women did not get the vote until 1920, hardly ran for office at any level until the 1960s, and at the end of the 1980s, remained a minor presence in governmental positions. Films reflected this absence of women in positions of political power. Unless the film was science fiction or utopian in its intention, (a rarity in American films), women appeared only in political movies as the wives of the politicians, the secretaries, the clandestine lovers, or the loyal followers. It is only when we broaden the definition of politics to mean power relationships—considerations of who is dominant and who is subordinate—that we can include women in a discussion of politics and the movies. Feminist Kate Millett coined the term "sexual politics" in the 1960s, thereby awakening a generation of thinkers and activists to the connection between sexual relations and power. Since then, the term politics has assumed many new meanings. Within this larger setting, politics becomes a relevant topic for women and the cinematic treatment of women's lives can be interpreted.

Whenever women appear, they do so in relation to others in the film, others who are superior to them in power, some who are inferior, and some others still who are equal. A new awareness, combined with a new measuring stick, enables the critic to study all women's roles in a movie from a political, i.e., power, point of view. This expanded definition of politics, of course, makes the task enormous, if not impossible. The saving grace, though, is that dominant cultural values prevail in all movies and women's roles are determined by those values. Whether we look at melodrama, adventure, or comedy, we find cultural expectations upheld. There are few surprises. Since the dominant cultural values assume that all major power positions have been, and therefore, should be occupied by men, it remains unusual, exceptional, and unique to see women in central roles of power in American life and film.

But the subject is still complicated; power is a complex and multi-faceted phenomenon. Are we discussing intellectual power, financial power, political power, status power, or sexual power? All of these powers, some of them, or only one of them? These questions must be actively analyzed and answered. The common-sensical assumption, when applying these questions to women and power, would be that women have little, if any, power. Only sexual power, both an asset and a deficit within our culture, would apply to women. Women as Eves, temptresses, who beguile and lead innocent males astray is an old image in Western culture, and not a desirable one at that. Indeed, American movies have a long tradition of featuring sultry beauties as sexual predators.[1] Generally, these women received their comeuppance. Greta Garbo, Rita Hayworth, Elizabeth Taylor, just a few of the most famous sex goddesses of earlier years, always received punishment for their sexual attractiveness. If they were the mistresses of powerful men, they ended up alone, on a back street, seduced and abandoned. Their virtues were always deemed vices; their loyalty, beauty, and excitement were viewed suspiciously, and in double standard America, only the men could indulge in passion and never pay a price for their self-indulgence.

Women as sexual power brokers offer little new insight into the larger subject of women and politics in the movies. The formulas within which that subject has been explored were drawn from literature and have had a long and successful life in film and television. The images and the outcomes are rather predictable. Their popularity and the endurance of the image, however, clearly speak to important values/vices/ambiguities in American thought and action; but they remain within the very narrow definition of power previously available to women. After all, Paradise was lost, according to this mythic image, because of woman's sexual power. The fascination with Eve, however, the pull of the illicit, has never abated. Many of the most interesting women film stars built whole careers on variations of that theme.

Greta Garbo, the ultimate romantic heroine, always looked tortured because of the problems in her love life. As Camille, the gorgeous courtesan, she is predeterminately doomed. She is loved, admired, and the recipient of public affection from all, but she must die because of her dissipated and unconventional lifestyle. Bette Davis, especially in the films of the 1930s (before she became the quintessential bitch in the 1940s and 1950s) was usually the gun moll, the whore, the illicit love, whose marginality prevented her from achieving society's greatest reward for women—marriage.

In *Marked Woman* (1937) one of Davis' finest, she played a night club hostess (a euphemism for prostitute) who stood up against the mob owners of the club. She ended up with a slashed face, one of the meanings of marked woman in the film. But she had the opportunity at the movie's conclusion to begin a new life with the aid of the crusading district attorney (played by newcomer Humphrey Bogart). She chose to walk away with her sister whores. She knew, as did the audiences, that she could not change her class or her background. Contrary to the American Dream, 1930s determinism required her to accept her fate as a marked woman and to fade away into the mist.

Although, as wit Oscar Levant has said, Doris Day accomplished the impossible when she went from playing whores to virgins (only in America), most Eves never redeemed themselves, though they may have had more fun than the sweet, virginal Marys. Until quite recently, American movies confirmed the view that women's only hope and claim to power in American culture could be within the province of a successful marriage. Marriage to a wealthy and powerful man conferred status and deferred power upon the wife. Joan Crawford made a career, again in the 1930s, out of being the beautiful but poor woman who used her beauty and charm to marry a rich man. *Mannequin* (1938) is an excellent example of that theme. Thanks to millionaire Spencer Tracy, she escaped an upbringing of poverty, a first marriage to a poor man, and uncertainty, and achieved financial comfort and assured social status. While the poor-girl-who-makes-good theme is fraught with danger (after all, the woman runs the risk of being labelled a golddigger), it can occasionally be carried off successfully. It was also treated humorously in the 1950s with *How to Marry a Millionaire* and *Gentlemen Prefer Blondes*.

In all of these cases, however, women's accession to power was based upon the skillful use of their sexual allure and alleged feminine wiles, traits culturally deemed suspect and somehow unfair. A fine line had to be drawn; a "respectable" woman used her charms discreetly to win over the desired catch while the Eve more blatantly sought her prize. Though sexuality and physical beauty are human traits, they are defined culturally as primarily female powers that are used unfairly in the game of love and life. When men use these very same qualities, a different set of criteria is applied. Men are acting out their natural instincts while women practice cultivated deceits. Surely, more of a commentary on cultural attitudes than on human qualities.

What about the rare times when women possessed some of the other kinds of power, such as financial independence and intellectual self-confidence and competency? How did Hollywood treat women who were decision makers, who received public respect for their roles in society, and who clearly enjoyed the fame and glory accompanying that power? What about movies that featured women as experts in male-defined skills? There have been such movies throughout film history. Seen as exceptional, nevertheless there have been times in movie history when there were sufficient quantities of such movies to describe them as a genre—the independent woman film—and the Golden Age of Hollywood, 1930-1945, was the period when such films flourished.

There were many career women films with women playing doctors, nurses, lawyers, writers, designers, and journalists. There were also many comedies in which aristocratic women led carefree lives precisely because of their financial independence. During the silent era, tomboy adventurers were a prominent type of heroine; the Perils of Pauline serials and the Nancy Drew adventures featured young women experiencing the mystery, excitement, and adventure usually reserved for men. But maturity, presumably, reined in the women and they became lovesick heroines and victims in melodrama.

There are two interconnecting forces that must always be examined when discussing the independent woman genre in Hollywood movies: the social times in which the movies are made and the endurance of the image of a powerful woman. If, as I will argue, the latter image has had a continuous life in American movies, it is only in periods when the current climate of opinion positively supports that image that it flourishes. Otherwise, it is a mere flicker, an occasional film, an occasional star, who plays a strong, spunky woman in a film that becomes known for its exceptional treatment of women. In recent times, and I am anticipating my later discussion, Meryl Streep can play an unusually powerful woman in one film followed by a woman-as-victim or woman-overwhelmed-by-love role.

The price of possessing power, it should be hastily added, has always been high: independent women rarely retained both power and the hero at film's end. It was one or the other, and most heroines chose the hero. Whether the strong-minded heroine was Katharine Hepburn, Barbara Stanwyck, Joan Crawford, or Bette Davis, they found the weight of traditional sex roles too much to overcome permanently; temporarily, they could exhibit freedom, self-assertion, creativity, and public success, but ultimately, they gave in to society's demands for conformity. But the temporary period represented the bulk of the movie and the capitulation only occurred at the end. To most of the women in the audience, and to audiences since, the film's message of independence and power for women overwhelmed the final moment's retreat.

While the Golden Age of independent women on screen was succeeded by a Dark Age, there have been continuous examples, however few, until the present era of that image, with the notable exception of the so-called liberated 1960s. As film critic Molly Haskell has written, from a woman's point of view, that decade ". . . was the most disheartening in screen history." It is indeed a major irony that the period that witnessed the emergence of the women's liberation movement also witnessed the absence of strong, rich portrayals of women on screen. The very turbulence of the times and the public confrontation of the women's liberation theme seemed to frighten Hollywood rather than inspire it to express it on film. But each subsequent generation of women film stars produced some notable examples of independent women on film, movies that matched their formidable personalities.

II

Hollywood filmmakers during the Golden Era sometimes rose above the Eve stereotype to blend it with other human qualities and to create richer, more complex portraits of women, women who could be characterized as powerful in areas other than sexual allure. *Woman of the Year* (1942), the first movie in which Katharine Hepburn and Spencer Tracy starred together, offered a fascinating illustration of how creative adaptation of images, combined with a great script and great actors, could produce an inventive and novel view of women. It also offered audiences an opportunity to witness women in positions of public power. A brief summary of the plot is called for.

Modelled after the real-life story of journalist Dorothy Thompson, Hepburn plays Tess Harding, international journalist, speaker of many languages, party giver, and converser with the elite. Tracy is Sam Craig, the sportswriter on the same newspaper for which Tess Harding writes her brilliant political commentary. Done as a comedy, role reversal becomes the comic tool. Harding as a careerist, an admittedly unusual role for a woman, is hardworking, driving, and serious. Craig's work means baseball games and barrooms, seemingly frivolous and unimportant. While he is thoughtful, considerate, conventional, she initiates the romance, pursues it, and finally wins him over. He insists upon wearing formal garb at their wedding; he calls his mother, gets a recipe book from her, and assumes that the marriage would be traditional. No way. Once she has him, Tess behaves the way a man acts after he has conquered his woman: she ignores him and goes about her business of living an exciting professional life. They learn, at one point in the movie, that they both had been in Chicago at the same time, he for a football game and she for a political meeting, but neither discover this fact until they both return to New York. He is upset that she did not call him at the press room to arrange a meeting while she can not understand why he is so perturbed. The critical moment and turning point of the film comes when Tess surprises her husband with a Greek refugee boy whom she has agreed to raise; her motives, however, are not maternal—as co-chairwoman of the Greek Refugee Committee, she felt obligated to be the first to volunteer her home for a needy child. Her husband objects because of her motives and because he wants a child of their own. But he relents and the child is taken into their home. The maid, however, becomes the child's caretaker as Tess continues unperturbed in her hectic schedule of reporting, writing, and travelling. The night she is to receive the Woman of the Year award Sam refuses to go, and unbeknownst to her, returns the child to the orphanage. He moves out the same evening. Tess then goes to the country for a weekend to witness the marriage of her diplomat widower father to her maternal aunt who had raised her and had epitomized the independent social-welfare type woman. She asks her aunt whether her life has not been a satisfying one; her aunt, articulating the moral of the movie, declares that all of her good works could not replace the love of a man. In old age, her life-long goal of marriage has been finally realized. Tess returns to the city early the next morning and lets herself into her husband's bachelor apartment. The final scene, considered a comic classic in film history, shows Tess Harding, the super-able political columnist, burning the toast, watching the water boil out, and cereal sputtering all over the stove. She is utterly incompetent in the kitchen. Her clatter brings her husband to the kitchen. Tess, reduced to tears of frustration, yields to her husband. They agree that she should not be reduced to Mrs. Craig but should retain her identity as Tess Harding Craig.

Ostensibly, the case for a woman's career seemed to be vindicated in *Woman of the Year*. Tess Harding does not abandon her career at the end of the film. However, how she will reconcile both roles remains unexplained and unexplored. How, indeed, is she to pursue a time-consuming career and keep house and raise children? Further, what possible attraction could homemaking hold for a woman who witnessed historically important events in the making? Tess Harding has a maid and cook which free her from these chores. Is she supposed to fire her domestic help and assume her tasks? What is to happen to her mind and imagination? In a spirit of egalitarianism, does her sports columnist husband agree to share the household chores so that she can continue her career? None of these questions are answered; indeed, they are not even asked in *Woman of the Year*.

Love conquers all in this movie as it did in all the others. Tess Harding's failure in the kitchen is rendered comically. This able, competent woman is viewed as a bumbling idiot where it really counts in our culture for women—in the kitchen. Her husband's love provides her with the needed support and comfort to overcome all obstacles. But during the course of the movie, for over an hour at least, Tess Harding operates in the public arena effectively. She is a powerful woman, until the challenges of domesticity defeat her.

Hepburn's reputation was based upon her career women or aristocratic lady roles. In both cases, she displayed supreme self-confidence during the movie (except briefly in *The Philadelphia Story*) and she was able to mature, though as she aged, the dowager roles obviously increased. But in her prime, she showed competence in the law court (*Adam's Rib*), on the golf course (*Pat and Mike*), and in an airplane (*Christopher Strong*). The public realm, of course, was the male-defined realm. If a culture deems some activity unworthy and useless, it has no power value. So that we continue to return to the fact that both sexes have generally accepted the division of power or rather that power belongs in the public domain, a territory dominated by men. While the woman rules the home, the man controls the pocketbook (until recently) and so has power over purchasing in the home as well.

When Hollywood wanted to venture into daring terrain, they often used sex role reversals as a comic technique. As already suggested, this allowed filmmakers to broach forbidden subjects with impunity. Rosalind Russell, who played twenty-three career women roles in the late 1930s and 1940s, also was an expert comic actress. In *Take A Letter, Darling* (1942), she plays a successful advertising executive. As A.M. MacGregor, she is a no-nonsense careerist whose partner, played by Robert Benchley, spends all of his time playing games in his office. A.M., however, needs a male secretary to act as her escort when she has to entertain clients, since the wives of her clients look unkindly on "business" dinners between their husbands and the attractive A.M. Fred MacMurray, an unemployed artist whose independent income has dried up, desperately needs a job. Though very reluctant, he accepts the position after being reassured that it is strictly business. A nice piece of sex role reversal. Throughout the film, references are made to the unusual situation: a successful woman business executive and a male secretary; neither knows how to behave in these extraordinary circumstances. At one point, A.M. says "A woman in business faces many problems that men don't face; in fact, one of them is men." After asking him whether he finds her attractive and receiving a negative reply, she gives him a raise. But the undercurrent of attractiveness, of physical appeal between them, continues to manifest itself. He assures himself that she is a "beautiful brain, beautiful clothes, no temperature, no pulse." Just as Tess Harding is not a woman at all, because she has neither the maternal nor the domestic instinct, so A.M. is not a woman because she displays no temperament, no emotion.

The plot takes many comic turns with each of them becoming involved with other partners only to fall into each other's arms at movie's end. How they will resolve their differences (he wants to go to Mexico to paint) is not attempted. After all, the implicit message in this most Hollywood of productions is that love is a solution to all of life's problems. When the couple embraces before the final curtain, the shared assumption is that knotty problems disappear. Perhaps it is no accident that this movie, like *Woman of the Year*, came out during the war and offered solace to all viewers. Traditional values will be preserved, held in check, and become functional once the troops return and true love can resume its natural course. But during the course of the film, audiences were treated to women decision makers, women bosses, and men who listened when women spoke.

Both *Take a Letter, Darling* and *Woman of the Year* illustrate the close and intricate connection between American cultural events and movie topics. In the 1930s and through World War II, strength in women was a valued trait. The struggles of the Depression required women to keep the home fires burning, the family together, and the creditors at bay. When war preparations were being made, women became primary recruits for the twenty-four-hour-a-day defense factories. Suddenly, a new image, Rosie the Riveter, became a popular and desirable one for women. Imagine women working a heavy duty crane. During exceptional times, exceptional things were demanded of everyone, including women. Thus, filmic depictions of strong women, even self-sufficient women, were acceptable. The successful careers of Hepburn, Davis, Russell and Stanwyck attest to the audience acceptance of this new image of women in film. Women in power, however, were seen as temporary expedients, necessities in difficult times, surely not desirable patterns for permanent adoption. For a brief historical moment, during the depths of two crises (the Depression and World War Two), women were given permission to enter the public realm where various forms of power were exercised.

But since 1945, there has largely been a return to status quo ante crises. The romantic Eve and the sweet Mary have returned and have dominated filmic images of women. As already suggested, the 1960s largely ignored women and as film critic Pauline Kael noted, the romantic duo of the 1960s became Newman and Redford. So even in the sacred realm of love and romance, women were replaced by buddies. The 1970s promised a change in the dismal state of affairs that had dominated the 1945-70 period but the promise went largely unfulfilled.

The careers of Jane Fonda and Barbra Streisand offer interesting evidence to support this generalization. Fonda, whose film career began in the early 1960s, played all of the primary images of women: she was the sweet teenager in *Tall Story* (1960), followed by a series of Eve-like roles including *Walk on the Wild Side* (1962), *The Chapman Report*

(1962), *Any Wednesday* (1966) and finally *Klute* (1971) when she won the Academy Award for her portrayal of a high class prostitute who goes to a psychiatrist to work out her problems. From no power as a Sweet Mary to the display of sexual power/powerlessness as an Eve, Fonda became an established star. During the early 1970s, however, she became politically active, travelled to North Vietnam, and lectured around the country against the American involvement in Vietnam. As a result, she was labelled box office poison.

It was not until *Fun With Dick and Jane* in 1977 that her film career got back on track. In a comedy, very much contradicting her earlier image, Fonda showed audiences her lighter side and was rewarded with box office approval. In the late 1970s, she made a number of movies that depicted her as the Independent Woman, reminiscent of the image and genre of an earlier period. In *Julia* (1977), *Comes A Horseman* (1978), *China Syndrome* (1979), and *Electric Horseman* (1979) she played a writer, a rancher, and two reporters respectively, all roles that would have been familiar to Barbara Stanwyck, Katharine Hepburn, and Rosalind Russell. So Fonda's late seventies films qualify as positive examples of the fragile continuation of the Independent Woman film genre. Because women in their forties remain physically attractive (and Fonda, of course, has created a mini-industry with her physical fitness videos and books), she could play attractive and desirable heroines at a point in her career when earlier generations of women stars would have been considered over the hill.

Fonda's screen career is an interesting case in which to discuss the relationship between women and power. When a real-life woman exhibits power, she is often treated with derision; because of Fonda's cinematic popularity, her anti-war speeches and actions received a lot of media coverage. Because she took an unpopular position, her fans turned against her, or at least Hollywood showed no interest in producing her films. The 1970s, in sharp contrast to the 1930-1945 period, experienced a different kind of cultural shock; Americans had to come to terms with a losing and unpopular war precisely when a large number of young people began declaring their liberation from traditional college curricula, the draft, sexism, and various other forms of oppression. Jane Fonda became an individual and a symbol whose presence was unwelcome on the silver screen. She stood for too many aggravating real-life issues. The happy and simple (minded) resolutions of Hollywood movies of the 1930s no longer worked. The power of women, once exposed, could not be hidden anymore. Perhaps Hepburn and Russell accepted their reduced status goodnaturedly in 1942 but audiences knew that Fonda would not be able to, nor would she be credible, in stereotypical Eve or Mary roles. By 1977, the U.S. had left Vietnam and Americans had become more comfortable with the idea of feminism. Indeed, the feminists had softened their image as well and the career roles of Fonda seemed to fit in with the new realities of the late 1970s.

Besides the cultural anger and the split opinions over Vietnam, in the late 1960s and early 1970s, Hollywood did not know how to deal with the women's liberation movement. In *Up the Sandbox* (1972), for example, Barbra Streisand brought the feminist heroine of Anne Roiphe's novel to life on the screen only to encounter indifference from her usually loyal audience. The daily fantasies and imaginings of a housewife-mother, difficult to translate to the movies, contributed to the movie's lack of success. But surely the general topic also put off many people. Who wanted to watch a woman complain about the confining nature of her domestic life? When questioned by feminists as to why so few movies were being made on the women's liberation movement, Hollywood producers mumbled and claimed that the subject was too controversial and current to be depicted on film.

The following year, however, Streisand discovered the magic formula for success. She took no chances. In addition to a marvelous musical score, a strong script and director, she starred with Robert Redford as her leading man. *The Way We Were* (1973) became a big box office success while dealing with a very important social theme. The most exciting aspect of the film, from the feminist perspective of course, was the fact that the central character was a woman coming of age on a college campus during the 1930s; the movie showed her grow, fall in love, mature, and reject the man of her dreams because his politics were too conservative. With the backdrop of New Deal politics at the beginning of the movie and the blacklisting of leftists in Hollywood near the end, the love story of Streisand and Redford provided the exciting center. *The Way We Were* becomes a rich, unusual example of a movie that combines at least three genres: the romance, the independent woman film, and the social consciousness film.

Katie, the Streisand character in the movie, exhibits a rare kind of human power—intellectual power to sway people to her causes. Though usually unsuccessful, the power of her idealistic words moves students and friends. The very idea of seeing a heroine act as the chief speaker for humanistic and socialistic ideas in a serious film marks *The Way We Were* as an exciting, albeit exceptional, departure from most formula films. The acting power of Streisand allows audiences to take her seriously and to consider the worthiness of her thoughts. She performs ably as a woman reformer, a type rarely projected on the screen, and one with few imitators. Indeed, one of its worthy predecessors was Hepburn's portrayal of a women's rights activist in *A Woman Rebels* (1936), a film that was not warmly received by audiences in that era.

The multitalented Streisand returned to comedy movies as well as melodramas. Her most ambitious recent film project, *Yentl* (1983), a movie she produced, directed, and starred in, captured many of the themes of the independent woman genre. Accompanied by a lush musical score, Streisand plays a Jewish girl in a traditional shtetl (ghetto) in Eastern Europe early in the century. As a daughter of a learned man, she is expected to be obedient, dutiful, and guided by her father's directives. When he dies, Yentl decides to pursue her lifelong yearning for scholarship; she disguises herself as a young man, travels to a yeshiva where no one knows her, and becomes a student in a male-only setting. When one of her fellow students falls in love with her (as does that student's fiancé), the plot becomes very complicated. She resolves the problem by sailing for America.

The power of learning, held in great esteem in Judaism but generally accorded only to men, is a powerful theme and one which *Yentl* portrays sensitively and effectively. Though audiences liked the movie and it became a major success in foreign markets as well as on video cassette, the critics panned it and the Motion Picture Academy ignored it on Awards night. Was Streisand guilty of *hubris*? Was she arrogant in her invasion of the male domain? After all, Hollywood studio executives, producers, and directors are still overwhelmingly male. Had she insulted their comfortable establishment? Many feminists thought so. Though the viewer surely had to suspend disbelief to accept Streisand as a young man, and assume her fellow students also did the same, the renderings of the yeshiva, the family home scenes, and the musical thoughts of *Yentl* made the movie an absorbing and entertaining movie experience, at least for this writer.

The interweaving of current events and movie subjects keeps intruding itself upon our consciousness. Just as strength was an admired trait during the stressful thirties, so women's independence became a much discussed and stressful topic in the 1970s and 1980s. Try as they might, movie makers could not entirely ignore the subject. True, they preferred resolutions that upheld the status quo. Hepburn fell into Tracy's arms. But in the more open 1970s and 1980s, could that ending hold? Streisand left Redford and sunny California in *The Way We Were* for ardent, crusade-oriented New York. Yentl left the student she loved for America rather than reveal her true being to him and thereby upsetting and outraging him and the community. In both cases, Streisand preserved her independence and integrity. She did not subsume her beliefs, compromise her principles, or abandon her causes. In order to go on learning, this time as a woman, Yentl sailed for New York and freedom. The theme of women's independence was not compromised at the film's end. This is a major difference from the genre films of the Golden Era.

While we can applaud the preservation of integrity in recent films depicting women of power, they are few in number and often far between each other. Whereas Rosalind Russell played in twenty-three career women films, Hepburn did almost an equal number, as did many other strong women stars of the earlier period, there are fewer women stars and fewer films of that type in recent years. The economics of moviemaking, of course, plays a major role, but the priorities, based upon values and attitudes, also contribute. Crime and adventure movies, after all, continue to be made as do horror films. The fact that women's films, especially those that portray powerful women, are so few speaks to the continued unwillingness of Americans to consider the multiple meanings of women's independence.

It is not because there are no strong women stars. Coming of age in the 1970s were such actresses as Jill Clayburgh, Diane Keaton, Ellen Burstyn, Sally Field, Jessica Lange, Kathleen Turner, and perhaps this generation's Hepburn, Meryl Streep. Behind them is another generation of younger stars such as Debra Winger, Molly Ringwald, and Ally Sheedy. Yet few of them have starred in career women films or any kind of film that depicts powerful women. Surely there have been notable exceptions to this generalization. Meryl Streep's performance as Karen Blixen in *Out of Africa* (1987) qualifies as a stunning performance in an epic film (Redford present) about a woman who surmounts major obstacles while engaging in a great love affair.

Jill Clayburgh had a brief series of films in the late 1970s and early 1980s that fit into the independent woman genre. *An Unmarried Woman*, *Starting Over*, *It's My Turn*, and *First Monday in October* all dealt with innovative themes and women either struggling to become whole or already exhibiting qualities of autonomy. *An Unmarried Woman* (1974) was one of the first movies to deal with the emotional damage done to a woman after her husband walks out on her for a younger woman. The importance of female friendships is also effectively portrayed in this film, a subject that is usually absent in Hollywood movies. Women in romance movies are always rivals, never friends. She rebuilds her life and though a new romantic interest surely accelerates her cure, the movie deals sympathetically with the process of reconstructing her life after divorce. The multiple meaning of selfhood, the essential first step toward autonomy and power, was a theme many women expected Hollywood to explore during the 1970s. The fact that there were so few examples spoke volumes about their attitudes to women's struggles for power.

In *It's My Turn*, the least successful at the box office of these films, Clayburgh was directed by a woman, Claudia Weill, another distinctive feature. The movie deals with a successful career woman who is searching for a new lover in order to improve her personal life. While such a subject would be considered usual if the central character were male, the sex role reversal discomfited traditional audiences. *First Monday in October* tells the story of the first woman justice of the Supreme Court, a conservative who locks horns with the Court's leading liberal (played by Walter Matthau). In recent years, Clayburgh has been absent from the screen. The lack of strong, challenging scripts may well be the reason.

Because there have been so few movies portraying women in positions of strength and importance, they stand out when they do appear. *Aliens* (1986), starring Sigourney Weaver as the only survivor of an earlier exploration of an outer space colony, is an unlikely candidate for inclusion in the genre but it fits. Weaver displays the qualities most admired by men and women: she is a cool professional, capable of learning intricate information, calm under pressure, and loving when caring for the child, the only survivor they find upon their return to the colony. Weaver exhibits maternal, masculine, and human traits; she demonstrates the humanness of the intellect and all emotions. Perhaps because this film is categorized as a science fiction adventure, all roles become possible to members of both sexes. One of the most aggressive soldiers on the mission is a woman. *Aliens* offers audiences a satisfying opportunity to see a woman in charge who remains a warm, loving person, ever mindful of her enormous responsibilities. (She has to bring the spaceship back to earth with the wounded and survivors.)

III

In a recent essay on women's films, Molly Haskell suggested that there seemed to be more of a tendency to put strong women down today than had been the case in the 1930s and 1940s. The reason, she suggested, was that ". . . there are more of us who want to 'do it all' or 'have it all', and more areas in which to feel anxious and inadequate." This view would also suggest the complex interaction that exists between social reality and filmic reality. If the current generation of real-life women are experiencing more power, freedom, and influence in the marketplace and in the home, they are also feeling more tension and uncertainty about their ability to do it all. This anxiety and insecurity cannot be ably or simply described on film, so the subject is ignored on the screen. Indeed, Haskell suggested three ways that Hollywood has dealt with women's newfound power in recent years: they have ignored it, substituted nymphet films for women's movies, and used men to deal with domestic issues usually ascribed to women. *Kramer vs. Kramer* is the example given to support this argument.

Genre films, and most films fit into one formula or another, maintain their powerful and successful hold on audiences for good and legitimate reasons: they deal with universal, compelling themes. Love and marriage remain vital concerns for women and men; indeed, in the ill-defined and therefore perilous 1980s, romance becomes a more problematic subject than in the surer 1930s. Courtship patterns are nonexistent and the rules no longer exist. Sexual openness only complicates the problem. Thus, moviemakers show youth's anxieties and problems, with few happy resolutions. The teenager and young adult coming-of-age movies that have dominated in recent years reflect the concerns of this large moviegoing audience. This introduces another practical factor into the equation. While women and children went to the movies in the 1930s, and women dominated the audience during World War Two, the post-1970 audience is young men, ages 14 to 24.

The genres they are most interested in are adventure and sex comedies. It is the hero's problems and adventures they want to watch, not the young or older woman's troubles described in detail. Thus, the combination of a new demographic reality, a social period of confusion regarding personal relationships, and the economics of filmmaking, makes for fewer roles available for women and fewer still that depict powerful women.

Many actresses, when interviewed on the subject of the roles available for them, assert their right to play any and all parts. They interpret feminism to mean the right to play strong, weak, and/or indecisive women. The freedom to play any and all genres, then, rather than ideology, determines their choice of parts. Feminist Jane Fonda, when asked why she played a down and out drunk in *The Morning After* (1986) said: "... I was getting a little angry at the idea that all of my roles had to be role models or uplifting examples of exemplary behavior. I'm an actress. I like to play all kinds of women."

Have we come full circle? Or has the circle been eliminated? While strong women roles seemed compatible with cultural needs in the 1930s, that need was reinterpreted as dangerous strength in post-1945 America. Strength and independence became subversive qualities in a country committed to returning to domesticity. Since women's strength had been seen as a temporary necessity, indeed, turning adversity into survivability, it had to be returned to its mysterious reservoir, only to be taken out again in times of emergency. But the ideological revolution of the 1960s suggested that women's strength was a permanent necessity and though many people did not welcome or accept the message, it could not be entirely eliminated from public consciousness. Haskell suggested that women's coming-of-age stories needed telling as did women's struggles with both internal and external enemies. Neither heroine nor victim, women's lives needed cinematic presentations. But who would tell their stories? In the heyday of feminism, it was assumed that feminist-conscious actresses, writers, directors, and producers would only engage in film projects that portrayed women in their diversity; today it is not clear what that means. Some women are strong, others are weak; some funny and some serious and neurotic, just like men.

Whereas compensatory women's history writing has been replaced by an effort to recreate the historical circumstances under which women lived (which often results in a woman-as-victim portrayal), this viewpoint continues to draw criticism from other camps of feminist thought. So filmmakers, representing a variety of attitudes toward independent women, make various efforts, some weak and some strong.

Perhaps the major culprit is the taste of the dominant moviegoing audience, or is it the unexamined assumptions of the filmmakers, or maybe the confused message of feminism? Or perhaps all of these factors contribute to the poor showing women receive in American movies. Or perhaps they reflect the poor showing women still receive in American life.

NOTES

1. See June Sochen, *Enduring Values: Women in Popular Culture*, Chapter Three, "Filmic Images of Women" (New York: Praeger Publishers, 1987).

2. See June Sochen, "Mildred Pierce and Women in Film", *American Quarterly*, Spring, 1978.

3. Ibid.

4. Molly Haskell, *From Reverence to Rape* (New York: Holt, Rinehart, and Winston, 1974), p.323.

5. Molly Haskell, "Women in the Movies Grow Up", *Psychology Today* (January, 1983): pp.18-27.

6. Ibid, p.20.

7. Roger Ebert, " 'Morning After' Is Murder for Fonda," *Chicago Sun-Times*, Show Section, December 14, 1986, p.3.

LEATHERSTOCKING IN 'NAM
Rambo, *Platoon*, and the American Frontier Myth

Harold Schechter
Jonna G. Semeiks
State University of New York

"The figure and the myth—narrative that emerged from the early Boone literature became archetypal for the American literature which followed: an American hero is the love of the wilderness, and his acts of love and sacred affirmation are acts of violence against that spirit and her avatars."
Richard Slotkin

For a decade following the pullout of American troops from Saigon, the supercharged subject of the Vietnam War was handled warily—when it was dealt with at all—by the Hollywood movie establishment. To be sure, the occasional auteur would be allowed to try his hand at using Vietnam as a metaphor for Something Significant. *The Deer Hunter* (1978) and *Apocalypse Now* (1979) even did respectable business. But for the most part, cinematic depictions of America's most unpopular war were regarded as box-office poison.

That perception has undergone a complete turnabout during the past few years, thanks to the success of two films, *Rambo: First Blood, Part II* (1985) and *Platoon* (1986), both of which broke the magic $100 million mark which separates the megahit from the mere blockbuster. In terms of style, sensibility, and political viewpoint, it would be hard to conceive of two war movies more antithetical than this pair. A high-velocity action film in which Sly Stallone (equipped with only a survival knife, a sheaf of exploding arrows, and a state-of-the-art physique) returns to Southeast Asia on a mission to rescue captive MIAs, *Rambo* was widely denounced for its rampaging narcissism, rabid anti-Communism and shameless rewriting of our recent history (in this cinematic wish-fulfillment fantasy, America gets to go back and finish the war that the bleeding hearts and the bureaucrats wouldn't let us win the first time around). That a movie as violent and one-dimensional as *Rambo* became the top-grossing film of the year was, in the eyes of many critics, depressing confirmation of the troglodyte taste of the mass audience, as well as of its steadfast refusal to face the inglorious truth about our involvement in Vietnam.

As a result, the phenomenal success of Oliver Stone's *Platoon* left the pundits in a state of some perplexity. Before its opening, Hollywood insiders expected Stone's low-budget picture to be, at best, a *success d'éstimé*. According to the conventional wisdom, no movie as serious, not to say grim, as this searing, semi-autobiographical film could possibly attract a large audience. The reviews, many of which hailed *Platoon* not only as the first honest film about Vietnam but as the best movie about any war ever made, came as no surprise. But when the box-office receipts started piling up, the critics—who had already pegged the moviegoing public as a bunch of political neanderthals, based on their response to *Rambo*—had to search around for some convincing explanation.

Typical of these attempts was the *Time* magazine cover story on *Platoon* in which Richard Corliss, citing Jean-Luc Godard's dictum that "when a good film is also a popular film it is because of a misunderstanding," attributes the success of Stone's movie to its misperception as an action picture.[1] It seems to us, however, that if anyone has missed the meaning of *Platoon*—and of *Rambo*, too, for that matter—it is not the ticket-buying public but the critics themselves. In the end, the appeal of these movies has very little to do, we believe, with either their politics or pyrotechnics. Rather, it derives from their skillful retelling of an archetypal narrative that has always exerted a powerful grip on our collective imagination and that Richard Slotkin, in his indispensable study of the American myth of the frontier-warrior, calls "regeneration through violence." In spite of the striking stylistic difference between Stallone's comic-book fantasy and Stone's quasi-documentary film, each is, in essence, a modern day variant of this deeply compelling "myth-narrative"—an archetypically American frontier adventure transposed to the jungles of Vietnam.

II

To most first-time viewers—and to many combat vets as well, who have testified to the film's verisimilitude—the most striking aspect of *Platoon* is its air of authenticity. Unlike Coppola's Conradian epic or Cimino's paean to blue-collar buddyhood, *Platoon* has the texture of a film made by someone who was there. And indeed, the movie's intense realism is a reflection not only of Stone's own military experiences but also of the uncompromising standards of the movie's technical advisor, a former Marine drill instructor who subjected the actors to a few torturous weeks of survival training in the Philippine jungles before filming began.

No other movie has captured so convincingly the look and feel of the Vietnam war. The beautiful but perilous jungle is glimpsed up close, through the lowly grunts' eyes. Exhausted soldiers sleep in the driving rain, faces pressed into the mud. They pluck leeches and biting ants from their skin. Wounded in battle, they learn to stuff their intestines quickly back into their bellies. The violence of the Vietnam "conflict" is portrayed in all its savagery and lunacy. We see an American soldier slicing a souvenir ear from the corpse of an enemy soldier. Another shoots a peasant woman point blank because he is irritated by the sound of her weeping. Inexperienced officers draw down bomber attacks on their own troops, and disgruntled G.I.s casually discuss "fragging" their leaders. With the exception of those characters in the film who are crazy or brutal enough to like Vietnam, it is clear that the soldiers strive for only one thing: to do their time, like convicts, and get out. In all these ways, *Platoon* recalls not the romanticism or jingoism of films made about earlier American wars but rather the grim realism of a documentary like Peter Davis' *Hearts and Minds* or a quasi-journalistic work like Michael Herr's *Dispatches*.

There is no doubt, then, about the fierce authenticity of *Platoon*. Nor about Stone's skill at making the dangers, discomforts, and outright horrors of Vietnam intensely real and palpable. Still, the average American moviegoer is not known for a willingness to spend five bucks at the local multiplex for the pleasure of experiencing two hours of living through hell. Though the film's uncompromising accuracy unquestionably contributes to its impact, its phenomenal popularity—its power to attract a mass audience—must be traced to another source.

Stone himself provides an important clue in the *Time* magazine cover piece on his movie, where he recalls a comment made by his father shortly before the latter's death, "He said, 'You'll do all right. There'll always be a demand for great stories and great storytellers.' "[2] We take it as axiomatic that (to modify Godard's formulation) when a good movie becomes, that it is because whatever other virtues the film may possess its dominant characteristic is a strong, compelling storyline. *Platoon* is built around such a plotline; it is, in fact, a cinematic version of a story that has been a favorite of American audiences since our fiction began.

It is not to detract from Stone's achievement to say that he is, at base, a pop entertainer, adept at embodying significant issues in the form of slick, briskly paced narratives. His artistic ambitions (or pretensions, depending on your point of view) are made clear in *Platoon*'s various allusions to classic works of American fiction, among them *The Sun Also Rises*, *Billy Budd*, and—most explicitly—*Moby Dick* ("Barnes was at the eye of our rage" says the protagonist in one of the film's periodic voice-overs. "And through him, our Captain Ahab, we would set things right again").[3] The true fictional antecedents of *Platoon*, however, are not the literary masterpieces that the screenplay so self-consciously invokes but rather those quintessentially American fables, running from Charles Brockden Brown's *Edgar Huntly* through James Dickey's *Deliverance*, centering on civilized heroes who undergo a deep inner transformation through their descent into a terrifyingly savage wilderness.

These are the stories which embody the motif that Slotkin (deriving the phrase from William Carlos Williams' meditation on Daniel Boone) calls "regeneration through violence." A specifically American variant of the universal hero-myth (whose features have been made known to the larger public by the work of Joseph Campbell), this motif involves a respectable, law-abiding individual—a solid citizen—who, in Slotkin's words, "embarks on a quest that takes him, figuratively or literally, back in time into a primitive world and downward into his own consciousness, until the basic or primitive core of the psyche is revealed" (308).

This formula precisely matches the action of *Platoon*. Chris Taylor, the hero and narrator of the film, is a fictionalized version of Stone himself, a freshly scrubbed youth from a privileged background who drops out of college to experience firsthand "the war of his generation." In comparison to the underclass "grunts" and social misfits who make up the rest of his outfit, Chris, cleancut and bookish, seems like a slumming preppie. In short, like Brown's Edgar Huntly and Dickey's Ed Gentry, Chris is representative of civilized values and beliefs, a sober and reflective individual who has never known madness or violence.

The basic pattern of the quest, as Joseph Campbell defines it, is "separation—initiation—return."[4] Following the archetypal formula, *Platoon* begins with the hero's passage from "the world of common day"[5] as we see Chris disgorged from the womblike hold of a military transport plane. Indeed, precisely because his life has been so sheltered, Chris' departure from "the World" (as the G.I.s refer to the United States) is an even more radical separation from normalcy than that of his mates, whose lives, we are led to believe, have been grim even in America. It is significant that, for all the similarities between the filmmaker and his fictional surrogate, in actuality Stone had been living in Asia for two years before joining the army. In this film, however, he has Chris Taylor arrive in Vietnam straight from the stultifying comforts of his upper-middle class life, thus heightening the initiatory character of the narrative.

The second stage of the adventure—the passage into and through the heart of darkness—likewise assumes a typically American form in *Platoon*. Like so many of his fictional forebears, Chris undertakes a night journey into a barbaric wilderness, here represented not by the deep forests of the American frontier but by their latterday counterpart, the impenetrable jungles of "the Nam." That Stone, in conceiving the film, saw it from the start as an archetypal rite-of-passage story is made clear in his preface to the published screenplay of *Platoon*. Discussing the real-life prototypes of the movie's antithetical father figures, the valiant Sergeant Elias and his nemesis, the scarred and soul-dead Sergeant Barnes, Stone writes:

> It was from these roots that the essential conflict between
> Elias and Barnes grew in my mind. . . . And I would act

as ... the observer, caught between those giant forces. At first
a watcher. Then forced to act—to take responsibility and a
moral stand. And in the process grow to a manhood I'd never
dreamed I'd have to grow to. To a place where in order to go
on existing I'd have to shed the innocence and accept the evil
the ... gods had thrown out into the world. ... To move from
this East Coast social product to a more visceral manhood.[6]

The film itself underscores this thematic intent with various references
to underworld journeys and rebirths. At one point, for example, as Chris
sits in a jungle downpour composing one of the various letters to his
grandmother that serve as a running commentary on the action of the
film, he describes his experience in archetypal terms, as a process of
descent, self-discovery, and transformation:

Well here I am—anonymous all right, with guys nobody really
cares about . . . They're the backbone of this country,
grandma, the best I've ever seen, the heart and soul. Maybe
I've finally found it, way down here in the mud. Maybe from
down here I can start up again—be something I can be proud
of, without having to fake it, be a fake human being. Maybe
I can see something I don't yet see, learn something I don't
yet know."

The trip to the underworld is portrayed even more explicitly in a
later scene, where Chris is inducted into the realm of the "heads"—the
"hippie, dope-smoking" members of the platoon whose "progressive"
values are actively antagonistic to those of their right-wing brothers,
"the lifers, the juicers, and the moron white element," including hard-
core killers like Barnes and the psychopathic Bunny. Stone's stage
directions describe Chris' first trip into this shadowy lair as a classic
descent into Hades, complete with threshold guardian, initiatory guide,
and lord of the underworld:

INT: UNDERWORLD HUTCH—NIGHT

King leads Chris down to a specially constructed cellar-like hutch dug deep into the ground on an isolated edge of the battalion perimeter. Ammo casings and canvas are piled over it, and sandbags surround it. From the outside very little sound can be heard as they go through a trap door made of ammo crates. Past a lookout pulling security (Adams), hitting a joint but alert. King motions to him, it's cool.

Inside is another world. Chris looking around, amazed it's like a private cabaret for 'heads' who are there cooling out . . .

To Chris it is a new world. And Rhah, the resident head, sitting there in all his finery puffing a huge burning red bowl in a three foot long Montagnard pipe, seems to be the lord of final judgement in this smoky underworld.[7]

"Whatcha doing in the underworld, Taylor?" inquires Rhah—to which Chris' guide, King, replies, "This ain't Taylor. Taylor been shot. This man Chris been resurrected."

Structurally, *Platoon* is a straightforward charting of its hero's "regeneration through violence." The narrative is organized around four combat patrols, each of which leads Chris deeper into the hell of the Vietnam jungle and one step closer to his ultimate confrontation with "the primitive core" of his psyche. Beginning with his maiden outing, when Elias empties the rookie's backpack of superfluous baggage, including several heavy, hardbound books, Chris is inexorably stripped of his civilized trappings and transformed into a killer.

The final stage of that metamorphosis is reached on the morning after the climactic firefight, when Chris coolly murders his brutal mentor, the desperately wounded Sergeant Barnes. In performing this cold-blooded deed, Chris (whom Barnes had earlier cut on the face, branding the boy with the mark of his own disfigurement) is acting in the spirit of Barnes himself. The hero has, in effect, become Barnes (or, to put it another way, he had discovered and released those dark, violent energies—that shadow self—symbolized by Barnes). This episode represents that culminating moment of the quest which Campbell describes as the hero's recognition of and identification with the father; it is "at-one-ment with the father" with a vengeance.[8]

By the end of the film, Chris' regeneration is complete. From a strictly civilized soul—the sort of young man who had never committed an act of violence, who had never (in Charles Brockden Brown's colorful phraseology) "imbrued his hands in the blood of his fellowmen"—he has been transformed into a wilderness warrior, a gun-toting avenger: i.e., into an archetypal American hero. In short, what we have in *Platoon* is a post-Vietnam reinvention of a central American myth. Chris' closing words, which we hear over the noise of the chopper that is bearing him out of the inferno he has entered and survived, reveal that, like all successful heroes of the quest, he is returning to "the World," ready "to teach the lesson he has learned of life renewed":[9]

> The war is over for me now, but it will always be there the rest of my days. As I am sure Elias will be, fighting with Barnes for what Rhah called possession of my soul. There are times since I have felt like the child born of those two fathers. But be that is it may, those of us who did make it have an obligation to build again, to teach others what we know and to try with what's left of our lives to find a goodness and meaning to this life.

III

Perhaps even more than *Platoon*, the much-reviled *Rambo* is a prime example of an all-American frontier adventure, a fact recognized by several commentators, including *Newsweek*'s Peter Goldman, who, in a 1985 cover story on the *Rocky/Rambo* phenomenon, observes of these characters that they "descend from a long bloodline of warrior heroes in American popular culture . . . .They date at least to the Minutemen, to Davy Crockett and Dan'l Boone."[10] Indeed, *Rambo* is nothing more nor less than a trendy incarnation of the traditional frontier hero—Leatherstocking on steroids—and the film itself simply an old-fashioned captivity narrative retooled for the Age of Reagan, with Reds substituting for redskins and enfeebled POWs for helpless white women and children.

Like many quest myths, *Rambo* opens in a wasteland—in this case, the sun-bleached rockpile where the hero has been sentenced to five years of hard labor for having wiped out the better part of a small-town police force in his previous screen appearance. *Rambo*'s "call to adventure" comes in the form of a visit by his Green Beret mentor, Colonel Trautman, who holds out the hope of a Presidential pardon if his prize pupil will agree to return to Vietnam on a one-man POW recovery mission. The adventure proper begins in the traditional way, with the hero making a descent (in this case a very literal one, via parachute) into a primitive, peril-filled wilderness.

Indeed, this return to the primitive commences even before Rambo hits the ground. As he leaps from the plane, his chute gets snagged in the hatchway. Heavily laden with a pack full of "ultramodern" equipment, Rambo dangles in the air, dangerously close to one of the engines, until he frees his knife and jettisons his gear. Thus, by the time Rambo reaches the jungle floor, he has completely shed his high-tech accouterments and must rely on the classic tools of the American Indian warrior: bow-and-arrow, sheath knife, and superior woodcraft.

This kind of reversion is a characteristic feature of the frontier hero myth, one that extends back to its earliest formulation in John Filson's "The Adventure of Col. Daniel Boone." Discussing Filson's seminal text, Richard Slotkin observes that "Boone's initiation into knowledge of the wilderness cannot be accomplished . . . while even one civilized amenity remains to him. He must be stripped to the barest essentials for survival in order to meet nature directly and without encumbrances."[11]

Indeed, many of the traits that Slotkin identifies as the defining features of Boone's character are equally integral to Rambo's: e.g., the hero's stoicism and solitude; his "love of exploit and violence for the sake of blood-stirring excitement"; his "career of semi-nomadic wandering" (when asked how he has spent his life since the war, Rambo replies, "I've moved around a lot"); his "kinship (with) the Indian" (Rambo is, we learn early in the film, the child of a German father and an American Indian mother); his "sense of identification with the land" Rambo is capable of merging so completely with the wilderness that, at one point, he renders himself invisible by blending into a mud bank.[12]

Like Daniel Boone—who is distinguished from the Indians by his "sentimental concern for women"[13] —Rambo displays a tender regard for the opposite sex which is in marked contrast to the brutish behavior of the enemy. Whereas the latter use women strictly as whores, Rambo not only exchanges a chaste kiss with the lovely Vietnamese woman who serves as his guide but also agrees to take her with him to America (whereupon—predictably enough—she is instantly struck by a bullet). Slotkin also notes of Filson's Boone that his "character . . . lies somewhere between the brutality of the savage and the passive orderliness of the good Quaker"[14]—a singular combination of savagery and spirituality that is also shared by Rambo (though this aspect of his character is not made explicit until *Rambo III*, which opens with a sequence in which we see our hero dividing his time between a Buddhist monastery and a Bangkok warehouse, where he picks up extra cash as a professional stick fighter).

The immense popularity of *Rambo*, however, has as much to do with its plot as with its protagonist. With the intuitive genius of the born storyteller, Stallone (who is credited as the primary writer of *Rambo*) has hit upon the perfect vehicle for his warrior hero—the captivity adventure. The movie contains all the major features of this favorite American genre: the singlehanded rescue of the helpless victims, the hero's own capture, torture, and escape, thrilling pursuits, awesome displays of the hero's wilderness skills, and so on. The primary difference between *Rambo* and a classic captivity film like John Ford's *The Searchers* is that the former dispenses with all those extraneous elements—thematic complexity, psychological depth, artful cinematography, characterization—that don't directly contribute to the action. Indeed, anyone seeking to understand why the traditional cowboy movie has become obsolete need look no further than *Rambo*. For an audience grown accustomed to this level of turbocharged entertainment—to the high-powered thrills, hyperkinetic pace, and nonstop, ratatat action of a *Rambo* or a *Road Warrior* or a *Terminator*—even the wildest Western has to seem woefully slow-moving and tame. Horses simply don't move fast enough, nor can six-shooters possibly deliver the requisite firepower. In short, what Stallone has done in *Rambo* is to create a state-of-the-art action movie by adapting the conventions of the captivity narrative to the demands (and attention span) of the contemporary audience.

To be sure, this accomplishment might seem like the worst form of pandering. But after all, *Rambo* is no more mindless than the most nineteenth-century dime novels, such as Edward Ellis' popular *Seth Jones*, or *The Captives of the Frontier*. In the end, the spectacular success of *Rambo*—like that of *Platoon*—says less about the morality or political leaning or even the aesthetic judgement of the mass audience than about the tremendous vitality—the continuing hold over our communal imagination—of the frontier hero myth. To his enemies, John J. Rambo might well be, as one character describes him, "your worst nightmare." But as his phenomenal popularity attests, he is also the incarnation of one of America's most cherished and enduring dreams.

Of course, for a business that likes to think of itself as "the dream factory," the film industry is notoriously bad at identifying the archetypal fantasies that make certain movies click with the mass audience. Following the success of *Star Wars*, for example, Hollywood churned out one futuristic flop after another (*The Last Starfighter*, *Tron*, *Capricorn One*, etc.), never realizing that it wasn't the supersonic action or state-of-the-art effects that made Lucas' film such a smash but rather its success as a piece of pop storytelling—an archetypal wondertale retooled for the computer age.

In the same way, Hollywood added up the combined box office receipts for *Rambo* and *Platoon* and (in a classic case of putting two and two together and coming up with five) concluded that the moviegoing public had suddenly developed an enormous hunger for films about the Vietnam War. The follow-ups released to cash in on this ostensible appetite met with a far less avid response, for the simple reason that they lack the mythic ingredient which gave *Rambo* and *Platoon* their irresistible appeal—i.e., the archetypal narrative that has enthralled the American imagination since the time of Mary Rowlandson.

Full Metal Jacket, for example, is essentially another black, Kubrickian comedy which uses a Vietnam context to explore that filmmaker's characteristic themes—the relationship between art and violence, the mechanization of modern culture, and so on—while both *Casualties of War* and *Born on the Fourth of July* deal with the moral heroism that repudiates violence. *84 Charlie MoPic*, a critically praised movie that nobody went to see, is distinguished mainly by its clever technique—a kind of simulated *cinema verite*—which gives the action a powerful sense of immediacy. Shot entirely on super-16 mm, as if through the lens of a handheld camera, the movie portrays the lives and shocking deaths of the members of an Army reconnaissance patrol from the point of view of a documentary cameraman, who is making a training film about them.

The first three of these films are impressive, often stunning, works by a trio of topflight directors (including Stone himself). The last, though much smaller in scale, contains a number of notable performances and powerfully affecting moments. Their failure to excite the kind of interest generated by *Rambo* and *Platoon* says nothing about their intellectual, political, or cinematic qualities. Rather it reflects the fundamentally mythic function of popular movies, which stand or fall, not on the basis of their aesthetic or ethical merits, but rather on that of their archetypal appeal, i.e., their power to communicate stories that audiences love to be told, stories we never grow tired of hearing.

NOTES

1. Richard Corliss, "Vietnam: The Way It Really Was," *Time*, January 26, 1987, p. 57.

2. Ibid., p. 61.

3. In his preface to the published screenplay of *Platoon*, Stone wrote of the actor Tom Berenger that he "is Sergeant Barnes, the Captain Ahab of the platoon . . . I want him to play someone with evil in his heart, but play him with an understanding that will shed light on Melville's line, 'O this lovely light that shineth not on me . . . '" (p. 7). Later, Stone describes the protagonist "as Ishamel, the observer, caught between those two giant forces" (9). The screenplay itself also contains a description of a Phantom jet fighter that compares the plane to "a giant white whale" (p. 123). See Oliver Stone and Richard Boyle, *Platoon & Salvador: The Original Screenplays* (New York: Vintage Books, 1987).

4. Joseph Campbell, *Hero With a Thousand Faces* (New York and Cleveland: Meridian Books), p. 30.

5. Ibid.

6. *Platoon & Salvador*, p. 9.

7. Ibid., p. 45.

8. See *Hero with a Thousand Faces*, pp. 130 ff.

9. Ibid., p. 20.

10. "Showing the Flag: Rocky, *Rambo*, and the Return of the American hero," *Newsweek* (23 December 1985), p. 62. Charles Molesworth makes a similar point, comparing *Rambo* to "the white man turned trailblazer who outstalked and out-primitivized the Indian in those movie westerns of three and four decades ago." See "*Rambo*, Passion, and Power," Dissent (Winter 1986), p. 110.

11. Richard Slotkin, *Regeneration Through Violence* (Middletown Connecticut: Wesleyan University Press, 1973), p. 284.

12. Ibid., pp. 307, 294, 308, 299.

13. Ibid., p. 284.

14. Ibid., p. 309.

PART III

Political History and Movie Culture

Heretofore the essays in this volume have been concerned largely with politics in the movies. But some contemporary film scholars are also interested in the myriad and subtle ways that the movie industry and movie culture have participated in politics throughout their history. Politics has been an integral part of the historical experience of the movies, in particular the responses of both industry and culture to the shifting and multiple realities of politics. The dynamic political culture of the United States is of interest as a crucible of political interplay between the movies and the changing political environment with which it must constantly contend. Further, it is clear that movie culture, and not only the cultural expressions in the films produced, is part of the "seamless web" of the larger political culture. As a student of American culture, Richard Maltby is interested in the "politics of the unstable text," the processes through which movies, and types of movies—such as the early 1930s gangster films—do in fact emerge. He aims at demystifying Hollywood's often self-serving "conventional history" through the discovery of the "conceptual significance" of a particular genre of popular film that held sway for a brief period of time. Further, the project of "historical contextualization" leads him away from "the primacy of the texts" towards the "material conditions under which movies were produced and consumed." In truth, this is likely a more difficult research task than simply examining the product of the industry, the movies themselves, since it involves developing a complete historiography of movie culture. But it does avoid the confusion which often occurs, namely focusing on the movies themselves as simply the most convenient artifact available, or writing a history of the "texts," the films produced, on the basis of a logic that reduces the entire process to "the history of its products." The careful historical reconstruction of what in fact happened demands the detailed analysis of the entire process, from beginning to end. Oftentimes the easy generalizations or conclusions drawn simply on the basis of the films alone are misleading or incomplete, if not downright wrong. This is not to say that the films do not constitute important historical evidence—surely the gangster films of the early 1930s do have something to do with the political and social climate of opinion extant in the Depression—but they have to be understood as only one piece of a larger puzzle that requires contextualization.

Maltby's work included here is an exemplar of such reconstruction, pointing out the important role of vested interest groups which surround and influence the movie industry. Such interests have a great deal to say about what kinds of movies are made, whether certain kinds can continue to be made, and what kind of didactic messages are to be included in films. Which groups are powerful enough to influence the movies, or are even interested in the form and content of films, changes over time, or in response to particular movies (*The Last Temptation of Christ*) or trends in the movies. Maltby's work reminds us that the political history of Hollywood must include the history of these active interests, and how changes in them and the film industry relate to changes in the larger political culture of the United States, and for that matter, changes in the larger movie culture that now transcends many national barriers.

Lary May's work expands the historical context of American movie experience even further. His work here deals with another palpable and observable aspect of the movies as a part of American political culture, namely what one might call the architechtonic context of movie culture. For changes in the very design of movie theatres is something that offers important insights into what both artists—in this case architects and those who influence styles of architecture—and moviegoers saw as appropriate design for the places where movies are watched. The specific historical juncture of the rapid change in political atmosphere after the stock market crash of 1929 and the advent of the New Deal witnessed a corresponding change in attitudes about, and the structure of, proper theatre design as an expression of social relationships and priorities. Changes in such design, May demonstrates, were not merely a matter of functionality or cost; rather there were considerations of political aesthetics, a socially conscious structure "emblematic of a new dynamic vision of public space." It is important to understand that a public area such as a movie house involves symbolic expression with political overtones. As the country moved quickly from one political era to another, so too did the transformation of public forms of expression such as movie theatre design.

May opens up vistas of inquiry into the motion picture and political culture that go far beyond movie theatre design. For as symbolic structures abound in complex societies such as the United States, so too are other forms of expression—lobby card art, marquee design, studio photography, costume design, movie magazine art, and so on—worthy of investigation. But in all cases the critical variable to understand is historical context, how a political culture transforms itself, and the relationship of that transformation to symbolic forms of expression that exemplify the political aesthetic of change. It might be useful to see such expressions as part of the dynamic "civil religion" of American political culture, which will be manifest in symbolic forms such as public ritual but also latent in forms such as movie theatre design. In any case, this is an area of the dynamic relationship between movies and politics that is relatively unexplored.

"GRIEF IN THE LIMELIGHT"
Al Capone, Howard Hughes, the Hays Code and the Politics of the Unstable Text

Richard Maltby
University of Exeter

"I'd rather the newspapers wouldn't print a line about me. That's the way I feel. No brass band for me. There's a lot of grief attached to the limelight."

Al Capone[1]

In his public pronouncements, Will Hays, president of the Motion Picture Producers and Distributors of America, Inc. (MPPDA) from 1922 to 1945, was inclined to say a small number of things over and over again: one of these homilies was that "No story ever written for the screen is so dramatic as the story of the screen itself."[2] It is an expectation that has become firmly ingrained in the writing of film history. Because of the place entertainment occupies in our lives, we seem to share the curious expectation that the history of entertainment must itself be entertaining. The 1951 MGM musical *Singin' in the Rain*, for instance, offers a history of Hollywood's introduction of sound, during the course of which Donald O'Connor discovers the principles of sound dubbing by standing in front of Debbie Reynolds and moving his mouth while she sings. Hollywood's history of itself offers history as entertainment, and in writing Hollywood history as a Hollywood story, film historians have at times echoed that sentiment. Until recently, the Hollywood history of the introduction of sound—that it was pioneered as a last desperate gamble by an almost bankrupt Warner Bros.—was universally accepted. Basing his revisionist account on documentary sources rather than anecdote, Douglas Gomery established not only the errors in the Hollywood version, but also the inadequacy of any explanation of what Hollywood was or how it worked that does not recognize the American film industry as an industry.[3]

Copyright © 1992 by Richard Maltby

Inadequate or not, the naive account is still regularly reproduced, because it corresponds to a Hollywood fantasy far more closely than the prosaic account of industrial practice does.[4] The fantasy of the Warner kids from the ghetto making good with an invention the big studios had turned down is a Hollywood story, the material for a biopic. In that sense it fits the mythological, *Singin' in the Rain* history of Hollywood, and accommodates the proposition that Hollywood's history must conform to the conventions of its own narratives. A mere demystifacatory demonstration of factual inaccuracy offers no adequate counterweight to that proposition. All the industrial pressures of Hollywood, both then and now, act against the revelation of a prosaic materialist history of the economic forces underlying the American cinema.

Writing a materialist history of the American cinema leads to the disconcerting realization that the production of movies was not by any means the major business of the American film industry. In 1931, investment in property, buildings and equipment used in production constituted ten percent of the total invested in the industry. Similarly, ten percent of the industry's labor force was employed in production.[5] The movie business was essentially a service industry, doing its business and making its money in exhibition. "Hollywood," "The Metropolis of Make-Believe," [6] was a disguise for the film industry, an invention of publicity agents to divert public attention away from the mundane, mechanical, standardized aspects of the industry's central operations towards its more attractive, glamorous periphery. The disguise has worked as effectively in diverting critics and historians as it did for contemporary audiences. The interest taken in the competition among female movie stars for the affections of an unattached male star deflected attention away from the monopolistic business practices in distribution and exhibition practiced by the companies for which they worked. In the same way, the interest taken in questions of censorship diverted attention toward the issues of the minutiae of movie content and away from questions of the regulation of the film industry in matters which were of more substantial importance, questions involving the regulation of the industry's trade practices by the federal government.

If the anecdotal history of entertainment has led to an undue emphasis on production, the collusion with the institutions of monopoly capital which that entails has been intensified by the manner in which film study has defined itself as an essentially critical, rather than historical, activity. Its primary concern has been with the interpretation of the text rather than comprehension of the industrial or cultural context. It is perhaps almost too easy to cite Andrew Bergman's exit line from his introductory four-page "Note on the Movie Industry and the Depression," "the most compelling evidence . . . lies in the films themselves. The preliminaries completed, we proceed to the black and white footage itself."[7] But the assumption that historical contextualization is a matter of a brief introductory statement, even when the critical project involves an enquiry into the ideological functioning of the text under investigation, is as implicit in the *Cahiers Du Cinema* text on *Young Mr. Lincoln*,[8] and in its many offspring, as it is explicit in Bergman. The early 1930s have been awarded a privileged place in the cultural history of Hollywood. Robert McElbane proposes that "nothing else was as central to American popular culture in that decade as the motion pictures . . . if any form of popular culture can shed light on a people's values, surely the Depression-era cinema is the most likely candidate."[9] Perhaps. But to insist on the primacy of the text as a piece of historical evidence as McElvane, following Bergman, does is to create a particular methodological problem if one is also claiming to be writing a social history of the movies. The history of the American cinema is not the history of its products any more than the history of railroads is the history of locomotives. The development of locomotives forms part of the history of railroads, but so, for example, do government land policies and patterns of agricultural settlement. To write a history of texts and call it a history of Hollywood involves denying the contextual significance of the material conditions under which movies were produced and consumed.

In the historiography of film studies the encounter between a critical concern with text and an anecdotal account of production history resulted, during the 1970s, in a cinematic equivalent of early twentieth-century literary history, an account which has in large part still to be rewritten. In works such as Colin MacArthur's *Underworld USA* or Jack Shadoian's *Dreams and Dead Ends*,[10] two essentially incompatible beliefs combined. On the one hand, it was held that film history, constructed as the history of a collection of texts, possessed its own separate system of causation, in the historical development of the gangster genre from one movie to another. On the other hand, it was also held that the movies were, by one means or another, reflections of the history of the culture, so that it was presumed that the gangster movies of the early 1930s tell us something about early Depression America. Most commonly, what they tell us is derived from Robert Warshow's observation that the gangster represented a left-handed version of the Horatio Alger myth[11]; for example, Shadoian's comment that,

> America invents the gangster as tragic hero against the grain of its democratic ideals-rapidly souring in the socioeconomic conditions of the depression;[12]

or Edward Mitchell's observation that,

> While retaining most of the surface trappings of the Horatio Alger myth, the gangster film denies its meaning at the source and returns to other, and conflicting, cultural convictions—chiefly, a pervasive sense of alienation and impending doom, a punishment that cannot be escaped for a fault that cannot be eradicated.[13]

There is a conventional history of Hollywood in the 1930s which marks July 1, 1934, as a watershed between the anarchic hedonism of a "pre-Code" era and the social and sexual conformism of "post-Code" movies.[14] In summary, this history proposes that the initial instigation for the Production Code came from within the industry, in part as a result of the introduction of sound, but that the Code adopted in 1930 lacked adequate enforcement mechanisms:

> At first the studios conformed to the provisions of the Production Code, but falling attendances at film theatres during 1932 and 1933 led to the deployment of more "daring" material.[15]

Producers unleashed a flood of sexually suggestive and violent films on the American public, and the MPPDA, without powers to enforce the Code, was unable to prevent it. The potentially disastrous effects of this attack on social standards were averted only by the entry into the fray of the one institution able to exert both the moral and economic power necessary to force the industry to put the public good before their private gain: the Catholic Church. The Catholic Church possessed an economic power much greater than that of any other reform groups because it could issue edicts to its members to boycott particular films or theaters or even to boycott the movies altogether. According to this account, in November 1933 the Catholic hierarchy began deliberating on how to reform the movies. In April 1934 they established the Legion of Decency, which had eight million members by June. Faced for the first time with this kind of threat, the producers immediately asked Hays and Martin Quigley, prominent Catholic editor of the *Motion Picture Herald*, to open negotiations with the Catholic hierarchy on their behalf. Those negotiations resulted in the Legion withdrawing its threat to boycott movies if the Code were properly enforced. A new regime was introduced in July 1934 with the implementation of the Resolution for Uniform Interpretation and the establishment of the Production Code Administration under devout Catholic Joseph Breen.

This conventional history is essentially derived from one source, Raymond Moley's book, *The Hays Office*.[16] It tells a story which conforms attractively to the pattern of a classical Hollywood narrative: it involves a small central cast of characters, all strongly motivated toward the achievement of a clearly defined goal, and it imposes a strict linear and chronological causality on events. This Hollywood history, with its climax in July 1934, has provided historians of film texts with a convenient device with which to divide the 1930s into periods of turbulence and order.[17] Accounts of the early 1930s note the existence of a vocal campaign complaining about the moral viciousness of Hollywood movies, and assume that Hollywood movies of the early 1930s must have been morally vicious—or at least socially and culturally disruptive.[18] This assumption is then confirmed through a critical interpretation of a small group of films which are, in some undefined way, claimed to be representative. What is seldom observed is that the group of twenty to twenty-five films usually considered represent approximately one percent of Hollywood's total output of feature films during the period 1930 to 1934. With such small sampling procedures, any critical expectation is likely to be confirmed by the choice of texts. With little justification offered for the particular selection beyond its familiarity, "pre-Code" Hollywood is represented by "Some Anarcho-Nihilist Laff Riots" featuring the Marx brothers,[19] the subversion of dominant sexual ideology by Mae West and Marlene Dietrich, Warner Bros.' social conscience and a trio of gangster movies.

The classical Hollywood narrative of The Hays Office is read subversively, and the Happy Ending of July 1934 is understood ironically as the instance of repressive closure.

It may be instructive to scrutinize more closely the chronology and context of some of these texts, in an attempt to re-examine how we may regard such films as cultural documents. The conventional history tells us that the gangster film was "the first—and most enduring—of the popular genres of the Depression years.[20] It is identified as having a "classical" period between 1930 and 1933/4,[21] and the films of this period are regarded as being particularly instrumental in the Catholic Church's action:

> Hollywood's evolving sexual mores generated less public consternation than did its portrayals of gangster films between 1930 and 1933 increasing pressure on Hays and the MPPDA to enforce its Production Code.[22]

Certainly, underworld or gang pictures comprised one area of great concern for the MPPDA. Together with the representation of sex, the representation of crime was the issue most likely to draw adverse comment from the press and reformers. The principal anxiety was engendered by the prospect of juvenile imitation of criminal activities, whether in details of behavior or more generally. In May 1929 the MPPDA produced a lengthy refutation of evidence produced by the economist Roger W. Babson suggesting that there was a link between movie-going and juvenile crime, and the Association was also assiduous in chasing down court cases in which a judge or a defendant blamed the movies, and publishing evidence contradicting their claims.[23] Middle-class anxiety was typically focused on, but not limited to, the movies. In 1929, Progressive reformer Jane Addams expressed concern about "the effect of all this law-breaking upon the young. There is no doubt that a spirit of adventure natural to boys in adolescence has been tremendously aroused by the bootleg and hijacking situation. It is as if this adventurous spirit were transferred from the Wild West in to the city streets."[24] In July 1931, an echo of that sentiment came from an unexpected source—Al Capone himself.

> "You know, these gang pictures—that's terrible kid stuff. Why, they ought to take them all and throw them into the lake.

They're doing nothing but harm to the younger element of this country. I don't blame the censors for trying to bar them . . . these gang movies are making a lot of kids want to be tough guys and they don't serve any useful purpose."[25]

Using Thomas Schatz's distinction between the classic gangster film and the diluted versions released later in the decade—that "the gangster hero's position within the genre's narrative structure [is] as the organizing sensibility through whom we perceive the urban milieu,"[26]—I can identify nineteen films including program pictures from minor studios which fit his criteria for classicism,[27] all released between September 1930 and May 1932. This assessment approximately corresponds to that made by the Studio Relations Committee in September 1932, when Jason Joy observed that "throughout the whole period when the gangster theme was being used on the screen, only 23 pictures could possibly be classified as gangster pictures."[28] Schatz's observation that "the gangster film enjoyed possibly the briefest classic period of any Hollywood genre,"[29] is, in fact, an understatement. The classic gangster film as conventionally identified was the product of one production season, 1930-31, and constituted a cycle comparable in duration and scale production to movies with a newspaper background produced in the same season, or imitations of *Back Street* made the following season.

The cycle was inaugurated by four films released late in 1930, of which only one, *The Doorway to Hell*, the first version of the Capone biography, enjoyed substantial box-office takings. Its early season success, followed by that of *Little Caesar* in January 1931, triggered a series of sequels. Warner Bros. released *The Finger Points* in February; Columbia, *The Last Parade* in March. *City Streets* (Paramount) and *The Public Enemy* (Warners) were released in April, *Quick Millions* (Fox) and *The Secret Six* (MGM) in May. For reasons which are discussed at some length below, *Scarface* was not released until May 1932. This release pattern indicates the typical response by the major producers of rapidly imitating a particularly impressive box-office success. None of the films released after April 1931 except *Scarface* performed with any notable success at the box-office.[30] What should perhaps be considered, then, given the (usually unsubstantiated) claims for the extraordinary success of the "genre" was why so few such films were made. Why, after the success of Robinson and Cagney in gangster roles, did Warners team them in a comedy-drama, *Smart Money*, for release in June 1931? Why was this followed, for Cagney, by roles as lower class urban figures on one or the other side of the law but nowhere near gangsterdom (*Blonde Crazy*, *Taxi*), and for Robinson with a variety of roles which settled on no performance archetype (*Five Star Final*, *The Hatchet Man*, *Two Seconds*, *Silver Dollar*)? The answers to such questions lie in a series of concentric contexts within which public response to the movies' representation of organized crime during the twenty months under discussion must be placed.

II

> "I'm just a business man. I've made my money by supplying a popular demand . . . Why should I be called a public enemy?"
> Al Capone[31]

As Al Capone never tired of arguing, organized crime was a left-handed version of American capitalism; the big bootleggers of the late 1920s were figures in the mould of the previous century's robber barons.[32] One of Capone's first biographers, Fred D. Pasley, subtitled his book, "The Biography of a Self-Made Man," and described him as "the Horatio Alger lad of Prohibition."[33] But the spectacle of gangsterdom was a phenomenon of the 1920s; in May 1929 the criminal oligopoly was stable, if not respectable, enough to hold a convention in Atlantic City, at which the main items for discussion were "disarmament, peace, and amalgamation on a national scale."[34] As importantly for its public image, organized crime was discovering, in the years immediately after 1929, that the publicity it had attracted during Prohibition was bad for business.

Prohibition had not created organized crime, and if anything crime in the 1920s was marginally less prevalent than it had been in the previous decade.[35] But Prohibition had provided it with, if not respectability, at least a basis by which publicity-conscious criminals might court public attention. Beginning with the funeral of Big Jim Colosimo in May 1920, big gangster funerals became media events, photographic fodder for the burgeoning tabloid press, while police raids and gangland wars supplied the melodrama on which the tabloids and sensational magazines thrived. In the second half of the 1920s Capone courted the press as if he were running for office instead of buying elections,[36] and the tabloids, in particular, responded. Owen Garrison Villard, editor of *The Nation*, noted that in October 1926 the *New York Daily Graphic* devoted ten times as much space to crime reporting as it did to foreign news.[37] "Poring over the stories of gangster killings," wrote Frederick Lewis Allen, their readers "found in them adventure and splendor and romance,"[38] and for much of the urban working class in the 1920s, Capone appeared an heroic figure: daring, stylish in his yellow and purple suits, "the gamin from the sidewalks of New York, who made good in a Big Shot way in Chicago."[39] At the end of an interview with Capone in January 1931, Mrs. Eleanor "Cissy" Patterson, editor of the *Washington Herald*, gushed, in precisely the way that made provincial Protestant culture most anxious,

> It has been said, with truth, that women have a special kind of sympathy for gangsters. If you don't understand why, consult Dr. Freud.[40]

The press creation of "Scarface Al Capone" was itself a site in the battleground over the institutions of representation during the decade, and one exacerbated by the spread of the urban daily press; between 1925 and 1930 rural subscriptions to city newspapers doubled.[41]

The celebrity Capone attracted was in part the cause of his downfall; precisely at the point when he seemed to have overcome all his rivals, he became too prominent to go about his business unhindered by the law. With Chicago's Mayor "Big Bill" Thompson (who proclaimed himself "wetter than the middle of the Atlantic Ocean"[42]), he became the target of aroused middle class reform sentiment and changing press and public attitudes. The St. Valentine's Day massacre in 1929 was, in a notable apocryphal phrase, "lousy public relations."[43] Immediately after the Atlantic City convention in May 1929, possibly in an attempt to evade both rival gangsters and a grand jury, Capone connived in his own arrest for carrying a concealed weapon. To his astonishment, however, he was sentenced to the maximum term of one year's imprisonment.[44] By the time of his release in March 1930, a marked change had come about in press attitudes. Their new heroes were federal agents, Eliot Ness and his Untouchables. The Chicago Crime Commission coined the term "Public Enemy" to identify the twenty-eight leading figures in Chicago's underworld. Capone was named Public Enemy No. 1, and the phrase was taken up by newspapers across the country. In June 1930, *Chicago Tribune* reporter Jake Lingle was murdered, provoking a national press campaign against outlawry that was not diminished by the revelations of Lingle's extensive connections to organized crime. Two weeks after the killing the *Chicago Tribune* carried an editorial headlined "End the reign of Gangdom":

> The killers, the racketeers who exact tribute from the businessmen and union labor, the politicians who use and shield the racketeers, the policeman and judges who have been prostituted by politicians, all must go."[45]

The murder of Jack Zuta in August provided, for the first time, clear bookkeeper's records of the scale of graft among Chicago's public officials and police. Throughout the second half of 1930 there were extended raids against Chicago speakeasies, gambling joints and brothels. Beer was no longer openly trucked through the Chicago streets, and many important members of the Capone organization were immobilized by the high bail set against them when they were charged. By the end of the year several, including Capone's brother, had been convicted of tax evasion. In pursuing a grand jury investigation into labor racketeering in November 1930, Chief Justice John P. McGoorty of the Chicago Criminal Court said of Capone,

> His most formidable competitors have been ruthlessly exterminated and his only apparent obstacle toward undisputed sway is the law . . . the time has come when the public must choose between the rule of the gangster and the rule of the law.

By January 1931, when the Wickersham Committee reported indecisively on Prohibition, the weight of public opinion was firmly in favour of repeal, compelled by the wets' argument that Prohibition was unenforceable and served only to aid organized crime. Such sentiments reflected a broader shift in public attitudes, particularly toward representation:

What had departed was the excited sense that taboos were
going to smash, that morals were being made over or
annihilated, and that the whole code of behavior was in flux.
The wages of sin had stabilized at a lower level.[46]

In March 1931, New York's flamboyant Mayor Jimmy Walker, as
gaudy a symbol of Jazz Age urban decadence as Big Bill Thompson,
was charged with malfeasance and negligence of civic duties, the day
after Capone was indicted for income tax evasion in Chicago. A week
previously, Collier's magazine had published an article entitled, "How
to Wreck Capone's Gang."[47] Press coverage of Capone in 1931 was
preoccupied with his sequence of court appearances, the result of a
concerted campaign of harassment by Federal and State law
enforcement agencies in Illinois and Miami, and with Capone's litany
of denial that he was still active in the rackets. In April, Thompson was
decisively defeated in the mayoral election by Democrat Anton J.
Cermak, who was actively committed to purging Chicago of Capone,
and of plays and films with gangster themes, if not of gangsters. In the
aftermath of his election, the local press echoed the new determination
to improve the city's national image: "Chicago not Crime
Ridden—Proud Claim by New Mayor"; "Chicago Crime is Ebbing—It
is Better and Safer Place."[48] At his trial in July, Capone pleaded guilty
to the tax evasion charges, but when, to the consternation of his lawyers
and the surprise of the press, Justice Wilkerson declared that he would
not be bound by the minimum sentence agreed to by the District
Attorney in exchange for the guilty plea, he revised his plea to not
guilty. Capone's trial began on October 6. On October 17, he was found
guilty on five counts of tax evasion, and a week later sentenced to a
total of eleven years' imprisonment. His parting comment to the press
was,

It was a blow below the belt, but what can you expect when
the whole community is against you?[49]

The gangster achieved a fictional prominence, in books and in the
movies, at precisely the time when the metropolitan civic corruption
celebrated in the previous decade was under trenchant attack,[50] when
the public image of Capone and other gangsters was veering rapidly into
decline, and at precisely the moment when organized crime chose to

avoid publicity.[51] W.R.Burnett's *Little Caesar* was published in 1929, Dashiell Hammett's *Red Harvest* in 1929 and *The Glass Key* in 1931. Between 1929 and 1931, seven books devoted wholly or partly to Capone were published, interweaving fact and fiction in the conversion of a no-longer-acceptable celebrity into a mythical figure who, in one account, was reported as declaiming, "Sentimentality is the main danger which threatens us in life. One either has to rid oneself of it or one is entirely in its power."[52] This at the same time that *The Daily Northwestern*, the Evanston campus newspaper, was commenting on Capone's attendance at a football game, where he had been booed from the stadium by students:

> Get this Capone: You are not wanted at Dyche Stadium nor at Soldier Field when Northwestern is host. You are not getting away with anything and you are only impressing a moronic few who don't matter anyway.[53]

and that Judge Lykle of the Chicago Felony Court declared, "Capone has become an almost mythical being. He is not a myth, but a reptile who deserves to be crushed."[54]

III

The classical gangster film depicts the rise and fall of a rugged individualist who calls himself a businessman. That narrative was borrowed from other institutions of representation and dramatized at the moment when the downfall of its most publicly prominent representative was being realized. Capone's demise provided the movie biographies with an ending, which they could then embellish. The gangster narrative became an overtly fictional form at precisely the moment when its closure could be established. *The Doorway to Hell* concluded,

> The Doorway to Hell is a one-way door. There is no retribution—no plea for further clemency. The little boy walked through it with his head up and a smile on his lips. They gave him a funeral—a swell funeral that stopped traffic—and then they forgot him before the roses had a chance to wilt.

Importantly, these films were all overtly retrospective accounts of the excesses of the 1920s as seen from the perspective of the worst years of the Depression. In all of them a strong element of criticism of their central character is present, couched in a rhetoric comparable to that used by press editorials:

> The end of Tom Powers is the end of every hoodlum. "The Public Enemy" is not a man, nor is it a character—it is a problem that sooner or later, WE, the public, must solve.

Critics have noted the disparity between such stated intentions and the effect produced by the performances, particularly, of Robinson and Cagney, of legitimizing the gangster's anti-social position. From this critical perspective, occasionally endorsed by production anecdotes, it is argued that the rhetoric contained in such captions is an empty and largely cynical gesture, to be disregarded in the service of a critically imposed internal coherence for the text. A more detailed consideration of the cycle's censorship history provides grounds for reconsidering this position. The strongest criticism of *The Doorway to Hell* was reserved for its casting of Lew Ayres (now most familiar for his role in *All Quiet on the Western Front*, or as Dr. Kildare) as the Capone-style gang leader. On November 15, 1930 the criminologist Dr. Carlton Simon, who had been hired by the MPPDA to report on the possible dangerous or beneficial effects of crime movies, made a point of emphasizing the dangers of casting a sympathetic actor such as Ayres in the central role, suggesting that young audiences might view him as a "hero-villain," which might be dangerous.[55] *Little Caesar* had already been shot, so the casting of Edward G. Robinson was not directly influenced by these comments; Robinson had already played similar roles in his first two films for Universal and in Warners' *The Widow from Chicago*. However, it seems more likely that the decision to cast James Cagney as Tom Powers rather than Edward Woods had more to do with pressure from the Studio Relations Office than with director William Wellman's claim that he decided Cagney would do the part better.[56]

Certainly the *Little Caesar* press campaign made clear the approach they wanted exhibitors to take:

> All your campaign should be geared to the theme of the picture. Do not in any way attempt to glorify the gangster or

racketeer. In fact it would be well to stress the helplessness of gangland to the law. Follow the ad copy and illustrations in this press sheet to the letter and you will be on the safe side.[57]

In preparing *Public Enemy*, Darryl Zanuck recognized the need to convince state censor boards of the studio's sincerity. Presenting the script to Joy, he argued,

> ... as you know better than I, *Doorway to Hell* is not being cut by the [censor] boards other than ONE or Two small eliminations, and I believe that this is because it has a strong moral tone and that is THE FUTILITY OF CRIME AS A BUSINESS OR AS A PROFIT. This theme in *Doorway to Hell* is emphasized by the last title in the picture and I believe this is why the picture has not been mutilated by the censors. In *The Public Enemy* we also have a strong moral theme, to wit, if there is pleasure and profit in crime or the violation of the Eighteenth Amendment, that PLEASURE and that PROFIT can only be momentary as the basic foundation of law violation ultimately ends in disaster to the participants.
>
> Also a SECONDARY theme which is that—PROHIBITION is not the cause of the present crime wave—mobs and gangs have existed for years and years BECAUSE of environment and the only thing that PROHIBITION has done is to bring these unlawful organizations more noticeably before the eye of the public. REPEAL of the Eighteenth Amendment could not possibly stop CRIME and WARFARE. The only thing that can STOP same is the betterment of ENVIRONMENT and living conditions in the lower reasons [sic] .... I feel that if we can sell the idea that crime is not profitable, IT ENDS IN DISGRACE OR DISASTER and that ONLY BY THE BETTERMENT OF ENVIRONMENT AND EDUCATION for the masses can we overcome the widespread tendency toward lawbreaking—we have then punched over a moral that should do a lot toward protecting us as I feel we have been protected in *Doorway to Hell*.[58]

The "environmentalist" position, then, provided Warners with a neutral stance on the more urgent question of Repeal; endorsing the "wet" position might have caused problems with Kansas censors, for example. In his comments on the script, Joy endorsed Zanuck's overall position while arguing that the role of the police should be enhanced:

> We know that you are trying to balance the ethical and moral values so as to leave the audience with the conviction that "justice prevails" in fact as well as in intent. Perhaps this would be a bit stronger if Mike did not seek to avenge the death of his brother . . . we are sure that the moral lesson which you are attempting to depict will aid you strongly in the controversy with the censors.[59]

By the time *Public Enemy* was in distribution, however, there was a growing volume of exhibitor complaints that audiences had surfeited on gang films and were complaining of the numbers of them. On April 14, the day after six scenes had been eliminated from *Public Enemy* before it was deemed acceptable for release in New York, Lamar Trotti reported the gist of a lengthy conversation with Dr. James Wingate, then head of the New York Censor Board, to Hays. Wingate was of the opinion that pictures showing police doing their job efficiently were suitable and even beneficial in establishing a wholesome regard for the law. However, when crime films showed the police as ineffectual, they added to what Wingate felt was the dangerous break-down in respect for law which had been brought about by Prohibition. This more substantial anxiety underlay his concern about movie representation. Nevertheless, he felt that Public Enemy told

> "a story that ought to be told." He thinks that people should know that racketeering exists, and he mentioned the revelations in the Crain investigation to show how far racketeering has gone in this country. He thinks it is a 'grave government problem' which if properly presented in pictures will be helpful."[60]

Censor Boards throughout the country were following New York in looking with decreasing charity on gangster and crime films, and the industry was preparing to distance itself from them. Hays had already taken action to discourage further production, declaring in his Annual Report to the MPPDA on March 30,

> The handwriting is now plainly on the wall that America is largely through with the post-war preoccupation with morbidity and crime in literature and drama. The orgy of self-revelation which marked such a large portion of modern authorship is passing . . . The motion picture screen in recent months has done much to debunk the American gangster in films dealing with current crime conditions. Nothing could prove more forcibly the success of self-regulation in the motion picture industry than the manner in which subjects have been invariably handled. The insistent message flashed upon the screen has been: "You can't get away with it." In other films, the deadly weapon of ridicule has been trained upon the gangster and his kind—ridicule that removed from the bandit and the gunman every shred of false heroism that might influence young people. But the fact remains that too many such films, however well treated the theme may be, tend to over-emphasize the subject matter. Furthermore, the fact is becoming evident that the American public is growing tired not only of gangster rule, but of gangster themes in literature, on the stage, and on the screen. I am glad to note, therefore, the decreasing importance of such themes in the production programs of 1931.[61]

At the same time, the MPPDA took measures to protect films already in distribution. Criminologist August Vollmer was hired to provide authoritative comments to declare their conformity with the Production Code. After seeing *City Streets*, *The Finger Points*, *The Last Parade*, *Public Enemy*, *Quick Millions*, and *The Secret Six*, "through the eyes of a policeman," he wrote Hays,

> I can only come to the conclusion that they are not objectionable but in many respects altogether otherwise. In some instances, they carry quite a powerful lesson . . . . *The Public Enemy* should make the potential gangster hesitate because it shows very clearly the effect gangster life has upon his immediate family. Whether a picture of this type has any tremendous amount of influence one

> way or the other is debatable .... To me the most striking part of the entire picture was ... the conclusion because it focuses the attention upon the problem and not upon the individual gangster, and makes perfectly clear that the gangster problem cannot be solved entirely until the factors that produce the gangster are eliminated. This conclusion is thought provocative and in that respect has educational value.[62]

Hays had developed what he felt was a defensible position, which he expressed to those who accused the movies of breaching the Code. Denying that any member of the MPPDA would willfully produce a picture that deliberately glorified gangsters, and using statements such as Vollmer's for evidence, he argued that

> the efforts of the press to expose the menace of the gangster, and the public sentiment aroused through the dramatization of this problem focused on the screen, have done much to uphold the forces of law and order. Hamstrung by public apathy or frustrated by the fear of witnesses to testify, the police often found themselves powerless to cope with the situation. Today the honest and competent police officer is assured that a strong public opinion, marshalled by the press and the film, stands squarely behind him ... whatever the divergence of lay opinion on the subject, accepted scientific judgement is practically unanimous in the finding that films which have dealt with the subject of crime within the social safeguards imposed by the motion picture Production Code were deterrents, not incentives, to criminal behavior.[63]

The argument was twofold: the movies' narratives conformed to the Code and provided a moral lesson, while the central performance "debunked" the gangster, rendering him unappealing to even an impressionable audience. Such a position conditioned the MPPDA's response to the few gangster movies remaining in production, including Howard Hughes' *Scarface*.

IV

Hughes undertook *Scarface* in the wake of financial success of *The Doorway to Hell* and *Little Caesar*. The production was announced in early March, 1931, with Capone's biographer F.D. Pasley named as scriptwriter. From March until late May, when a final script was submitted, MPPDA officials attempted to dissuade Hughes from producing the film, pointing out the scale of public objections to gangster films, and the comments by official censor boards that they would not pass any more gangster films. On June 4, Joy wrote to E.B. Derr, production manager of Hughes' Caddo Company, that the script contained a considerable number of unacceptable elements, of which the most important concerned the presentation of Camonte as heroic and sympathetic.

> It is inevitable that the audience's sympathy will be won by him because the only crime for which he is taken is one which the audience will consciously or unconsciously condone, namely the killing of the man who betrayed his sister. In addition, there is the fact that Camonte is shown as a home-loving man, good to his mother and protecting his sister . . . All of this is the more dangerous because of the resemblance to Capone, who so far has succeeded in defeating the law. It is probable that many will regard the use of the almost identical name and character the same as featuring an actual criminal and crimes in newsreels . . . . Would it not be possible to give Camonte's mother some strong lines at the proper place in the story indicating that she was utterly opposed to that kind of business and emphasizing the fact that a life of crime always ends badly not only for the criminals themselves, but for those who love them and are dependent upon them.

It was also necessary, Joy argued, to change the ending, which then depicted Camonte, "spurred on by his proud sister," in a gun battle with the police which ended with a final "gesture of bravado when he deliberately walks into the police gunfire. In this sequence he is one against many and braver than any." This danger would be avoided by rewriting the final scene "so that Camonte becomes a cringing coward, while Guarni, the policeman, becomes even more a fearless and efficient policeman who would be able to walk into Camonte's blazing arsenal to capture him alive." Joy insisted on the unprecedented scale and vehemence of public criticism of the current cycle of crime films.

> There is a vast growing resentment against the continued production and exhibition of this type of picture. Some of the people, especially those in places of authority, are almost fanatical in their desire to stop the further flow of these pictures. Personally, I believe that they are unconsciously motivated by their desire to rid the country of gangsters, but the actual release of their energy is upon the picture itself.[64]

During production Joy was in regular discussion with Derr and Hawks over modifications to the shooting of various sequences, but the real obstacle came from Hughes' desire to make the picture "as realistic as possible." Hughes only allowed Hawks and Derr to modify the treatment after Joy had told him that the picture as initially shot stood no chance of passing any censor board and therefore of playing in more than twelve percent of the English-speaking market.[65] The changes Joy proposed included the suggestion that "the idea of a protective brother-sister relationship" be changed "to that of jealousy . . . and to imply a situation in which *Scarface* was planning to use her for ulterior motives."[66] Movie gangsters were not permitted to have happy or even conventional families, but Tony's "incestuous impulses towards his sister" remained unnoticed in the critical discourse about the film until 1968.[67]

Before shooting was completed, however, the already high level of criticism directed against gang films by a press anxious to transfer public opprobrium away from their own representation of crime was intensified by the accidental fatal shooting in July of Winslow Elliott, aged twelve, by William Gamble, sixteen, in Montclair, New Jersey, while Gamble was allegedly acting out scenes from *The Secret Six*.[68] The killing provided anecdotal confirmation of claims by such figures as New York Police Commissioner Edward P. Mulrooney that gang pictures encouraged juvenile crime.[69] The Protestant religious press exploited the incident to encourage support for Senator Clarence Dill's resolution for a congressional investigation of the motion picture industry, and the operations of the MPPDA in particular.[70]

Scarface was previewed by the SRC on September 8, when Hughes was informed that a new ending, in which Camonte "turns yellow" must replace the existing shoot-out with the police. By this stage, Hughes was primarily concerned with protecting his investment, in modifying the film so that it could at least be released, preferably in time to coincide with Capone's upcoming trial. A further substantial modification, part inspired by the Gamble-Elliott killing, involved the insertion at this stage of the production of an anti-gun theme,

> which, we believe, gives it a right to live in spite of the prevalent, panicky opposition to gangster themes . . . . What Hawks has done is to insert in about ten places in the picture scenes and dialogue pointing up the idea that *Scarface* is a killer as long as he has his guns. When he first gets hold of a machine gun there is a dramatic scene that fairly knocks you out of your seat emphasizing the fact. Then at the end he is caught. Without his gun he goes yellow, becomes a cringing, crying, pleading rat.

These sequences, together with "a strong, forceful foreword," provided the basis for Joy's defence of the movie as "worthwhile propaganda as well as entertainment." *Scarface*, he argued, demonstrated in its narrative that

> As long as a gangster has access to guns, either pistols or machine guns, he is a bold, bad-man, menacing society and mocking at law and decency, but once robbed of his guns he is a yellow rat who will crawl into his hole. For the first time, therefore, a gangster picture strikes at the very heart of what more and more people believe to be the answer to the gangster problem, namely the passage and enforcement of more stringent anti-gun laws.[71]

On September 29, the Board of Directors of the Association of Motion Picture Producers (AMPP), the West Coast subsidiary organization of the MPPDA, passed a resolution prohibiting any further production of "gangster" films.[72] By that date, Joy claimed to have seen

Scarface in various forms twenty times, and told Hays that Hughes had agreed to turn over supervision of the advertising campaign to the SRC. Nevertheless, the New York censor board indicated in early October that it would not pass this version. When the film was viewed by Hays and other industry heads in early November 1931, under the Jury system established by the 1930 Resolution for Uniform Interpretation of the Code, there was general agreement that it remained unacceptable. Further deletions, and further revision of the brother-sister relationship, were ordered, and the ending was revised so as to show Camonte's subsequent trial and execution. A final version, with all these emendations, was approved on December 24, 1931. All that remained to be settled was a modification of the title, eventually agreed as *Shame of the Nation*.[73]

Scarface was not the only film Hughes was having difficulty with. His other current production, *Cock of the Air*, a World War One flying story similar to *Hell's Angels*, had encountered similar problems with the Studio Relations Committee and with the New York Censor Board, which had rejected it. Hughes had spent $100,000 on revisions and retakes on each film to make them acceptable, and at the end of the year he had two films which he regarded as "cut up until they weren't any good any more."[74] Having taken substantial losses on at least three of his four previous pictures,[75] Hughes seems to have decided in early 1932 to quit the picture business, undoubtedly to the relief of the MPPDA, since he had been by far the least co-operative producer with whom they had dealt. However, the headaches over *Scarface* were not yet over. By February 1932, United Artists, the company through which Hughes was releasing the film, were effectively prepared to cut their losses. Believing that the film would not pass any censor board, Joseph Schenck, President of UA, wrote to Hays advocating that Hughes be allowed "to get what he can out of the picture in the spots where there is no censorship and where local authorities permit him to run it."[76] Although he continued negotiating with the Studio Relations Committee about releasing an acceptable version, Hughes and his press agent, Lincoln Quarberg, devised a publicity campaign for the film, in keeping with Schenck's strategy, emphasizing *Scarface*'s challenge to censorship authority. On March 2, 1932, there was a press screening at Grauman's Chinese Theatre in Los Angeles. The version shown was the one seen by the SRC on September 8, 1931. Having abandoned his involvement with production, Hughes was testing the MPPDA's authority as well its patience. Schenck and UA, however, had more to lose; there was no question of UA's releasing any version other that agreed to in December, which was still held to be in conformity to the Code. The publicity brought by Hughes' press campaign made even that version increasingly difficult to support. In late March the December version was rejected by the New York and Massachusetts censor boards. Although Caddo issued press releases claiming that Hughes was bringing a court action to challenge the New York censor board, and insisting that the film would be released uncensored, it was in fact undergoing further editing revisions under the supervision of Lewis Milestone, including the insertion of the scene in which the newspaper editor denounces criticism of his reporting of gangster activities. Those revisions finally produced a version acceptable to the New York board in early May. At the same time that Quarberg was putting out press releases claiming that New York had passed the original version in preference to fighting Hughes in the courts, [77] Hughes was contacting Hays asking the MPPDA not to contradict Caddo's publicity.[78]

When eventually released, *Scarface* grossed $600,000, which Balio estimates may have been enough for the film to break even.[79] To that extent, Hughes' publicity campaign may have been successful in at least limiting his losses on the project. The film's release continued Protestant protest against movie representation of crime, which was kept alive as an issue by the publication, in the September 1932 edition of McCall's Magazine, of the first synopsis of Henry James Forman's *Movie-Made Children*.[80] But, as Jason Joy explained in his valedictory observations to Hays in September 1932, concern about the representation of crime had by then almost entirely given way to concern over the representation of sex. The Legion of Decency campaign in 1933 and 1934, preoccupied as it was with sex and sacrilege, exhibited no concern at all with the representation of crime.

The problem created by the gangster film, then, took place in a much more specific period than that accorded it by conventional histories, and in relation to a quite specific set of external events. The films themselves were part of a wider discourse of condemnation of gangsterdom, enacted at the moment when gangsterism appeared to be on the wane. That discourse, in its various public forms, was a subject of controversy, but during the period in which the films were released, both press and film versions of the discourse were anxious to be seen as firmly repudiating any glamourization of organized crime, and identify that practice as a phenomenon of the previous decade. At the point at which it became clear that the movies could not sustain the contradiction between the necessary condemnatory attitude and the performative appeal of the gangster protagonist, the industry abandoned production in the face of public opposition.

One more conclusion may perhaps be drawn about the problems of writing textual history. After its initial release, *Scarface* developed a mythology of its own. With the exception of a couple of bootleg prints, *Scarface* disappeared from public view until 1979, when Hughes' Summa Corporation sold rights to it and all other Hughes productions to Universal.[81] Although it is not possible from the existing documentation to identify all the differences among the four versions of *Scarface* produced between September 1931 and May 1932, it is clear enough that the text with which we are currently familiar corresponds exactly to none of them. It contains the additional material shot for the May 1932 version, but otherwise appears most closely to resemble the October 1931 version, which was never put into general release. For whatever purpose and at whatever date this version of *Scarface* was constructed, the text which is currently available to us to analyze is not that seen and argued over by audiences in 1932. Any judgments we may care to make about the cultural history of the period based on an examination of texts need to be tempered by the cautionary recognition that the texts concerned were far more malleable than we now commonly give them credit for. Censorhip was one cause, among several, for the inherent instability of cinematic texts; the Production Code was one instrument among several which sought to standardize production, distribution, and exhibition procedures. An incidental effect of this was to increase the stability of Hollywood's film texts, but they remained vulnerable to other destabilizing forces, from "political censorship" to incidental physical damage to perverse interpretation.

V

The circumstances surrounding the production of gangster films provide an example of the co-operative development, between the SRC and the studios, of codes of representation which would prove acceptable to the various audiences the movies had to address. Rather than being misrecognized as an anarchic golden age, the early 1930s may best be seen as a moment in which the industry was developing narrative and other textual practices by which it could recuperate the contradictions between the two opposed terms that were central to the debate over the cultural function of the movies: "sophistication" and "innocence." The industry's aim was to find a way to undercut its moralistic opponents through a formula which would appeal to audiences with both "innocent" and "sophisticated" sensibilities. This involved devising discursive systems in which "innocence" was inscribed into the text while "sophisticated" viewers were able to "read into" movies whatever meanings they pleased to find there, so long as the producers could, effectively, use the Production Code to deny their responsibility. It was the impossibility of adequately resolving this contradiction in the case of the gangster protagonist that ensured his marginalization after 1931.

What needs to be considered in tandem with this history of textual instability, however, is the censorship of the history of censorship produced by the construction of an "official" history of the MPPDA by Raymond Moley. Like the Warner Bros. publicity department's account of the introduction of sound, Moley's official history of the MPPDA is not so much inaccurate as full of holes, empty spaces where facts that do not fit have been omitted. Most importantly, it diverts the discussion of industry self-regulation, and the function of the MPPDA, into a concentration on the censorship of film content that subsequent writers have repeated. At the same time, its one real deception is the claim that the Code was a dead letter between 1930 and 1934.[82] Moley's account has been accepted in part because he had access to the internal documentation of the MPPDA, and in part because other accounts from participants have told compatible stories.[83] In part, the *a prior* assumption about Moley's trustworthiness has come from the heavy reliance film history has placed on secondary sources, because its primary conern has been with writing about texts. There has been, as a result, little inquiry into the historiography of The Hays Office.

Moley's book is an official history of the MPPDA, commissioned as part of the industry trade association's defense campaign against the Department of Justice anti-trust suit begun under Assistant Attorney-General Thurman Arnold in 1938. The need for the book's publication was initially averted by the 1940 Consent Decree signed by the Big Five, which halted the Department of Justice suit. That suit was renewed in August 1944, the same year that Mae D. Huettig's critical account of the industry, *Economic Control of the Motion Picture Industry*,[84] which was based on research undertaken by the Department of Justice,[85] was published. These events provoked the publication of Moley's book, which is written as a defense of business self-regulation, and

> with no mission except the limited one of showing one industry's effort to maintain a measure of self-government and to save a great popular art from the hand of political interference and control.[86]

That mission, in 1939 and again in 1945, was hardly an abstract one: the entire structure of the American film industry, and with it the studio system and the Classical Hollywood Cinema, was dependent upon the vertical integration of the major companies which were represented by the MPPDA.

The issue resolved by the Paramount decrees in 1948 was the same issue as that raised by the Federal Trade Commission's first anti-trust complaint against Famous Players-Lasky in August 1921, the legal issue which had led to the founding of the MPPDA. That issue, the question of whether the majors' monopoly control of the industry constituted an unfair trade practice, remained a matter of active legal and Congressional debate throughout the period spanned by Hays' Presidency of the MPPDA, and it would hardly be an understatement of the case to suggest that it was Hays' extraordinary political skills which held the wolverine forces of free market competition at bay, and kept the Classical Hollywood Cinema intact, during those years. Even if Moley is incorrect in attributing Calvin Coolidge's maxim that "what America needs is more business in government and less government in business" to Hays,[87] that maxim was certainly what Hays practiced on behalf of the movies.[88]

Raymond Moley, too, was some way from being an unbiased reporter. A conservative advocate of the government-business co-operation which underlay the policies of the First New Deal, and one of the principal Brain Trust architects of the National Recovery Administration, he subsequently became disaffected with the leftward drift of the New Deal, and left the administration in mid-1936. From then on, as editor of *Today* and *Newsweek*, Moley was a persistent and increasingly vehement critic of the lack of coherence in Roosevelt's economic policies. At the same time that he worked on *The Hays Office* he was writing *After Seven Years*, his major critique of the New Deal.[89] Some of his strongest condemnations were reserved for the administration's attempts to blame corporations and the "curse of bigness" for the business collapse of 1937, and for the "trust-busting" initiatives—including the original suit—which followed it. *The Hays Office* was the second publication he had written for the MPPDA; in 1938 he had produced *Are We Movie Made?*, a rebuttal of Henry James Forman's summary of the Payne Fund Studies, *Our Movie-Made Children*.[90]

VI

Like a great number of other industries in the 1920s, the film industry established a trade association—the MPPDA—as a mechanism for standardizing business practice and promoting its political interests. The emphasis on its activities in relation to censorship and "self-regulation" that is so much part of Moley's and subsequent accounts is absent from both contemporary reports of its founding and its own extant documents from the early 1920s. One of the MPPDA's functions was the management of the industry's public relations, and its response to demands for censorship fell into that category. In addition to its Public Relations activities, The Association had three other principal functions which it chose to describe under the umbrella term of "self-regulation." Firstly, it sought to implement more efficient and more profitable systems of operation among the major companies, from the organization of the Central Casting Corporation, which regulated and standardized the employment and wages of extras, to the establishment of a Standard Exhibition Contract between its member distributors and independent theater-owners. Secondly, it maintained a large legal department, which involved itself extensively in the many litigations brought against individual companies and the "organized industry" as a whole. Private suits accusing the major companies of infringements of the anti-trust laws were frequently brought by independent exhibitors, and, indeed, by the Federal Trade Commission. Other suits, in which the industry as a whole was held to have an interest even though they were brought against an individual member company, also fell within the MPPDA's brief.

Thirdly, the MPPDA undertook the defense and protection of the industry in Washington and state legislatures. In any given year between 1925 andd 1940, an average of more than 250 bills affecting the motion picture industry (almost invariably adversely) were presented in state legislatures, while each Session of Congress in the 1930s saw the introduction of bills intended to tax theater admissions, establish federal censorship and/or prohibit block booking. From 1934 to 1940 there were four major congressional investigations of the industry. The industry's principal reason for choosing Hays in 1922 was his reputation as one of the most able political organizers in the country. His extensive network of contacts within the Republican administration during the 1920s was invaluable for the industry in securing it government cooperation, particularly from the State and Commerce Departments. The MPPDA's General Counsel, Charles C. Pettijohn, who organized the network of local lobbying activities, maintained an almost perfect record for preventing the passage of adverse legislation at a state and municipal level. It was the efficiency of Pettijohn's operation that prevented the independent exhibitors, who would have been the principal sufferers from such legislation, becoming any more hostile towards the major companies than they did.

In both Moley's account and MPPDA practice, questions of the censorship of film content became the primary focus in the debate over industry self-regulation. One reason for this was that, for much of the time, it was favorable ground for the Association. Hays maintained a constant critique of what he always termed "political censorship" as the best target on which to attack proposals for government control of the industry. This tactic also accorded with the industry's general strategy of concentrating public attention on the activities of production rather than other branches of the industry. But it was also the case that the content of motion pictures, and their influence on those who saw them, was a matter of widespread public concern during the 1920s and 1930s.

One way of understanding the crisis in representation during the early 1930s is to see in the calls for censorship "an awkward expression of demand":[91] a complaint that too much of one kind of product, and not enough of another, was being made.[92] Certainly the issue was frequently discussed in such terms: of what proportion of movies were suitable for children, for example; or of the problem of the overproduction of "sophisticated" material that was unacceptable or unappealing to small-town audiences. But the issue of audience demand was most often couched in moralistic terms, which attached it to the continuing cultural debate over the control of both the institutional and semiotic systems of representation.

Over a broad range of cultural issues in the 1920s, a battleground was being staked out over which an increasingly uncertain, insecure Protestant provincial middle-class sought to defend its cultural hegemony, its command of public life, from the incursions of a modernist, metropolitan culture which the provincials regarded as alien—a word which was often, but not always, a synonym for Jewish. The movie theatre was a site at which an establishment WASP culture, which recognized itself as rural and suburban, felt its values endangered by a newer, urban, immigrant, largely Jewish and Catholic culture. The movies were a particularly threatening representative of that culture both because they were apparently owned by aliens, and because their advertising (which was all many of their reformers saw of them) suggested that their permissive representations of sex and violence were designed to cater to the baser instincts of "morons," a term widely used to refer indirectly to the immigrant working class. During the 1920s this issue commonly became expressed in the opposition of "Broadway vs. Main St." Its articulation provided the Catholic Church with an opportunity to act as a moral and cultural broker between the city and provincial Protestant morality.

By mid-1922, within six months of the founding of the MPPDA, Hays had developed a strategy to contain the threat posed to the industry by the lobbying power of nationally federated civic, religious, and educational organizations. The aim was to "make this important portion of public opinion a friendly rather than a hostile critic of pictures," and the strategy was the same one the MPPDA would consistently employ: to provide previewing facilities for representatives of participating organizations, and financial assistance in distributing their lists and reviews of recommended films. This policy, which became known as the "Open Door" in 1924, was essentially a containment exercise: cooperating organizations gave publicity to the movies they approved, and made private complaint through the MPPDA about those of which they disapproved.[93] Naturally, Hays had a cogent explanation of how such a system would produce greater benefits than public criticism. That explanation relied on and contributed to the mythology of Hollywood as alien and sophisticated. Audiences had to be educated to want "better movies," and producers in Hollywood had to be educated to recognize this demand. Repeatedly this was couched in the language of the industry maturing, "growing up," and in the process moving away from its initial "alien" influences in production to come under the sway of those among whom, as Hays was inclined to put it, there was "little difference of opinion between what is fundamentally right and what is fundamentally wrong."[94] In 1924, specifically in answer to claims by Protestant reform groups that the industry was dominated by a handful of aliens, the MPPDA demonstrated that the "active managers" of companies controlling ninety percent of production were of non-Jewish origin.[95] But the mythology of alien standards in Hollywood was necessary to Hays as an explanation for mistakes or slips. The MPPDA, representing the "organized industry" as a whole, needed to be seen to be aligned with Main St. rather than Broadway. Hollywood and its producers had to remain the scapegoat villains of this scenario, always being represented as unable or unwilling, without some form of compulsion, to recognize that decency was in their own best interests.

No organization co-operated more fully with Hays' "support the best, ignore the rest" strategy than the Motion Picture Bureau of the International Federation of Catholic Alumnae. The Legion of Decency was far from being the first large-scale activity relating to movies undertaken by the Catholic Church. Under the auspices of the National Catholic Welfare Conference and with the approval of Archbishop Hayes of New York, the IFCA began a bi-monthly reviewing service in 1923. By late 1929 they were reviewing approximately 200 films per month, and their reviews were carried by 42 newspapers, 113 Catholic newspapers, and seven radio stations. The IFCA was firmly aligned with the MPPDA over questions of industry organization and in particular over repeated proposals of Protestant reformers that the industry be subject to Federal Regulation both of film content and business practice.

By 1928 it was widely recognized within the industry that some form of prior censorship at the point of production by the new technology of sound, particularly sound-on-disc systems which showed censorship mutilation very clearly by losing sychronization. The compilation by a committee of studio executives of the "Don'ts and Be Carefuls" out of existing state and foreign censorship practices, and the establishment of the Studio Relations Committee under Col. Jason Joy in 1927, were moves in this direction. Sixty percent of distributor rental income was derived from territories under some form of state or municipal censorship,[96] and in late 1928 the MPPDA started to explore the possibility of working with existing censor boards to produce a more uniform practice regarding deletions. The Association also attempted to organize Protestant activity along similar lines to the IFCA, but this proved disastrous. A dispute over the MPPDA's financial support of the Protestant organization involved, the Church and Drama Association, led to accusations that the MPPDA had been trying to buy support of the Federal Council of Churches of Christ in America. In June 1929 these charges were taken up by the Episcopalian journal *The Churchman*, which began a vitriolic personal attack on the officers of the MPPDA, and revelled in repeating accounts of Hays' discomfiture in testifying before the investigation into the Teapot Dome affair. *The Churchman's* attack was initially and primarily concerned with a critique of the business practices of the industry and the MPPDA, and hardly at all with movie content.[97] At this stage, however, what Hays regarded as a thoroughly unholy alliance began to develop between the Protestant reformers who saw themselves as heirs to the paternalist social legislation of Progressivism and Prohibition, and the independent exhibitors.

VII

In 1931 there were approximately 14,500 theatres operating in the United States. 2,250 of those theatres were in circuits or chains owned by or affiliated with the Big Five major companies. Another 1,200 were run by circuits unaffiliated with the majors. Together they made up approximately twenty-five percent of the theatres, but they also represented almost fifty percent of the seating capacity of all theatres, and they paid something like seventy percent of rental fees to distributors. The remaining 11,000 which were owned and operated as independent, individual concerns on much the same basis as the corner drug store thus actually produced only thirty percent of the distributors' income.[98] Half the people who went to the movies in the U.S. saw them in independently owned theatres—"Mom and Pop" theatres servicing small towns and suburban areas, but their seeing movies was a matter of peripheral economic importance to the major companies. Indeed, under certain circumstances, it was to the majors' economic disadvantage, and the economic interests of the major distributors and the small independent exhibitors were therefore frequently in direct opposition to each other. For the distributors, servicing the small exhibitor could significantly interfere with their maximizing profits.

MGM distribution executives cited an example, in the small city of St. Joseph, Missouri. When they sold their pictures exclusively to a first-run theatre, they earned an average of $500 a picture. In a subsequent season, they also sold the pictures to a smaller and cheaper subsequent-run theatre, from which they earned an average of $22.50, but it resulted in their income from the first-run theatre dropping to $100 per picture.[99] In 1932 two companies whose product was most geared to first-run exhibition, United Artists and Loews/MGM, began to propose schemes for differential distribution, in which both movies and theatres would be divided into classes, and only Class A theatres with higher seat prices would play Class A movies. This would have introduced a notion of differential access to Hollywood's output, in a spirit contrary to the generally proclaimed industry position of cinema as universal mass entertainment.[100] In practice, cinema attendance was concentrated in the middle and lower-middle income groups in the major metropolitan centres, particularly in the most densely populated areas of the country in the industrial North-East; as much as forty percent of the American population hardly ever went to the movies. But the idea of universal mass entertainment was absolutely central to the industry's rhetoric, particularly when it was necessary to defend its business practices. Pettijohn expressed the point in a typical manner in July 1932:

> the greatest part of this business is the fact that the humblest theater in the land can show the same production with the same 40-piece symphony orchestra accompaniment that is shown at the Roxy theatre in New York. Pictures will die when they can't be shown at the littlest as well as the biggest motion picture theatres of the country.[101]

The conventional solution adopted as long-standing practice by distributors was to use the bulk selling techniques of block booking and blind buying as the most economical and efficient way of selling movies at marginal profit to these smaller theatres. In defending these practices, which greatly reduced the exhibitor's choice of what he screened, distribution executives claimed that it was the only way they could be serviced at a cost low enough to ensure that they stayed in business. By similar means they defended their protection and clearance arrangements by which subsequent run theatres had to wait for periods of time before showing a particular movie at lower prices: "$10 rentals are possible only because some one ahead of you first paid big prices," argued Sidney Kent of Fox to the Motion Picture Theater Owners of America in 1932.[102] The exhibitors' grievances, on the other hand, were rooted in their belief that the major companies used their control over the distribution of profitability within the industry to dictate terms to small exhibitors, forcing them to buy more movies than they needed, and to show films the exhibitors regarded as unsuitable or unappealing to their communities. In a variety of ways, the introduction of sound had worsened relations between distributors and exhibitors, and in 1929 a trade association for independent exhibitors, Allied States, was set up to provide a counter-voice to the MPPDA, a voice arguing in favour of federal regulation of the industry.

By the late 1920s, an impressive moral reaction was building among a vocal section predominantly of the non-metropolitan WASP middle class to what were then seen as the excesses of the post-war decade. The impetus given to this moral reaction by the Crash coincided with the spread of sound cinema out of the major metropolitan centres into the majority of neighborhood and local theaters during 1929-1931. The success of sound cinema, against prevailing economic trends, seemed to confirm the widespread conviction that movies were a major source of influence on the behavior, attitudes and morals of their audiences. The introduction of sound also brought about major changes in movie content, involving a greatly increased reliance on material from the stage. Throughout the decade Broadway had been castigated for its "realism" and its "sophistication," particularly in its representation of sexual mores and improprieties. With the coming of sound, and Hollywood's increasing adaptation of Broadway plays, provincial morality perceived that the threat had moved much closer to home. Broadway's dubious dialogue and "sophisticated" plot material was now playing on Main Street for the children to see.

Local exhibitors received the brunt of these complaints. They had long excused themselves to local reform groups by arguing that block booking meant that they had no control over which films they showed, since they were obliged to show the whole of the block they had bought from the distributor. They could not, therefore, accomodate community taste. As part of a tactic for gaining more widespread support for the abolition of block booking, Allied States promoted this argument among reform groups, generally taking the line that the monopolistic activities of the major companies, aided and abetted by Hays and the MPPDA, obliged the well-intentioned but powerless independent exhibitor in upstate New York or the small-town Midwest to show "sex-smut" regardless of his own or his community's preferences. Out of their own self-interest, they took up the call for community control, convincing the Protestant opinion-makers that the only way to secure decency on Main St. was through Federal regulation of the industry's monopolistic practices. The *Churchman* took up the argument, and within a year it had been adopted as a broader front by the whole spectrum of the Protestant press, including the widely circulated liberal *Christian Century*. The movies were indicted by a failing Protestant culture for the cultural changes of the 1920s and the threat they posed to a normative, consensual, religious-based social and cultural value-system. As the movies had been a prominent success in the 1920s, they were a prominent target of the general questioning of business morality that followed the Crash in the early years of the Depression. The Protestant attacks on the industry, and on Hays himself, combined a critique of the movies' moral content with an even more savage critique of the ethical bankruptcy of the industry's business methods, in forcing immoral product on exhibitors.[103]

At the core of the dispute was not movie content, but the threat of legislation. Believing itself to be just and equitable, the "organized industry" feared the economic consequences of federal regulation of its trade practices. There was an absolute, ideological divide between those groups of Protestants, Progressives, and Prohibitionists in favour of government intervention and regulation, who frequently compared regulation of the film industry to regulation of the Food and Drug industries, and those allied to the dominant forces in the industry, who denounced federal regulation as socialistic. For all industry parties, the issues of monopoly control and trading practices were economically much more important than questions of censorship. But questions of censorship were of greater public interest and concern, and were easier to understand. They could also, if necessary, be resolved at less risk to the majors' monopoly interests. The MPPDA's awareness of this encouraged it to displace the by now public but essentially internal battle over the industry's distribution of profits onto another arena.

There was an enormous increase of attention paid to youth in the 1920s, and not merely with the celebrations of the Jazz Age. An important educational lobby debated both the potential and actual effects of the movies on youth groups which constituted more than thirty percent of the audience. The League of Nations was taking an active interest in questions of motion pictures, youth and education. Among other activities it established and funded an academic journal, the *International Review of Educational Cinematography*. Given the growth of parent-teacher organizations during the decade (*Parents Magazine* had a circulation of two million by the end of the decade), the organized force of this concern was not limited to a few educationalists. It is in this context of concern about the effects of movies on young people that the publication, in 1933, of the Payne Fund Studies, needs to be located.

The Payne Fund Studies were the result of a five-year research program established in 1928 by the Motion Picture Research Council. There were twelve of them, collectively titled *Motion Pictures and Youth*. In conventional and received film history, they are communally dismissed as unreliable, inadequately researched and using dubious methodology—all the charges that were brought against them by Moley in his first work for the Hays Office, *Are We Movie-Made?*[104] At the time of their publication, however, they were widely taken not only as authoritative accounts of their subject areas, but, in several cases, as ground-breaking pieces of sociological or psychological research, and they were, indeed, undertaken by some of the most eminent figures in the field of educational psychology at the time.[105]

The picture was, however, somewhat complicated by the attitude of the MPRC, which was itself hardly an unbiased body. Its director, the Rev. William H. Short, was an ardent and vituperative critic of the movies, whose 1928 book, *A Generation of Motion Pictures*, clearly revealed a strong vein of anti-Semitism underlying his critique. While the Payne Fund Studies did gain academic respect—and, indeed, were far from universally hostile to the movies—the major contribution to the wider public debate was made by Henry James Forman's *Our Movie-Made Children*, a popularization and sensationalization of the Studies published in May 1922 and widely synopsized, extracted and reviewed in the popular magazine press. Forman's book made Short's intentions much clearer than the Studies had done, in producing a sustained attack on the movies, and incidentally on the organization of the industry and the Hays Office.

The motion picture producers tended to regard the emerging alliance between independent exhibitors and the articulate spokespeople of small communities which were of no real and economic importance to them as bogus and dishonest. Hays and the MPPDA had constantly to remind them that these communities possessed a good deal of political influence which could be used against the industry. The MPPDA's counter-moves began in September 1929 with a conference on "The Community and the Motion Picture," which brought together what Carl Milliken, Secretary of the MPPDA, referred to as "our Public Relations Family," to applaud Hays' unusual homilies on "Better Pictures," establish a Committee on the Use of Motion Pictures in Religious Education, and endorse the appointment of Mrs. Alice Ames Winter, a former president of the General Federation of Women's Clubs, as a representative of "the women of America" to the Studio Relations Committee in Hollywood. The Commissioning of the Production Code was part of this same defensive process. It was typical of Hays that, when faced with an unholy alliance of small exhibitors, small-town Protestant conservatism and Progressive reformers wanting to extend Federal Regulation, he should seek to forge an equally unholy alliance between Big Business and Big Catholicism. Effectively, by 1930 the MPPDA could not recruit a sufficiently authoritative protestant voice to endorse its program of self-regulation, so it turned to the Catholic Church as one of its oldest and most faithful friends.

In some respects the Catholic Church, dominated as its hierarchy in the 1920s was by second- or third-generation Irish-Americans, clearly better integrated into the dominant cultural value-system than more recent waves of immigrants, was ideally situated to mediate and negotiate this site of cultural conflict. The issue was not to be resolved through the mechanisms of Congressional investigations and legislative lobbying, the conventional political methods employed by earlier Protestant reformers. The experience of Prohibition had failed—and was seen widely proclaimed to have failed—as a Great Experiment in legislating morals. *Christian Century* complained in 1932 that it was the only weekly still advocating the retention of Prohibition, which is perhaps indicative of how difficult it might have been to make a convincing case for regulatory legislation. But the public issue provoked around censorship was not susceptible to resolution simply by a reform of content or by the development of an efficient regulatory procedure, such as took place between the acceptance of the Production Code in February 1930 and the passing of the Resolution for Uniform Implementation in June 1934. What was needed, in addition, was a sufficiently public act of atonement and propitiation by the "organized industry" to an identifiable moral authority, an act which would silence, if only temporarily, the legion of Protestant reformers demanding federal regulation.

Ideologically, the Catholic Church was firmly located on the same side as the industry, opposed to legislative regulation. But it was also empowered by a sense of moral certainty which it, alone among the religious groupings of the inter-war period, appeared to possess. Where Protestants seemed to see themselves as losing their grip on their own religious traditions, and on America, Neo-Thomism provided Catholics with the means, as William Halsey puts it, "to think of themselves as the saviors of American ideals."[106] Catholics, far more effectively than any other group, could maintain a nineteenth-century instrumentalist view of culture—as serving to demonstrate how people ought to behave, rather than what they did. As one Catholic writer, James Gillis, put it in an open letter to Theodore Dreiser, "Be decent, be clean, and America will seem less tragic."[107]

This Catholic response to what it denounced as Neo-Humanism was strongly developed across a number of cultural fields between 1928 and 1935, and a small group of leading Jesuit intellectuals were prominent in its articulation. The involvement of the Catholic clergy with the movies needs to be seen as part of this general project of confident Catholic cultural assertiveness, which found expression in the Catholic Action movement.

The Papal Encyclical *Quadragessimo Anno*, published in 1931, was a call to initiate Catholic social activism, under the banner of Catholic Action. Histories of Catholic social reform have tended to describe the American program of Catholic Action as a failure, and at the same time they have tended to downplay the connection between Catholic Action and the Legion of Decency, which is usually viewed as something of an embarrassment. But the effects which appeared to be produced by the Legion in 1934 fitted precisely with the goal of the Catholic Action campaign David O'Brien in *American Catholics and Social Reform* describes as "The role of Catholic Action" being "to train Catholic laymen in the knowledge and practice of their faith so they would diffuse the spirit of the gospel throughout the world,"[108] and Michael Williams, editor of *The Commonweal* and the "Happy Wanderer of Catholic Action"[109] in his 1934 book *The Catholic Church in Action*, declared that "Catholic Action of today is simply the effort being made to increase the effectiveness, heighten the power, and make more rapid the world-embracing influence of the Church at a time of universal social crisis."[110] The Summer Schools for Catholic Action were begun among the Sodalities in 1931 by Lord. The Catholic press heralded the Legion of Decency as "The Outstanding Achievement of American Catholic Action,"[111] and it was endorsed by the Papal Encyclical "Vigilante Cura" of July 1936.

The MPPDA in late 1929 began to offer the Catholic Church an opportunity for large-scale participation in the industry's process of self-regulation, most visibly in having Father Daniel A. Lord, S.J., editor of *The Queen's Work* and the leading figure in the revival of the Catholic Sodality youth movement, prepare a "Suggested Code to Govern the Production of Motion Pictures."[112] In June 1930 Joseph Breen was hired to work out of the Chicago offices of Martin Quigley's trade paper, the *Motion Picture Herald*, promoting endorsements for the code among the Catholic hierarchy in the U.S. and more generally disseminating knowledge of it around the Catholic world. Although there were one or two exceptions, the majority of the Catholic hierarchy were clearly convinced by the arguments of the industry's good intentions and the likely benefits to emerge from their cooperation. As early as October 1930 Breen was sending copies of his personal correspondence with members of the hierarchy and other senior figures in the Catholic Church to Milliken and to Hays. These included his correspondence with Monsignor Joseph Corrigan, Rector of the Catholic University of America, the man who in September 1933 suggested that the Apostolic Delegate Cardinal Cicognani should make a public pronouncement on the movies. It was this act which precipitated the Catholic action of early 1934, leading to the establishment of the Legion of Decency. The historian of the Legion, Father Paul Facey, wrote in 1944 that

> behind the apparent spontaneity of the Legion of Decency campaign was the conscious activity of a few men who labored, first, to provide a solution for the problem of movie

morals, and then to provide pressure to make the solution work.[113]

It seems increasingly difficult to avoid the suggestion that one of those men was Will Hays, and that the "organized industry" acquiesced in the limited Catholic attack on it in order to protect its more fundamental economic interests.

The real danger the industry faced was from the passage of legislation outlawing block booking and imposing federal control, a danger that grew more acute as the Protestant reform faction grew stronger. By the beginning of 1934 it was evident that the reform movement would neither succumb to persuasion, nor could they any longer simply be dismissed as a crackpot minority. The industry could redeem itself publicly only by an overt act of penance, and the Catholic Church provided it with an opportunity through the Legion of Decency. How much overt collusion between the two organizations was involved in that is far from clear. Very significantly, the Legion never took up the issue of block booking—occasional priests who introduced it as an issue in their denunciation of the movies were in most cases reprimanded by their bishops, and there is certainly some evidence that the MPPDA offered to enforce the Code (which they were doing anyway) in exchange for the Legion's restricting its concern only to questions of morality.[114] The Legion managed very effectively to steal the thunder of the Protestant reformers and claim the glory of reforming the movies for themselves and Catholic Action. The industry managed to concede the public pressure, and at the same time to separate the issues of trade practices and profitability from the question of morals, and to discredit, by comparison to the Legion, the Protestant reform groups. Both parties found a great deal that was convenient in this arrangement, and it is hard to believe that the transactions were entered into without some expectation that making the movies morally pure enough for Catholics to attend would not also provide important incidental benefits for both reformers and reformed.

No fundamental shift of MPPDA policy toward the Production Code occurred as a result of these negotiations, and the apparent changes in Code operation introduced in July 1934 were in fact mainly cosmetic. Certainly there was a further tightening up of practice, but there had been at least three of those since September 1931, as the Code was implemented with gradually increasing efficiency and strictness, and as a machinery of implementation was developed on an *ad hoc* basis of precedent. The evidence suggests that the real turning point in policy came in March 1933 and was brought about by the bank holiday and fears of what the Roosevelt administration might do. As the treatment of *Scarface* indicates, the mechanisms of self-regulation were operative well before 1934, at least in those areas where the industry recognized vocal public concern. But one of the lessons that the "organized industry" learned during the early 1930s was that refining this machinery did not constitute a sufficient response to public protest. To be convincing, self-regulation had to be as public as every other aspect of this most publicized industry; and Will Hays knew as well as Al Capone how much grief there was to be found in the limelight.

NOTES

Much of the research for this article was undertaken during the academic year 1983-84, in which I held an American Studies Fellowship from the American Council of Learned Societies. Further research has been facilitated by awards from the British Academy and the University of Exeter. I am greatly indebted to the Motion Picture Association of America, and to its Secretary, James Bouras, for permitting me to consult documents in the MPA archive in New York; to Sam Gill, Archivist of the Margaret Herrick Library of the Academy of Motion Picture Arts and Sciences, Los Angeles; and to Karen Rench of the Indiana State Historical Society, Indianapolis. Many colleagues—among them David Bordwell, Kristin Thompson, Janet Staiger, Lea Jacobs, Robert Sklar, Guiliana Muscio, Francis Couvares, Mick Gidley, Anthony Fothergill, Karen Edwards, Michael Wood—have helped me clarify my ideas on censorship through discussion; but my greatest practical and intellectual debt is to Ruth Vasey, for exploring the research material used here with me, for organizing and explaining it to me, and most of all for her boundless enthusiasm.

1. Quoted in Andrew Sinclair, "Epilogue," Fred D. Pasley, *Al Capone: The Biography of a Self-Made Man* (London: Faber, 1966 [first published 1931]), p. 322.

2. e.g. "Mr. Hays' Foreword" to Will Irwin, "Will Hays' Ten years in the Movies," *The New Movie Magazine* (September 1932), p. 20.

3. Douglas Gomery, "The Coming of Sound to the American Cinema: A History of the Transformation of an Industry," Ph.D. dissertation, University of Wisconsin-Madison, 1975. Douglas Gomery, "Writing the History of the American Film Industry: Warner Bros. and Sound," *Screen* 17, No. 1 (Spring 1976).

4. e.g. Michael Freedland, *The Warner Brothers* (London: Harrap, 1983), pp. 28-45.

5. *Motion Picture Almanac* (Chicago: Quigley Publishing Company, 1931), p. 11.

6. Title in *A Star is Born*, prod. David O. Selznick, 1937.

7. Andrew Bergman, *We're in the Money: Depression America and Its Films* (New York: Harper, 1971), p. xxiii.

8. "John Ford's *Young Mr. Lincoln*: A Collective Text by the Editors of *Cahiers du Cinema*," *Screen* 13, No. 3 (Autumn 1972), pp. 5-43.

9. Robert S. McElvane, *The Great Depression: America 1929-1941* (New York: Times Books, 1984) p. 208.

10. Colin MacArthur, *Underworld USA* (London: Secker and Warburg, 1972). Jack Shadoian, *Dreams and Dead Ends: The American Gangster/Crime Film* (Cambridge, Mass.: MIT Press, 1977).

11. Robert Warshow, "The Gangster as Tragic Hero," in *The Immediate Experience* (New York: Atheneum, 1970), pp. 127-133.

12. Shadoian, op. cit., p. 22.

13. Edward Mitchell, "Apes and Essences, Some Sources of Significance in the American Gangster Film," *Wide Angle* 1, No. 1 (1976), reprinted in Barry Keith Grant, ed., *Film Genre Reader* (Austin: University of Texas Press, 1986), p. 165.

14. Recent versions of this history can be found in, e.g., Pam Cook, ed., *The Cinema Book* (London: British Film Institute, 1985), p.7; John Izod, *Hollywood and the Box Office* (London: Macmillan, 1988), pp. 105-106; Edward de Grazia and Roger K. Newman, *Banned Films: Movies, Censors and the First Amendment* (New York: Bowker, 1982), pp. 32-45.

15. Cook, op. cit., p. 7.

16. Raymond Moley, *The Hays Office* (Indianapolis: Bobbs-Merrill, 1945).

17. Robert Sklar, *Movie-Made America: A Cultural History of American Movies* (New York: Random House, 1977), pp. 175-194.

18. Edward Buscombe, "Bread and Circuses: Economics and the Cinema," in Patricia Mellencamp and Philip Rosen, eds., *Cinema Histories, Cinema Practices* (Los Angeles: American Film Institute, 1984), p. 8.

19. Bergman, op. cit., p. 30.

20. McElvane, op. cit., p. 209.

21. Thomas Schatz, *Hollywood Genres* (New York: Random House, 1981), p. 99.

22. Ibid., p. 98.

23. "A Letter to Roger W. Babson from Carl E. Milliken, Secretary, Motion Picture Producers and Distributors of America, Inc." dated May 7, 1929 (New York: MPPDA, 1929).

24. Quoted in Allsop, *The Bootleggers* (London: Hutchinson, 1961), p. 340.

25. Al Capone, July 29, 1931, quoted in John Kobler, *Capone: The Life and World of Al Capone* (London: Coronet, 1973), p. 313.

26. Schatz, op. cit., p. 99.

27. see Appendix for list.

28. Memo, Joy to Hays, Motion Picture Association of America Archive (hereafter MPA), New York, 1932, Production Code file. Roger Dooley claims that there were "more than thirty clear-cut examples, plus many marginal items" in 1931, but he positively identifies only eleven. Roger Dooley, *From Scarface to Scarlett: American Films in the 1930s* (New York: Harcourt Brace Jovanovich 1979), p. 293.

29. Schatz, op. cit., p. 82.

30. Allen Eyles, *That Was Hollywood: The 1930s* (London: Batsford, 1987).

31. Quoted in Allsop, op. cit., p. 476.

32. Andrew Sinclair, *Era of Excess: A Social History of the Prohibition Movement* (New York: Harper, 1964) p. 222.

33. Pasley, op. cit., p. 317. In his introduction to the 1966 edition, Andrew Sinclair observes, "Al Capone was to crime what J.P. Morgan was to banking, the first man to exert national influence over his trade." (p. 3).

34. Kobler, op. cit., p. 246.

35. Geoffrey Perrett, *America in the Twenties: A History* (New York: Simon and Schuster, 1982), p. 398.

36. ibid., p. 395.

37. *The Forum* April (1927).

38. Frederick Lewis Allen, *Only Yesterday: An Informal History of the 1920s* (New York: Harper, 1964 [first published 1931]), p. 224.

39. Pasley, op. cit., p. 317.

40. Quoted in Kobler, op. cit., p. 297.

41. "Recent Social Trends in the United States: Report of the President's Research Committee on Social Trends" (New York: McGraw Hill, 1933), p. 537.

42. Allsop, op. cit., p. 261.

43. Sinclair, op. cit., p. 229.

44. Marvin Gosch and Richard Hammer in *The Luciano Testament* offer an alternative explanation, suggesting that Capone's arrest was the result of a communal decision taken "for the good of the organization of the underworld," at Atlantic City: "The bloodletting in Chicago had brought a public outcry and pressure on the underworld all over the country. A sacrificial lamb was needed to ease the heat. Capone was to be the lamb." (London: Pan, 1975), p. 113).

45. Quoted in Allsop, op. cit., p. 219.

46. Allen, op. cit., p. 290.

47. Col. Robert Isham Randolph, "How to Wreck Capone's Gang," *Collier's* (March 7, 1931). Randolph was the Chairman of the Chicago Association of Commerce Subcommittee for the Prevention and Punishment of Crime, better known to the press as the Secret Six.

48. Quoted in Allsop, op. cit., p. 265.

49. Quoted in Allsop, op. cit., p. 377.

50. Judge Samuel Seabury's investigations into civic corruption in New York filled the press with allegations of connections between Tammany Hall and organized crime during the winter of 1931-32, and led to Jimmy Walker's resignation in September 1932.

51. "[Luciano's] regulations gave his men an image the antithesis of the one portrayed in the press of the day and later popularized in the scores of Warner Brothers [sic] movies of the early 1930s. Luciano's men were ordered to dress neatly and conservatively, like office workers, to avoid wide-brimmed hats, loud shirts and ties, garish suits completely. ('Let Capone and his Chicago guys to that. We won't.')" Gosch and Hammer, op. cit., p. 76.

52. Jack Bilbo, *Carrying A Gun for Al Capone*, 1931, quoted in Allsop, p. 381. One of the books, *Jake Lingle of Chicago on the Spot* (New York: Dutton, 1931), was written by Chicago *Tribune* reporter John Boettiger, who later married President Roosevelt's daughter Anna. Immediately on Roosevelt's inauguration, Boettiger was employed by the MPPDA as a special assistant to Will Hays.

53. Quoted in Kobler, op. cit., p. 293.

54. Quoted in Allsop, op. cit., p. 424.

55. Carlton Simon to Hays, November 15, 1930, *The Doorway to Hell* Case File, Production Code Administration Archive (hereafter PCA), Margaret Herrick Library, Academy of Motion Picture Arts and Sciences, Los Angeles, California.

56. Quoted in Shadoian, op. cit., p. 44.

57. Quoted in Bergman, op. cit., p. 6.

58. Zanuck to Joy, January 6, 1931, PCA *Public Enemy* Case File.

59. Joy to Zanuck, January 26, 1931, PCA *Public Enemy* Case File.

60. Trotti to Hays, April 14, 1931, PCA *Public Enemy* Case File.

61. Will Hays, Annual Report of the President of the MPPDA, March 30, 1931. MPA, 1931, Meetings file.

62. Vollmer to Hays, April 20, 1931, PCA *Public Enemy* File.

63. Hays to Joseph Melillo, Secretary of the Hoboken Lions Club, June 11, 1931, PCA *Public Enemy* file.

64. June 4, 1931, Joy to E.B. Derr of Caddo. MPA, 1932, Caddo, *Scarface* file.

65. Joy to Hays, November 3, 1931. MPA, 1932, Caddo, Scarface file.

66. Joy to Hays, March 5, 1932. MPA, 1932, Caddo, *Scarface* file.

67. Arthur Sacks, "An Analysis of Gangster Movies of the Early Thirties," *Velvet Light Trap* 1, p. 8. The only film in this period in which incest was a matter of serious concern to the SRC was *The Barretts of Wimpole Street*.

68. *Literary Digest*, Jul. 25, 1931, pp. 20-21.

69. *Christian Century*, May 13, 1931, p. 641.

70. *Christian Century*, August 12, 1931, pp. 1015-1016.

71. Joy to Hays, September 30, 1931. MPA, 1932, Caddo, *Scarface* file.

72. This resolution is referred to in an unsigned memo dated September 29, 1931, in the MPA Archive, 1931, Production Code file. In a Letter to Hays on September 5, 1935, Breen noted, "In September 1931 . . . the Board here, by formal resolution, agreed to call a halt to what was then generally referred to as 'gangster' films. The effect of this, as you know, was very satisfactory." (MPA, 1936, Production Code file) On August 7, 1939, in a letter to Hays, Breen referred to it as "the Special Agreement adopted in

September 1931, against the production of gangster films" (MPA, 1939, Production Code file). The relevant wording, listed in the "Regulations re Crime adopted for a clearer and more exact interpretation of the Code" would appear to be: "Action suggestive of wholesale slaughter of human beings, either criminals, in conflict with the police, or as between warring factions of criminals, or in public disorder of any kind, will not be allowed." ("Regulations re Crime in Motion Pictures," December 20, 1938. MPA, 1938, Production Code file) It is, however, possible that some other wording was used to differentiate gangster pictures from crime films.

73. Joy to Hays, March 5, 1932. MPA, 1932, Caddo, *Scarface* file.

74. Hays memo March 10, 1932, Caddo, *Scarface* file.

75. Tino Balio, *United Artists: The Studio Built by the Stars* (Madison: University of Wisconsin Press, 1976), p. 111.

76. Joseph Schenck to Hays, February 26, 1932. MPA, 1932, Caddo, *Scarface* file.

77. May 8, 1932, RKO Archives, Los Angeles, Censorship file.

78. Hughes to Hays, May 12, 1932. MPA, 1932, Caddo, *Scarface* file.

79. Balio, op. cit., p. 111.

80. Henry James Forman, "To the Movies—But Not to Sleep," *McCall's Magazine*, Vol. 29, No. 12, pp. 12-13, 58-79.

81. Joseph McBride, *Hawks on Hawks* (Los Angeles: University of California Press, 1982), p. 44.

82. Moley, op. cit., p. 75.

83. Will H. Hays, *The Memoirs of Will H. Hays* (New York: Doubleday, 1955); Martin Quigley, *Decency in Motion Pictures* (New York: Macmillan, 1937).

84. Mae D. Huettig, *Economic Control of the Motion Picture Industry* (Philadelphia: University of Philadelphia Press, 1944).

85. I am grateful to Guiliana Muscio for this information.

86. Moley, op. cit., p. 8.

87. Ibid., p. 5.

88. A summary account of anti-trust suits can be found in Simon Whitney, "Antitrust Policies and the Motion Picture Industry," in Gorham Kinden, ed., *The American Movie Industry: The Business of Motion Pictures* (Carbondale: Southern Illinois University Press, 1982), pp. 161-204.

89. Raymond Moley, *After Seven Years* (New York: Harper, 1939).

90. Raymond Moley, *Are We Movie-Made?* (New York: Macy-Mascius, 1938).

91. Martin Quigley, editorial, *Motion Picture Herald* (May 14, 1932), p. 9.

92. e.g. *Motion Picture Herald* (April 16, 1932), pp. 9-11.

93. "The Open Door," MPPDA pamphlet (New York, 1924, 1927).

94. Will H. Hays, "The Motion Picture—1930," speech delivered February 1, 1930, published as a pamphlet by the MPPDA, p. 4. Will H. Hays Archive, Indiana State Historical Society, Indianapolis.

95. J. Homer Platten to Hays, November 26, 1924, National Motion Picture Conference file.

96. Figures derived from *Motion Picture Almanac* (Chicago: Quigley Publishing Company, 1931).

97. e.g. "Moral Waste of the Movies," *The Churchman* (August 17, 1929), pp. 8-9.

98. MPPDA, An Open Letter to Roger W. Babson from Carl E. Milliken, p. 4.

99. Motion Picture Herald (May 14, 1932), p. 11.

100. ibid., pp. 10-11.

101. *Motion Picture Herald* (July 2, 1932), p. 36.

102. *Motion Picture Herald* (March 19, 1932), p. 10.

103. e.g. Fred Eastman, "The Menace of the Movies," *Christian Century* (January 15, 1930), pp. 75-78.

104. e.g. Gerald Mast, *The Movies in Our Midst* (Chicago: University of Chicago Press, 1982), p. 346. Mast only quotes Forman. A more balanced account, which nevertheless does not fully recognize the innovative nature of the much of the research, is in Garth Jowett, *Film, The Democratic Art* (Boston: Little, Brown and Co., 1976), pp. 220-229. The best short account of the studies, which does accord them the respect they deserve, is Shearon Lowery and Melvin L. De Fleur, *Milestones in Mass Communication Research: Media Effects* (New York: Longman, 1983), pp. 31-57.

105. e.g. Kimball Young, review of Herbert Blumer, *Movies and Conduct* and Henry James Forman, *Our Movie-Made Children*, *American Journal of Sociology* (September 1935), pp. 250-255.

106. William M. Halsey, *The Survival of American Innocence: Catholicism in an Era of Disillusionment, 1920-1940* (Notre Dame: University of Notre Dame Press, 1980) p. 5.

107. James Gillis, "Sutsum Corda," *The Catholic News* (New York) (February 6, 1932), quoted in Halsey, op. cit., p. 106.

108. David J. O'Brien, *American Catholics and Social Reform* (New York: Oxford University Press, 1968), p. 21.

109. Redmond A. Burke, "Michael Williams: Happy Wanderer of Catholic Action," *The Catholic Literary World*, 15 (1944), quoted in Halsey, op. cit., p. 29.

110. Michael Williams, *The Catholic Church in Action* (New York: Macmillan, 1934), p. 341.

111. Gerard B. Donnelly, "The Outstanding Catholic Achievement," *America* (June 5, 1935), pp. 298-300.

112. Authorship of the Production Code, and indeed the stability of the text of the Code, are complex issues which will be more fully explored in my *Reforming the Movies: Hollywood, the Hays Office, and the Campaign for Film Censorship, 1922-1939* (New York: Oxford University Press, forthcoming).

113. Paul W. Facey, S.J., *The Legion of Decency: A Sociological Analysis of the Emergence and Development of a Social Pressure Group* (New York: Arno, 1974), p. 46.

114. e.g. George Schaefer to Hays, May 23, 1934. Will H. Hays Archive, Indiana State Historical Society, Indianapolis.

APPENDIX:
GANGSTER MOVIES, 1930-1932, BY YEAR OF RELEASE

1930
RKO *The Pay Off*

Paramount *Street of Chance*

Warner Bros. *The Widow From Chicago*
 The Doorway to Hell

1931
Universal *Reckless Living*
 Homicide Squad

Paramount *City Streets*

MGM *The Secret Six*
 A Gentleman's Fate

Warner Bros. *Little Caesar*
 Public Enemy
 The Finger Points

United Artists *Corsair*

Fox *Quick Millions*

Columbia *The Last Parade*
 The Guilty Generation

Tiffany *Hell Bound*

1932
MGM *The Beast of the City*

United Artists *Scarface*

DESIGNING MULTI-CULTURAL AMERICA
Modern Movie Theaters and the Politics of Public Space 1920-1945

Lary May
University of Minnesota

When our society was established this "natural" process of Americanization continued in its own unobserved fashion, defying the social aesthetic and political assumptions of our political leaders and tastemakers alike. This, as I say, was the vernacular process, and in the days when our leaders still looked to England and the Continent for their standards of taste, the vernacular stream of our culture was creating itself out of whatever elements it found useful, including the Americanized culture of the slaves. So in this sense the culture of the United States has always been more democratic and American than the social and political institutions in which it was emerging.
    Ralph Ellison, *Going to the Territory* (1986)

A certain type of life has inspired the modern world. It is our life, but it is particularly America's. And our life is the motion picture. There is a natural affinity between modernist art and the photoplay theater which it would seem the architect and the exhibitor cannot ignore.
    George Schutz, "Modernistic Art: Its Significance
    to America and the Photoplay." (1929)

Early in the Great Depression the Anglo-Saxon tastemakers that Ralph Ellison saw as so central to American life entered motion picture exhibition, seeking to generate a fusion between high and popular art. Their brainchild was the International Music Hall in Rockefeller City. Designed by Raymond Hood and Edward Stone, the building drew on art deco motifs derived from international fairs and exhibitions, particularly in France. Radiating a monumental streamlined style, the entire structure was composed of angular steel, glass, and chrome that unified the interior as well as exterior. The street front engaged rather than retreated from the world of machines and speed, and the circular marquee and exterior motifs wrapped around the corner, giving form to one of the busiest intersections in New York City. The step-back volumes receding up the skyscraper provided a sense of push-and-pull that gave the whole a quality of dynamism. Inside, the auditorium contained a proscenium arch that radiated out into the audience, and the sculptures and murals used classical motifs to dramatize the age of electronic communications, and airplanes. To its designers, the Music Hall blended into the business complex of Rockefeller City, creating amid hard times a vision of hope and renewal. As Will Hays, the head of the motion picture producer association, proclaimed at the opening ceremonies:

> This is not a dedication to a theater—it is a reaffirmation of faith in America's indomitableness and fearlessness. (It) rises like a Pharos out of the blinding fogs of irresolution and bewilderment to proclaim that leadership has not failed us ... the bravest declaration of faith in their country's stability that the Rockefellers, father and son, America's most useful citizens—have yet offered. Let us rise and salute them and all their works.[1]

In many ways, such rhetoric might seem to be another example of show business advertising and self promotion. Yet there was more to it. And it was not hard to find: it emanated from the patrons and artists who financed and designed Rockefeller City and the Music Hall. The patron that Hays praised so lavishly was the son of perhaps the most powerful industrialist of the nineteenth century. Like the men he assembled in New York City to build his business complex, John D. Rockefeller, Jr. inherited the tradition of Victorian self-denial and service that defined the world of Anglo-Saxon elites. Yet as he began to take over his father's enterprises, he was shocked by the ruthless world of laissez-faire business practice that led to militant labor strikes, and worried that the revolution in manners and morals encouraged the wide defiance of Prohibition laws and civic disorder. By the twenties he had established non-profit foundations and welfare programs, and exhorted corporate reformers to guide the nation into a new realm of moral virtue and progress. In the midst of the nation's greatest economic crisis, his patronage of Rockefeller City culminated a long list of civic endeavors, a project that would be, as the opening program stated, a spiritual ideal, a "Taj Mahal," elevating humanity to "new heights . . . banishing ignorance and illiteracy."

Transferred into the aesthetics of Rockefeller City and the Music Hall, this civic idealism received its best expression in the internal memoranda that the design team commissioned to explain the meaning of the artistic symbols—the sculpture, reliefs and murals—that united the various buildings into one "understandable story." Written by Hartely Alexander, a professor of philosophy from the University of Nebraska, the memorandums described how in earlier times the endless "beckoning of the geographical frontiers has had a vital effect on the growth and shaping of American life." As long as there were opportunities for Anglo-Saxon farmers and craftsmen to own land, the people could create in the New World a republic grounded in reason and moral virtue. The major "story of two centuries of American civilization can be spoken of in terms of its unfolding of physical frontiers . . . to the Pacific Ocean." The rise of the machine age, however, had brought a series of perils: the revolution in manners and morals, the immigration of Southern Europeans, and class conflict at home and abroad. Yet under the guidance of enlightened elites, Rockefeller City arose as a twentieth century "city on a hill," providing

> the first clear expression in our economic life of a new social ideal, that is, of human welfare and happiness centering on the work that we do, and not on some incidental wage: if a whole population, such as Rockefeller City will possess, can be lifted into a finer life in their working and leisure hours, then the economic democracy of America will have begun its answer to the Bolshevik challenge. In all of these phases, then,

Rockefeller City is a builder's enterprise, and it is appropriate to announce its theme as Homo Faber, Man the Builder.²

No one was better able to transfer these aims into a new architectural style than the man Rockefeller chose to head the design team, Raymond Hood. Raised in an atmosphere of strict Protestant self-denial and temperance, Hood started his career as a prominent designer working in the Beaux Arts tradition. Within this school, the function of architecture was not just to create a building for different functions. Rather, the artist should present in the civic arena—that space between private life and the state where citizens voluntarily gathered for commercial or voluntary purposes—a set of historically derived symbols and ideals, serving thereby to inspire the values so necessary for self-governance in a republic. Yet by the twenties, Hood began to fuse together historical and modernist principles. As that combination unfolded in the Radiator Building, and then culminated in the bold display of steel and glass in the Daily News Building, Hood and his illustrator Hugh Ferris argued that the architect's task was to compose the various materials of the machine age into a dynamic vision of order. Carrying these goals into the construction of Rockefeller City, Hood and his design team coordinated several different buildings around modernist and classical beaux arts principles. The integration of Rockefeller City around a single modernist motif, with its nightclub, skating rink, radio center, business offices and entertainment sites brought that vision of urban planning to fruition, promising to set a model for the nation.³

On opening day, however, the verdict was less clear. The office complex that housed wealthy businessmen seemed well on the way to success. Yet at the International Music Hall where the ordinary patrons cast their ballot, the judgment of the public was quick and instantaneous: Rockefeller and his theatrical manager, S.L. Rothafel, the "Napoleon of Broadway," had met their "Waterloo." In the opinion of trade journalists, the hopes that the Music Hall would set a national trend emulated throughout the country had turned into the "world's biggest bust." Audiences did not like the show, and not enough paying customers covered the operating costs. The roots of this disaster were all too evident. Across the country theatre managers and critics found that fans had transformed themselves from a passive audience into a public, one that made choices and judgments concerning popular images and styles. One result was that attendance declined at the downtown

Designing Multi-Cultural America 187

theatre palaces and patronage at nondescript, neighborhood theatres experienced a business upsurge. Yet rather than the Music Hall providing a trend that would revive the theatre palace, critics observed that it simply perpetuated in modern dress the old limitations.[4] These "faults of design" were long and numerous. Inside the monumental interior of the Music Hall, for example, the auditorium contained over 6,000 seats, complete with several ascending balconies that continued the traditional playhouse practice of dividing patrons by class and status. Most of the reliefs and murals represented their stories within the canon of classical Greek mythology, but the average fan lacked the education to understand their meaning. Conspicuously missing were portrayals of the workers and ethnic minorities whose labor had built this monument to America and whose patronage was so necessary for its commercial success. Symbolic of that oversight, S.L. Rothafel decided to forego sound films altogether, since he disliked the dialects informing the new gangster and social problem genres. Instead, "Roxy" presented a live panoramic symphony that glorified elite pioneers from the Dutch to the Rockefellers of today. Critics and fans complained that such history lessons provided "one long multiplication table" narrated by a figure who resembled the "Almighty Himself." And to top it off the admission price to see the "Almighty" was too high. Beset on all sides, the Board of Directors reluctantly fired the famed Roxy, returned to film showings and lowered prices. Only Rothafel seemed to realize that an era was ending, as he told a reporter in 1933.

> I'll be back in April, after a trip South, and go to work and settle all this stuff that is going around about me. Oh, I've heard the things they've been saying. They're all wolves, this Broadway crowd. They're glad when somebody who has always stood for something in the theater stubs his toe . . . I'm sick of it. These sophisticated, worldly wise, narrow faced, stare-eyed low life that hang around Broadway! I used to walk down Broadway in the old days. Now I never walk there when I can help myself. I feel like I ought to go home and take a bath when I do. The whole street exists by shots in the arm of excitement and filthy excitement and filthy scandals and rumors.[4]

Though the International Music Hall would eventually be refurbished and undergo a name change to become a profitable sightseeing attraction in New York City, it never set the nationwide trend for theatre design that was the fondest dream of its builders and motion picture executives in 1932. Nor would Rothafel, the "Napoleon of Broadway" ever return in triumph to the "Great White Way." The lessons that might be learned from this dual tragedy were as bright as the lights on the Music Hall marquee. Trade journalists, writers who proudly paid less attention to artistic standards than the profit and loss equations of the market place, recognized that audiences now had minds of their own. In the midst of the Depression, fans rejected theatre palaces that offered a democracy of wealth derived from the standards of the rich. Both the lavish modern and historically designed theatre palace that were successful in the twenties now recorded a sharp decline in business due to their "faults of design." Early in 1933, however, the trade journals ran a series of polls and found that theatre owners were ready and willing to remodel in a fresh style. Yet two elements inhibited that well-calculated appraisal of the market. The first was the lack of an alternative style to replace the palatial mode, the other was the lack of capital. A ray of hope occurred from an unexpected source, making it possible to launch amid hard times a great boom in remodeling. Riding on the votes of immigrants and city dwellers, Franklin Roosevelt assumed the presidency in 1932. Almost immediately his pump-priming policies placed money in the hands of moviegoers, and more importantly, the New Deal Housing Act provided the fresh capital for small theatre owners—entrepreneurs who did not have their capital tied up in the mammoth theatre palaces—to innovate along new lines.[6]

At the forefront of the ensuing revolution in movie house design was a streamlined theatre identified with social and cultural renewal. Among the many advocates of this new style appearing in the trade journals, none was more visible than Ben Schlanger. Unlike the Anglo-Saxon elites that designed Rockefeller City, Schlanger was the son of Jewish immigrants who were part of that great wave of migrants from Eastern Europe that so aroused the fear of Hartely Alexander as he developed his civic themes for the Center. Yet it was to be Schlanger rather than Hood or Hartely who was to set the tone for theatres over the next twenty years. Repeatedly Schlanger promoted in numerous articles and speeches the conversion of movie houses from large (1,000-

3,000 seating capacity), lavishly ornamented theatres decorated in period motifs to smaller, 600-seat structures with sleek motifs characterized by glass, concrete, formica, asymmetrical volumes and a horizontal axis. Inside, the seating was on a democratic basis and artistic representation gave expression to the world of "today," namely to the historical memories and popular values of the local audiences. By 1934 these more egalitarian models were copied almost as unthinkingly as had been the earlier deluxe house. Yet that change was not seen as simply the rejection of a tired consumer item for a fresh look. At the core, their popularity was a rationale which saw the new theatre emblematic of a new dynamic vision of public space, one rooted in abundance, equality and the communal values of a multi-cultural people. As John Root Jr., the son of the famed Chicago School architect, wrote in praise of that transformation:

> Nothing can be better than experimentation if it is not aimless. But it must be towards the expression of the Twentieth Century in the United States, and not in terms of Chinese pagodas, Greek temples, Roman amphitheaters, Moorish palaces and Gothic cathedrals. We are going to see motion picture theaters contrived and staged for a democratic republic. We have a civilization of our own yet realized in the fine arts, but even in its partial manifestations more our own than anything the world has yet seen.[7]

Sixty years after these events, the ideological struggle swirling around the construction of competing movie house designs from 1930 to 1950 seems almost incomprehensible. The reason lies in the way historians and humanists have understood the relation between politics, architecture, and popular culture in the Great Depression. Traditionally students of American architecture separate questions of social and political ideology from style, focusing their attention on the formalistic innovations that characterized modernism. Generally in their concentration on innovative form they have ignored the ideological meaning—the values and social beliefs that undergirded these designs—or they have argued that modern architects in the United States—in contrast to the innovators in Europe—forsook ideology and concentrated instead on pragmatically solving functional problems for their business patrons. Complimenting this approach are students of popular culture, especially those influenced by the Frankfurt School sociologists who have seen that the producers of mass-produced art framed their work in the context of backward looking national myths and futuristic dreams of affluence that served the interests of business leaders. The culture of the thirties is thus seen as a seamless or escapist web of homogenous American myths, serving to distract attention from the major transformation in economic and political power that characterized the New Deal era. Synthesizing these two approaches have been scholars of modern design who argue that the machine styles informing the World's Fairs and consumer items reflected corporate reformers' successful efforts to appropriate artists and impose their values on consumers. Architects and modern designers, in the words of the historian James Allen, made it possible for capitalists to "gain hegemony over high culture by turning artists and intellectuals into its agents, thereby robbing them of their ability to criticize and pose alternatives to the kingdom of commerce."[8]

The problem with this analysis is not that it is wrong. The designers and patrons of the International Music Hall clearly envisaged modernism as a means to promote their ideological interests and civic goals. John D. Rockefeller, Jr. and Raymond Hood envisaged the fusion of the beaux arts and modernism as a means to revitalize faith in themselves and impose their values on the viewers. Here was indeed the self-conscious effort of educated elites to fuse modern architecture and popular art to ideological ends. Yet a theory which sees elites always successful in their goals cannot account for the fact that the Music Hall initially failed to make a profit, and never sparked a national trend. Nor can an analysis which posits a unified culture of Americanism account for the rise of a successful counter theatre style, one with a very different set of national symbols than promoted at the Music Hall. Instead of emanating from established businessmen, the small streamlined movie house was first promoted by marginal businessmen and architects responding to the needs of a new polyglot public. And above all, these outsiders found their efforts supported by the policy initiatives launched by the coming of the New Deal, a political movement that was often at odds with the corporate leaders and tastemakers who funded and designed the Music Hall.

The purpose of this essay is to explore how and why this transformation occurred. Its focus is on a single but extended relationship: the way in which the unprecedented success of the small, modern movie house was at one with the creation of an alternative vision of public space in New Deal years, one that contested at the popular level official views of social order. My aim is not to present a comprehensive analysis of theatre styles from 1920 to 1950. Rather I will trace the impact of stylistic changes on inherited views of civic life. Three assumptions frame this sequence. At the turn of the century, an official high culture dominated architectural conceptions of urban space and public building. It was promoted because it both identified Anglo-Saxon elites with the refinements of beauty and taste and justified their status and power in the new industrial order; that this universalistic vision of high culture also informed theatre design, but was dramatically altered with the rise of a new type of audience gathered in the movie house; and that in the legitimation crisis sparked by the advent of the Great Depression artists and audiences originating from marginal groups found an architectural language which gave representation and form to their own lives and the movie experience itself, a development that embodied a major change in public attitudes towards class and national values.[9]

Let us begin our story with what all contemporaries agreed was the determining factor informing innovations in theatrical design: the rise of a new style audience for the movies. Even before the advent of the thirties, architects and entrepreneurs catering to this market place began to erode traditional architectural practice. Commentators were quick to explore the reasons why this occurred. Like nightclubs and amusement parks, the early film industry was unique in that it was originally associated with patronage and entertainment styles of the lower classes. Early critics exhorted businessmen and artists to address the needs and desires of this new moviegoing audience. Yet they were also unable to define what sort of public had been brought into being. For the exhibition of movies provided a collective space markedly different from that where music, painting, and entertainment had been presented in the past. In the United States as in Europe in the late nineteenth century public architecture was visually determined from above. The educated leaders and artists had first to satisfy their elite patrons or select audiences who patronized subscription theatres, museums or symphonies, carefully separated from the more ribald and polyglot entertainments of the lower classes. The advent of the movie house, however, marked a removal of art from the ritualized hierarchies that characterized the production of high and popular art. Over and over trade journalists and critics saw the movies appealed to a polyglot audience composed of all classes and sexes. Inside gathered men and women from all ethnic groups and classes in the city, each with their eyes focused on the screen where images moved, challenging the conceptions of space and time that marked the more traditional categories of art and architecture. Here it seemed that the ranked Victorian world was dissolving or breaking down. Yet neither the patrons nor the managers knew exactly how to satisfy these new desires or give them public definition. In other words, the audience was a new mediating factor in the production of art, standing between the traditional relation of artists and patrons. But no one could clearly identify the nature of this new public, only that it had generated a set of questions that were not easily answered. What would be the nature of architecture and representation that would legitimize class mixing and the dynamic power of the movie experience itself? What architectural style would give form and meaning to an experience that challenged inherited definitions of public space and civic life?[10]

Though we are not accustomed to see it, these questions underscored the work of the early movie house architects. Each was aware that in catering to this new audience, they were fundamentally altering, even subverting, the older architectural practice. But in the quest for profits and commissions, they began to satisfy their demands. The career of the major theatre architect of the twenties, Thomas Lamb, illustrates the first stage of this process. Lamb was a Scottish immigrant who found his first success in designing lavish theatres for the wealthy. In 1905 one of his most representative buildings arose on upper Broadway: the Cort Theatre. In accord with the desire of Victorians to use art as a means of moral instruction, Lamb drew on the canon of historical functionalism to define the place of art in the civic life of the city: Gothic was appropriate for churches, classical Greek and Roman for civic buildings, Renaissance for the universities, Neo-classical and Baroque or Romanesque for the theatre. Working in this professional framework, Lamb made the Cort a refined neo-classical chateau which the opening program described as "inspired" by the French Kings at Versailles. The stable and balanced facade was on a side street where traffic slowed and was devoid of blaring ads. The box office resided inside glass doors to create an aura of exclusiveness separated from the diverse population of the street and the corrupting world of commerce. Inside, the murals and reliefs depicted French aristocrats and Greek and

Roman gods and goddesses at play, and the auditorium divided the spectators by status and income.

Nearly a decade later, however, Lamb turned his hand to designing the Capitol movie house in Times Square. In order to create a building that would uplift an arena where all the classes and sexes mingled, Lamb turned the Capitol into a monumental version of the Cort. Only now the neo-classical mode informed the widespread democratization, as it was called, of wealthy European standards. To attract the attention, Lamb proudly utilized several large electric marquees that could be seen for several blocks, and situated the box office conspicuously on the sidewalk where everyone had access. The interior contained an eclectic mix that challenged the traditional code of historical functionalism, complimented by colored lights and gold wallpaper. And since the manager found that moviegoers were unwilling to go upstairs to the several balconies, with their associations of inferiority and second class status, Lamb made the upper lobby even more luxurious than the lower level. To promoters these innovations dramatized something new; a monumental theater where "the vast wealth of our country has permitted the erection of costly buildings for the service of our communities. Tacitly we recognize that the old order has changed, that the palace of aristocracy is now the playhouse of democracy. Where royalty deemed it as its own particular right to revel in the created beauty of artists and craftsmen, the democracy is now privileged to enjoy its creation for its hour of leisure."[11]

Nowhere was that conflict between aristocratic values and democratic reception more evident than in the downtown movie houses of the nation's big cities, particularly in Chicago and New York. Amid the hotels and amusements of Times Square fans drawn to the glitter of lights and entertainment found movie palaces modeled on European palaces with plush interiors modeled on Romanesque, Renaissance, Baroque and Neo-classical motifs. (Fig. 1) Each name connoted royalty and a release from everyday life: The Uptown, Brooklyn Paramount, the Strand, Capitol, Rivioli, Roxy, or Rialto. Inside there were palatial lobbies, grand staircases, uniformed ushers, grand symphonies, historically accurate paintings and sculptures. The result, commented one manager, was an urban frontier where we have "collected the most precious rugs, fixtures and treasures that money can produce. No kings or emperors ever wandered through a more lavish world. In essence they are social 'safety valves' in that the public can partake of the same luxuries of the rich and use them to the same extent." As the Times Square "safety valve" became emulated in other big cities, the architectural critic Lewis Mumford noted that the generic term "Broadway" now stood as the "great compensatory divide of the American city. The dazzle of white lights, the color of electric signs, the alabaster architecture of the movie palaces, the aesthetic appeals of shop windows—these stand for elements left out of the drab perspective of the industrial city."[12] (Figures 2 and 3)

At the core of this lavishness, however, lay one central reality. In many ways the use of traditional styles and symbols provided a mask, serving to contain the experience of class and sexual mixing within the aura of an eclectic and hybrid architectural canon. Nonetheless, whatever new demands were evoked by a polyglot audience, a conscious representation of this new reality in structure and style was carefully avoided. Yet amid these "high hat" trappings, the key to profits was for the audience to see their own face either on stage or screen. The most famous master of this delicate balancing act was S.L. Rothafel, "Mr. Broadway,"the manager of five Times Square movie houses: the Rivoli, the Capitol, the Roxy, the Strand and lastly, the modernistic International Music Hall. Like many of the showmen who had "made it" in the marginal realms of commercial entertainment, "Roxy" was the son of poor Jewish immigrants from Eastern Europe. Finding initial success as the owner of nickelodeons, Roxy mixed together the ambience of refined, uplifting symbols with an eclectic mix of historical styles. Next he added a coterie of militarily-attired ushers—young men which Roxy advertised as future "captains of industry." In the orchestra pit he placed church organs as well as symphonies directed by European conductors who expurgated "jazz" from their classic compositions. And he framed the smart entertainment itself within lavish proscenium arches that served to contain the silent film inside the panoply of the best that civilization with a capital "C" had to offer.

The result was a hybrid form of entertainment that like the movement appearing on the screen questioned all static and eternal categories and symbols. The ensuing tension between artistic hierarchy and democratic reception sparked innovators like Roxy and his legion of followers to feature films starring former Italian immigrants like the erotic Rudolph Valentino and Dolores Del Rio stylized as noble Spanish lords and ladies, followed by a stage show featuring a chorus line of scantily clad chorus girls dressed in sparkling gowns who also displayed "plenty of flesh." To attract Catholic fans during the sacred week of Lent, he held Charleston contests accompanied by ragtime music derived from African-Americans. Down the street at the elegant Paramount, Duke Ellington's jazz band performed in a "Black and Blue" stage show, followed by the Jewish vaudeville queen Mae West singing spicy tunes about an "occidental woman" in search of "oriental love." Describing the look of romance and ribald fare informing that formula, the famed film director Fred Niblo noted that fans wanted to "be lifted out of reality into the glamorous world of entertainment. There they will admire the chic French gowns and handsome Italian Count, while the man admires the hero's skill and daring. They revel in foreign flavors. Similar situations may be equally as interesting in an American story, but they become triply romantic when placed in a foreign setting."[13]

Late in the decade, moreover, the demand for an architectural language that would be even more emblematic of this transgression of boundaries slowly appeared. By the late twenties, architects observed that the audience desire for constant change seemed endless. In response they began to create theatrical structures that were unique to the United States. As the mass audience in Europe maintained a strict loyalty to the western-derived architectural canon in their movie houses, Americans deviated from the norm by patronizing exotic theatres that drew on the designs of primitive and non-western peoples. This arose innocently enough when architects suffused the ceilings and side aisles of their theatre palaces with twinkling stars, blue skies, glimmering moons and palm trees evocative of Mediterranean villas. Seeking an even more romantic environment, managers built exotic theaters stylized on a "time when the world was young." A classic example of these "fantastic fairylands" emerged on upper Broadway in New York City where the facade of Loew's 175th Street combined in one eclectic whole Classical, Islamic, Mayan, and Indian motifs. At Loew's Thomas Lamb explained he wanted to cast a "spell of the mysterious and to the Occidental mind, of the exceptional . . . and conspire to create an effect thoroughly foreign to our western imagination . . . where the mind is free to frolic and becomes receptive to entertainment." Further to the west the spell of the mysterious came to focus on the Chinese and Egyptian theaters of Sid Grauman in Los Angeles. Upon the suggestions of his architect who recalled the manner in which saints' relics drew pilgrims to cathedrals in Europe and Asia, Sid Grauman placed in the entrance of his Chinese theater in Hollywood the hand and footprints of famed movie stars. Before entering, the fans touched the relics of the modern gods and goddesses, creating a fusion between art of the movies and the wish for secular salvation itself.[14] (Figures 4 and 5)

By the end of the twenties, these radical innovations were a constant subject of comment in the motion picture trade journals. All agreed that there had been nothing like the grand theatre palace in Europe or the United States. Yet divisions arose among managers and critics alike over the meaning of these innovations. Everything had been done to surround the movie house with the look of civilization and high culture. Yet the noted critic Thomas Talmadge viewed these same Mayan temples and flamboyant rococo monuments and concluded that the barnyard had erupted into the sacred halls of art. "Divorce the motion picture from vaudeville and jazz, separate the theatre from tawdry decoration and vulgarism and it will yet take its place among not only the educational and moral forces of this country, but with the other arts as well." Architects answered that their professional standards had been eroded by the "onerous" demands of the audience, and showmen observed that "In answer to the charge that these gorgeous shrines of entertainment are vulgar, the plea must be 'guilty'. Of course they are vulgar to the highly sensitive person and quite evidently it is not meant for him . . . . In other words the average picture exhibited today demands a jazzy interior and is better patronized than a refined picture in a refined house."[15]

What lay at the core of this debate, and the constant use of the metaphor "jazz" was the slightly disturbing thought that it was not elite patrons, architects, or even showmen who were in charge. Rather it was the audience itself. Placed on the defensive by this criticism, movie house architects answered that it was the "unprecedented" and "fickle" demands of the patrons that "forced" them to innovate so broadly beyond inherited standards. Explaining why the movie house was so flamboyant, for example, the manager of the Paramount theatres in New York City argued that their customers did not come to the "movies" for cultural uplift. Instead lavish theatres appealed to people like the "tired toil-worn father" or the "tired shop girl" who since their dreams had never "come true" wanted a release from "Puritan" codes. "People want to come and live for an hour in romance. They seek escape from the humdrum existence of daily life. Our modern civilization has crowded from their daily lives places where formerly they could get mental rest and imaginative release." In catering to that demand, one showman noted that "The poets sing for the reviewers of the literary supplements. The novelist writes for the circulating libraries and the educated minorities who have the imagination to make their own pictures out of words. The costly and expensive and wasteful stage serves a metropolitan few, and the opera is the withered flower of a medieval art that died." But "the motion picture industry is an expression through and by mechanism for the masses . . . this business serves the wishes of millions." In catering to that marketplace, everything was potentially fluid and up for grabs. As Samuel Katz, one of the most noted theater managers of the day, told a group of students at the Harvard Business School:

> our operations will be different from those of the ordinary chain stores or other lines of business in so far as we are selling an intangible something which we call entertainment. We appeal wholly to the people in their moments of relaxation and we have no gauges, no standards as to whether this food or that food will produce certain results. We appeal wholly to imagination and that provides interesting material to work with."[16]

So pervasive was the dissolving power of that "interesting material" that as the Depression struck, it eventually provided a final knock-out blow to the high culture standards surrounding the movie house itself. At first that change seemed barely noticeable, for even after the stock market crash of 1929, the films and theaters linked to the jazz age continued to show a profit. Yet hardly had the season of 1932 begun than promoters noticed that as unemployment reached record numbers and business failures spread, audiences turned away from urban amusements in record numbers. Soon red-faced industry leaders had to admit that recent years had "exploded the theory that the motion picture industry is largely depression proof." Formerly confident producers spoke of a "world turned upside down," as total theaters operating in the country dropped from 28,000 in 1929 to 12,480 in 1932, with the heavily mortgaged, overseated downtown "palaces" slowly locking their doors. With fans turning from the downtown theaters to cheaper houses in ethnic and working class areas, the average price of admission decreased from thirty-six cents in 1929 to twenty-four cents in 1933, and overall receipts declined over fifty percent. Finally, the industry's highly inflated attendance figures showed nearly a fifty percent decline from 110 million in 1930 to 60 million in 1932. And as the year 1931 passed into history, the editor of *Variety* wondered "whether the movie industry will ever again know the popularity of those peaks it reached in the silent film era and then with sound."[17]

Slowly and unwillingly producers realized that the "golden age of extravagance was gone," and in its wake they were "all out to sea" on why the formulas embodied in exotic stars and lavish theaters had failed. When executives asked their exhibitors what caused the collapse, they discovered that fifty percent of their lost profits came from the economic effects of the Depression. People simply did not have the money to spend at the movies, no matter how cheap. But what caused the other fifty percent? It was not that the deluxe theatres could not be wired for sound, or that formerly popular silent film stars failed to attract fans. As late as 1931 *Variety* reported that all the images associated with silent films retained their popularity: John Gilbert and Greta Garbo could talk, and small, "period style" theaters were very much available to all bidders. Rather, exhibitors complained bitterly that audiences no longer wanted the "regal trappings" praised by "arty and high-brow critics." Why? Amid hard times, the fans had lost faith that they could be "millionaires," with the result that they rejected the atmosphere of the "400," the select society crowd in New York City. In plain words, the monumental theatres were now falling flat, because "the times are eliminating the older class distinctions so far as the industry is concerned."[18]

Beset with troubles on all sides, industry leaders realized that they were living through what current political theorists call a legitimation crisis: a period when the values and norms that had formerly held a society together were undermined. Early in 1932 one analyst remarked that with older standards failing, the "business had to be reincarnated. Everyone knows it . . . but no one could predict what year." Another noted that "We must start lowering admissions and start catering to the masses who drifted away when we showed the type of product geared to the "high-brow" crowd. In the quest to give public meaning to low-brow desires, industry leaders focused as much attention on theatres as films. Indeed, it was critical given the large amount of investment that at the point of exhibition the right tone be struck.

Fortunately their wishes coincided with a major political change in the nation, namely the coming of the New Deal to national power. Almost immediately industry leaders of all political persuasions praised the Roosevelt administration's new pump-priming activities and state intervention that promised to solve the "underlying problems of the industry." Yet this was not just based on abstract hope. Almost immediately the trade journals praised the New Deal Housing Act which provided "23 million dollars" to remodel movie houses. Everyone also knew, moreover, that this money was not to be used to finance theatres in a cheaper mode of the old historical style. As John Eberson, the architect most noted for promoting the grand palaces of the twenties confessed, "In designing and building theaters in various communities, the day of the garish, ornate, non-functional elements which marked, even marred theaters of the past is gone forever."[19]

In searching for a new style all agreed that they could not return to the historical model that graced public buildings for over a hundred years in the West. Rather, as designer Paul Frankl argued in his book, *Machine Made Leisure*, architects must create an architectural language that would bridge the gap between the world of work and play, creating a style that would give form to the desire for social renewal sweeping the country. Out of that search came a growing self-consciousness concerning the ideologies resting at the basis of architectural form and structure. To Frankl, for example, the lavish movie houses like the Times Square Paramount and Roxy signaled what had gone wrong: a people proud of their machine making ability and republican virtue had been corrupted by the tastes and styles promoted by the wealthy who looked to Europe for their standards of taste. A wayward people had been punished by the advent of the Depression and an isolated leisure realm "degenerate in its oriental power." "Man had a long romance with the machine, but she had turned into a tyrannical mistress." Can she ever be turned into a willing wife? In answer Frankl saw that a new vision of republican "manhood" could be revitalized in the free space of leisure. At that center of that dream would be a machine-style theatre that would provide a utopian model for generating the larger public world. "We must," he argued,

> master the machine as an instrument for the creation of a new leisure. In so doing we are recreating our own values. We are establishing an end for which it is desirable to work, providing

of course that we may utilize leisure as a method of educating and developing the race . . . if the machine can be mobilized toward the realization of that happy state, toward the creation of a really good life, then its tortuous and tragic history will fully be satisfied and leisure will once more be a blessing and not a curse."[20]

Gradually, the architectural models appropriate for overcoming the contradiction between the world of work and play began to dominate the journals, displaying the heart of American genius: the production of technology. In what was to be a very nationalistic quest, the new architects saw themselves as part of a larger modernist movement that identified architecture with social and cultural renewal. Yet at the same time they tried to mediate between the three competing forms of the machine style that informed the building of stylish shops, department stores, world fairs and select movie theatres in the twenties. At one extreme was a style identified totally with the world of play: the art deco and nouveau designs that had characterized the construction of monumental movie houses like the Aurora and Pickwick theatres in Chicago or the International Music Hall in New York City. Geared to a prosperous audience who wished to lead what one contemporary critic called "happier lives," these lavish theaters not only assimilated the wavy and angular lines of the machine style to the older playhouse structure, but they were also located in stylish shopping districts far from the world of the working classes. As such the French Gaumont graced the Champs Elysees in Paris, the German Komode sat on the wealthy Kurfurstendamm in Berlin, and the International Music Hall displayed its monumental beauty on upper Times Square, near the museums and opera houses of the Fifth Avenue rich.[21] (Figures 6 and 7)

At the same time the Americans separated themselves from functionalists oriented purely to the world of work and public life. Rising to prominence in areas of revolutionary activity after World War I, the functionalists hoped to create a style that would provide an alternative to the buildings of the old capitalists and feudal regimes of Germany and Russia. Designers like Walter Gropius and Eric Mendelsohn of the German Bauhaus as well as the Russian Constructivists "got their chance," in the words of an admiring contemporary critic, as the old regimes fell after World War I and the "red flag was a sign for a major revolution that was to prove by no means exclusively a political and social one." The functionalists rejected the playful wavy lines of art deco and nouveau in favor of a theatre that embodied the international world of machines and mathematical order. Outside,the asymmetrical forms boldly displayed the productive possibilities of the new technology. Inside a theatre devoid of hierarchical symbols associated with aristocratic as well as middle class leisure, the audience was educated to understand and transform the world. So the main point of attention was the film which served less as a means of entertainment than as a means to teach the people the lessons of history and scientific laws. All in all, the modern theatres complimented the Marxist goals of building a new society in the wake of revolution, a process diametrically at odds with the playful modernist theatres of France and Germany.[22]

Yet as much as the new American architects shared both these aims, they also argued that their designs could not be an "aping or copying of European modernism, which is an imported idea with no relation to our daily life and habits." On one level this was a clear response to marketplace demands. The art deco Music Hall had failed to attract audiences, despite the fact that corporate reformers identified their design with social renewal. The more radical functionalist design had also failed to find audiences outside avante-garde theatres in New York and Chicago. Yet both forms of European modernism were deficient because they divided the world of work from play, promoting a high culture aesthetic removed from popular or national sentiments of the people. The architectural task of the future was thus to invent an American style that would combine the world of work with leisure, rooting that duality in the popular or national values of the American people. To accomplish that fusion, the new designers found their roots less in international than national soil, namely the work linked with Louis Sullivan, Frank Lloyd Wright, and John Root. Wright in particular saw his work emancipating the public from the feudal values of the rich. Not only had elites in his view used the machine to monopolize wealth, but they had used the fruits of production to construct historically styled buildings that imposed hierarchical values and images of scarcity on the "New World." In contrast to these "European" models Wright saw his designs realizing an open egalitarian ideal, one that would show how the machine could be used to promote American values and "democratic" abundance. Yet Wright and the

Chicago School architects had lost favor from the 1890s to 1930 as businessmen turned to the historical mode for their office buildings. Wright's designs, however, were now being revived in the world of commercial entertainment. In explaining why this effort would succeed, Joseph Urban observed that

> America is free from the influence of a dying royal conservatism and bureaucracy, which in Europe still crushes the vitality of the living with the weight of history and tradition. American life belongs to the future. America has the means and opportunity; has she the spiritual endowment comparable to the Greeks two and a half millennia ago? The age has yet to give proof of this. It lies with America to allow that great promise to perish or mature.[23]

Exactly what modernistic forms were appropriate for realizing that promise began after 1932 to dominate the "Better Theaters" section of the major trade journals. Among the several trend setters, none was more influential than Ben Schlanger. As he carefully diagrammed "changes in theatre planning factors" in the major trade journals, his principles provided core designs for managers and other architects all over the country. In his eyes, the American theatre of the "future" had to be more efficient, cheaper and geared to maximizing the demands of the commercial marketplace in the United States. Yet there was more to this effort than simply pointing out the need for a functional building. What Schlanger and his colleagues disdained were the "European" standards. Whether in modern art deco or historical guise, these were "fancy fakers." In the Depression they were particularly inappropriate since their overseating and waste as well as their glittering structure derived from the opera house or the legitimate stage that "hid the faults of design." As he explained, "These large, over-ornamented theatres commonly found in the big cities are intended to create a sumptuous feeling and to intrigue the beholder with their glittering cornices, excess ornamentation . . . and thus we have arrived at a combination of exhibition of palatial architecture in motion pictures. It is assumed that these places will be patronized irrespective of the quality of the performance given in them, but a trick stops working."[24] (Figure 8)

Repelled by the "tricks" of the past, Schlanger argued that the architect had to "slaughter" the "garish staircases, the grand lobbies, the overly ornamented side walls, the columns and pilasters, the classical murals and side reliefs." Stripped of excess, the new "movie house" would be much smaller, from 500 to 800 seats as compared with the 1500 to 3000 seats of theatre palaces and be affordable in price. Each part would merge into a unified whole, displaying the shiny materials of contemporary technology—steel, formica, chrome, and glass. Colors should evoke machine materials, and lights should be geometric and rounded, receding into the walls, creating a soft beam from beginning to end, displaying clearly the steel and cement that underlay the structure. The endless chrome rails would heighten the look of integration through clear lines, while on the floor the polished cement and figured rugs guided the fans smoothly from one area to the next. Further, the walls and rounded corners would blend together and the asymmetrical volumes would create a look of movement and dynamism throughout the whole. Finally, unlike in Europe, the streamlined box office and blazing marquee would be prominently displayed on the street, and fully engage modern art with the world of commerce.[25]

Furthermore, the new design advanced a model of how technology could yield the dream of abundance, releasing the people from a world of pure necessity. Indeed, at a time when politicians from Franklin Roosevelt to Huey Long castigated businessmen and speculators as nonproducers, Robert Boller drew on the republican tradition of American uniqueness to explain the significance of the new machine style. In Europe, he noted that "working class architecture" had never been able to flower because the larger society was dominated by monopolists and aristocrats who caused World War I and the Depression. The United States, however, was different. Here a corporate order had arisen to great power, but the architect's task was to create a building that would display the power of the machine to realize the people's dream of equality and affluence, free of excess and disorder. As the new theatre displaced older styles associated with the rich, trade journals glorified the new professionals who designed in accord with the public interest. "We architects," wrote a major advocate of that synthesis, "and you theatre owners and managers, have a great responsibility . . . . The public looks to us for specialized and wide intelligence in the building of their theatres. In the theatre the patron who has finished his days' work and is recreating himself in leisure, he is very impressionable; his impressions influence his nature and taste. We have a great deal of power in our hands."[26]

Just as architects used their power to present a model of abundance, so they saw the structure at one with the egalitarian values of the audience. A writer like Paul Frankl, for example, saw that the central ideals of a classless society had been realized in a long and perpetually expanding frontier where citizens could acquire free land and freedom from the tyranny and monopolists of Europe. On the frontier, the people organized themselves horizontally as equals. Yet with the end of free land in the 1890s, industrialists arose who, like feudal lords, used their power over machine production to construct skyscrapers and office buildings organized on a vertical or hierarchical basis. As the motion picture theatre imitated the cultural standards of the rich, Frankl feared that the movie fans internalized feudal standards, complete with graduated prices for better, high status seats. In contrast, exhibitors and architects during the Depression saw that fans no longer trusted the values of big business. To evoke the new egalitarian wishes in spatial terms, the modern movie house would be stripped of all status symbols and organized on a horizontal axis. The fans would pay the same price for every seat, and would mingle in local theaters that emphasized classless ideals.[27]

The designers also saw the look of dynamism surrounding the movie house satisfying the yearning for modern security. In some ways this evoked what Warren Susman has described as the central desire running through the mass culture of the Depression era: the wish for assurance to counter the chaos of the larger society. With their coordinated and flowing lines, the streamlined structures satisfied these desires in miniature. To encourage group cohesion, for example, the modern theatre was much smaller and more intimate than the deluxe houses. Inside the integrated auditorium the fans found themselves part of a compact and intimate community, secure from the outside world. Yet that aura of coordination was complimented by an aesthetic of movement and change. Instead of presenting a balanced and orderly facade, the modern movie house used rounded corners, flowing surfaces, asymmetrical blocks, stepped back volumes and box offices that engaged the movement of the thoroughfare. In other words, the new theatre evoked a world of security and abundance, but it was grounded in a dynamic style that gave the appearance of movement and improvisation, symbolic of a modern popular culture that was never contained in one formula.[28]

Above all, these several innovations converged to create a theatre that gave representation to film art itself. In that task, Schlanger was clearly influenced by the Film Guild Cinema in lower Manhattan. Designed in the late 1920s by the Austrian functionalist Frederick Kiesler, the Film Guild specialized in showing avant-garde productions to select New York audiences in an area "far from the Broadway palaces," namely the Bohemian art district of Greenwich Village. To immerse the audience inside the film frame, Kiesler eliminated the refined proscenium arch and excess ornaments, forging thereby a long and narrow auditorium that gave the appearance of a large lens. As one reporter wrote in 1929, "Picture yourself a dwarf inside a camera, for that indeed is what the auditorium of this theatre surely resembles." Images appeared on not just one, but three side walls. Each part of the interior could thus be "used as a screen for supplementary motion pictures, thus lending atmosphere to the piece that is being played on the regular screen . . . if 'Jeanne D'Arc' were being played, the auditorium could be bathed in flames, during the scene in which the heroine is burned at the stake by her British captors."[29]

Though Schlanger never surrounded the viewers with several flaming images, he did design theatres that were meant to heighten the full qualities of the "machine art." During the twenties, he implemented his ideas at two avante garde theatres, the Thalia and St. George Playhouse in New York City, where he pioneered what was to be his most widely emulated invention—the parabolic reverse floor. To insure that the viewer and the film experience blended together, he eliminated the proscenium arch, enlarged the screen and diminished the size of the auditorium to magnify the impact of the images. The colors of the side walls merged with those of the elevated front, insuring that the auditorium and stage became one unified whole. Schlanger also maximized uniform sight lines by creating a stepped back auditorium that was a long tunnel or elliptical space, with a lowered ceiling that insured that all eyes stayed focused on the front. And to give everyone the same, heightened view, he minimized side and center aisles and built the auditorium to recede downward from the stage, flatten out in the center, and then climb upward towards the projection booth. As he wrote, the "parabolic reverse floor design" required a "gradual simplification and omission of forms as they recede to the auditorium rear; the forms used should have strong horizontal direction, instead of vertical emphasis, fastening the eye on the screen focal point."[30] (Figure 10) By the mid-

1930s, Schlanger and his colleagues saw the horizontal theatre not only breaking down the division between life and art, but providing a perfect complement to the rise of a new style talking film and star. Indeed, after the initial crisis of 1933, trade journalists no longer complained of exhibition sites, films, and stars incongruous with audience demand. Nor did they bewail performers distant from the vernacular language and playful impulses of the populace. Instead, trend setting films starring Will Rogers and James Cagney, and directed by Frank Capra or John Ford, presented characters who freed communities from the values of monopolists and corrupt "stuffed shirts." Unlike traditional characters, these stars incorporated "high" and "low" characteristics that had formerly been separated into rigid artistic categories. Giving this new imagery a dynamic look were directors such as Busby Berkely and Lewis Milestone who put the camera on tracks and broke down the space between the fans and the characters on the screen. Recalling the impact of these images, one fan recalled years later that movies in the Depression years had become a "universal part of life making possible a heightening of psychological involvement so persuasive that the gulf between the audience and the screen is all but obliterated."[31]

Gradually a theatre that "obliterated the gulf between the audiences and the screen" became enormously popular. Whereas the small, streamlined theatre was one of several competing styles in the early thirties, it was by 1933 the "appointment" in which all new remodeling and building unfolded. The sumptuous theatre of the twenties by no means disappeared but the sleek modern theatres were constructed at the rate of about 500 a year throughout the Depression. Yet in the rapidity of that change, architects and managers catered to a new type of market demand. After 1932 entrepreneurs found that they had to make the theatre expressive of local values and traditions. Symbolic of the process at work was the simple act of naming. In the recent past, the theatre palaces radiated the aura of romantic high culture, removed from audience's daily lives. As such, they carried names like the *Granda* (a capitol in southern Spain), the *Tivoli* (town in Italy), *Rialto* (island in Vince), the grand and pastoral *Arcadia* (an ancient pastoral district in Greece), the *Alhambra* (a lavish palace of the Moorish Kings in medieval Spain) or the ever present *Palace*. In contrast the promoters of the small modern theatres rooted the names of their establishments in patriotic and local loyalties: *The Roosevelt*, *The Lincoln*, *The Pocahontas*, *The Washington*, *The Will Rogers* (in an ethnic neighborhood in Chicago, Illinois), *The Liberty, The Colonial, The Varsity, The Lake, The Peoples' Theatre*, or simply the *Community Theatre*. By the middle of the decade even the name of the *International Music Hall* was changed to *Radio City Music Hall* in accord with the trend towards identifying the movie theatre less with an international high culture than with local roots and American experiences.[32] (Figure 11)

Such inventiveness did not stop with a name. To create a synthesis between contemporary life architects merged the machine style with local materials such as sandstone in the Southwest or brick in New England. Examples of the new ethos were varied and plentiful. At the Trans Lux theatre chain that spread across New York City, large murals represented the work and play of modern urbanites. At the Newsreel theatres in New York City, artists ingrained a large camera in the floorway entrance, guiding the patrons to their seats, while on the auditorium walls murals appeared that dramatized the work of documentary filmmaking. At the Will Rogers theatre in an ethnic neighborhood in Chicago, the streamlined lobby displayed popular slogans of the famed Indian cowboy, coupled with reliefs that portrayed his current career as a roper, aviator, and film star. Further west in Kansas City, managers graced theatre walls with murals utilizing a flowing, regionalist style, representing the heroic myths and historical memories of the local populace. In Colorado Springs, Colorado, the architect named the modern theatre after a local Indian tribe, and filled the adobe walls of the Ute Theatre with a large mural dramatizing their history. On the far northern lakeports of Minnesota, the muralist for the Duluth Theatre pictured the construction of ocean vessels and agricultural production, activities that formed the work lives of a multi-cultural audience composed largely of immigrants from Southern and Eastern Europe. Finally, the Uptown Theatre situated in Minneapolis, Minnesota displayed a large side mural of the French explorers movement up the Mississippi in the seventeenth century.[33] (Figure 12)

Audiences were more than comfortable seeing their histories and everyday lives on the walls. In contrast to the twenties when the world of modern play was often at odds with the values of local voluntary groups, the movie house now provided a site where fans merged together popular expressiveness and civic life. Several related trends followed. The pattern began innocently enough as showmen attracted fans with lotteries, dish nights, amateur hours, and sing-a-longs. In this ambience, the Jewish comedian Larry Storch, for example, recalled that he got his start in the Depression era by imitating ethnic movie stars at amateur nights in the Bronx and Brooklyn. In Irish areas he would come out of the audience and imitate James Cagney, while in Jewish sections he gave impressions of local heroes like Edward G. Robinson or Eddie Cantor. Movie theatres also became the locale in small towns and urban neighborhoods for Rotary club meetings, high school graduations, and boy scout gatherings. Not to be outdone, Hollywood produced timed film premiers to coincide with local holidays and civic events, a trend which apparently began in 1932 when the stars for the musical *Forty-Second Street* toured the country and opened in Washington D.C. at the time of Franklin Roosevelt's inaugural. Later in the decade, films like *Santa Fe Trail* opened in Santa Fe, New Mexico, *Gone with the Wind* premiered in Atlanta, Georgia, and *Knute Rockne, All American* had its debut in South Bend, Indiana, along with official state holidays, with parades honoring film stars and the famed football coach.[34] (Figure 13)

At the core of all these several innovations, moreover, lay the "Americanization" and democratization of the new consumer culture. In the twenties the monumental movie house was clearly identified with the promise of affluence emerging in the United States. Yet at a time when Anglo-Saxon industrialists and opinion makers promoted an ethic of scarcity, the historically designed theatre linked that promise to a "European" high culture that was removed from the communal loyalties of the audiences. It signaled that upwardly mobile urbanites who shed their past would find open opportunity in a society where the fruits of mass culture were available, but also distributed within a social and cultural hierarchy. Indicative of that assumption, the period style movie house was organized on a basis of hierarchy, complete with better seats for the successful. Along these lines, the film palaces in the better sections of the city were "first rank" while those in poor sections were "run down" shabby edifices. By way of contrast, the modern theatre sat everyone on the same level, and identified the fruits of the machine age with local values and traditions of a multi-cultural audience. The slick modern theatre penetrated into rich and poor sections alike, symbolizing that an American standard of living was not something above the people, but an intimate part of their daily lives and expectations.[35]

Throughout the period, moreover, trade journalists perceived that the new theatre was at the forefront of vast expansion into new areas

Designing Multi-Cultural America

and regions. It is true, of course, that a mass culture—one that broke down the barriers between the sexes and classes—began at the turn of the century in the major cities. But in the 1920s those markets remained solidly urban. Conspicuously missing from producers' calculations were racial minorities and the rural sections, particularly in the South. During the 1920s, Prohibition played a symbolic role in that geographical division, for it signaled that the values of the metropolis were different from those of small towns and farm areas. In this context, movie houses in the cities ran twelve hours a day, seven days a week. Yet in the countryside, films were often displayed in a general store or converted auditorium that operated only on Friday and Saturday nights, with Sunday showings outlawed because of what the trade journals called "Puritan" codes. Producers were also known to cater to this "Puritan code" by aiming one style film for the cities, another for the rural areas, often with altered endings to fit rural tastes.

Yet after 1933 this pattern was reversed as the film industry spread rapidly across all parts of the nation. Stimulating this growth was the repeal of Prohibition which trade journalists saw as liberating a "public mind which had gotten used to denying itself all amusements except radio and bridge." By 1934 reports arrived of nightclub owners in formerly dry Minneapolis proudly celebrating the end of the "great mistake" with a "New Deal at the Golden Bubble" while theatre managers kept their businesses open on Sundays in all parts of the nation. In this context, the total number of exhibition sites in Atlanta, Georgia increased by thirty-nine percent and in the state as a whole by over twenty-five percent, with expansion occurring in what trade journalists called the "American Style." Similarly, theatres in small towns now showed films every night of the week, and social workers recorded not only major increases in film watching among the children of immigrants in the large cities, but the penetration of the modern theatre into working class neighborhoods. And even though racism was still a major part of American life, select dance halls like the Savoy and movie theatres in Harlem were also in the streamlined style, complete with murals that represented the experience and histories of African-Americans. The result was that wherever trade reporters went after 1933—to Italian, Jewish and African-American neighborhoods in New York City, to small towns in the midwest, to former Spanish villas like Santa Fe in New Mexico—they found a modern movie house that brought formerly isolated groups and experiences in contact. As one investigator wrote after touring the midwest,

> The Little Towner no longer need glance enviously in the direction of the Big Citian, because the talking picture has supplied the Big City to the Little Town . . . . Our Little Town is in touch with the world, hears the world speaking and sees the world in action.[36]

What was most remarkable about this transformation was that it not only spread across the nation amidst hard times, but it was unique to the United States. To state it another way, although all the nations in the western world had film industries, Ben Schlanger and his colleagues were alone among modern architects in finding a mass market for their product. One reason for this difference was the opportunity offered by a constantly growing market. During the period from 1920 to the early 1930s, the number of theatres in the America grew from 21,000 to 28,000. By comparison, in Germany they went from 2,826 to 5,000 and in France from 1,500 to 3,000. Yet the combined populations of these two countries were about the same as that of the United States. In addition, Schlanger's native land had more movie theatres than all of Europe, and demand for the movies by the late 1930s was even larger than it had been in the prosperous years of the 1920s. Part of the explanation lies in pure economics: this country was the most economically advanced, particularly after World War I devastated the European economies. Affluence was probably more widespread even in the 1930s, making it possible for urbanites in cities like New York to spend more of their discretionary income on moviegoing and amusements of all kinds.[37]

Beyond this economic cause, however, lies a more fundamental cultural and political reason for this difference. As George Mosse, Carl Schorske, Jeffrey Brooks and Jurgen Habermas have shown, most European countries industrialized within cultures where a hierarchical social structure and a homogeneous population was the expected norm. In this context, a popular reading material might spread that challenged the old regime, but public space was less identified with the breaking down of class and ethnic barriers than the retention of traditional standards and national images. Movie theatres retained the historical canon which signaled that aristocratic values and social distinctions still pervaded countries devoted to full scale modernization and capitalist enterprise. Further, these public standards were rarely destabilized because European producers and film distributors found their mass market horizontally across regions than vertically across classes, with the result that movie going did not become identified with a challenge to cultural distinctions and social barriers. Above all, in the United States during the Roosevelt era, the new architects faced a hostile state, for when the Stalinists and Nazis rose to power in Germany and Russia, they outlawed modern art of all kinds, and promoted as government policy a historically derived style.[38]

By the mid-1930s, the effect of these several European developments—the continuing popularity of the period style movie house, the absence of mass culture that broke down the barriers between classes, and the repression of modernists in Germany and Russia—was exactly the opposite of the situation in the United States. Yet what explains this difference? Although an answer to this problem can only be advanced in a tentative, outlined form, it does not appear that the small modern theatre gained popularity because it was promoted by corporate capitalists who used the machine style to establish their hegemony over public life. Instead the evidence presented so far suggests that the modern movie house gave expression to audience desire to contest the inherited values dominating public space in the nineteenth century. Indeed, ever since the 1890s urbanites feared that with the rise of a new corporate order, the treasured ideals of individualism and democracy were being lost. In search of new forms of play and egalitarian space, city dwellers turned to amusements that broke down the boundaries between the classes and sexes. Seeking to capitalize on that new experience, but unsure exactly how to give it form and meaning, the new theatre owner William Fox noted in 1912 that

> Movies breathe the spirit on which the country was founded, freedom and equality. In the motion picture theatres there are no separations of classes. Everyone enters the same way. There is no side door thrust upon those who sit in the less expensive seats. There is always something abhorrent in different entrances to theatres . . . in the movies the rich rub elbows with the poor and that is the way it should be. The motion picture is a distinctly American institution.[39]

Doubtless Fox was aware that mass amusements such as sports and nightclubs had also become arenas where the classes and sexes mingled. Yet there was validity in giving special attention to his own line of work. Only the movie house provided continuity between the high culture realms of the theatre, music and the visual arts, with all their associations in the Victorian era of hierarchy and elevation of tastes, and engaged with the new ribald world of popular culture. At first Fox and other theatre managers sought to contain this tension within an architectural canon derived from the Victorian past. Part of the reason was that during the twenties industry leaders had to devise ways to avoid wealthy moralists who wished to control their playful impulses in the name of older "American" codes. When the personal side of that aim failed in the twenties—indicated by the widespread visibility of a revolution in manners and morals, and the open violation of Prohibition laws, showmen catered to a divided experience. The large Hollywood studios built flamboyant theatre palaces in the historical mode that defined the promise of the new consumer culture in terms of the hierarchy and civilization promoted by wealthy tastemakers. But in order to appeal to a polyglot audience, managers also "jazzed up" the playhouse design with colored lights, box offices on the street, blazing marquees, and eclectic mixing of styles from different lands that would have been anathema in contemporary Europe or the American past.

Given that these experiments were confined to an isolated leisure realm, they could not provide the means to question the larger corporate order. The legacy was a mass culture caught between the potentials of a new life and a new consumer culture still dominated by traditional Anglo-Saxon codes of Americanism. Yet when established institutions were discredited in the Depression era, audiences rejected the monumental historically styled theatre as well as the attempt by wealthy tastemakers who built the International Music Hall to use modernism as a means to revitalize corporate values. In the ensuing competition for an alternative model cultural reformers within the film industry were aided by the coming of the New Deal to national power. Not only did the administration of Franklin Roosevelt mobilize immigrants and launch attacks on monopoly capital, but they ended Prohibition and provided the funds which made it possible for managers to remodel and expand into new markets and regions.

Still the alliance between New Dealers and small theatre owners was not simply fortuitous. At a time when social movements challenged established economic and political institutions, theatre managers and trade journal critics found that the audience had become a "public" that rejected the artistic values and symbols associated with cultural elites. The culmination of that trend came where we began our story, with the failure of the Radio City Music Hall to make a profit during its first five years of existence. In response, designers like Ben Schlanger advanced a new architectural language which offered a utopian ideal of a classless machine world, coordinated and rooted in egalitarian symbols. Soon the smooth glimmering lines of that small, modern theatre graced the Main Streets and Broadways in hundreds of small towns and cities across the country, with its lighted marquee beckoning customers with a reinvention of the republican dream—an America that validated widespread abundance and the vernacular experiences of a multi-cultural people. As this gave public meaning to the world of play and consumption, it also suggested that reform in the New Deal era may very well have succeeded not because it was at odds, but at one with the struggles informing the popular arts of the Great Depression and World War II years.[40]

FIG. 1. The facade of the Uptown Theatre in Chicago, Rapp and Rapp architects, 1925. A classic example of the "theatre palace" of the twenties. Built in Spanish Renaissance style to replicate "Castles in Spain," the Uptown was advertised as a "Palace of Enchantment, Not for Today—but for ALL TIME." Together the slogans symbolized the theatre palaces' distance from the machine society, linking it to the historical canon of a European derived high culture. (Courtesy of the Theatre Historical Society, Chicago, Illinois)

Designing Multi-Cultural America 215

FIG. 2-3. The interior of the Brooklyn Paramount in New York City, Rapp and Rapp architects, 1924. A typical example of the theatre palace interior. Notice the divided seating, the separate balconies and box seating, complimented by baroque motifs coupled to statues of classical gods and goddesses. In order to divide the fantasy world from the audience, the stage and screen was prominently framed by an elaborate proscenium arch. (Courtesy Museum of Modern Art/Film Stills Archive)

FIG. 4. Grauman's Chinese in Hollywood, California, Meyer and Holler, architects, 1927. The pinnacle of the exotic theatre that found popularity only in the United States during the twenties. The Chinese allowed the fans to enter a fantasy world even more divorced from European standards than earlier movie palaces such as the Uptown or the Brooklyn Paramount pictured in Figures 1, 2 and 3. (Courtesy, Museum of Modern Art/Film Stills Archive)

Designing Multi-Cultural America 217

FIG. 5-6. Pickwick Theatre, Park Ridge, Illinois, Zook and McCaughey, architects, 1929. Typical of French derived art deco theatres that found a limited patronage by the late twenties. The Pickwick appealed to an affluent clientele in a Chicago suburban shopping district. Notice the merger of art moderne motifs with the structure of the monumental theatre palace. Inside the geometric motifs fused with the symbols and icons of Mayan and Aztec civilization, creating ironically both an exotic and modern style divorced from the world of "today."

CHANGES IN THEATRE PLANNING FACTORS	
(A) THE OLD	(B) THE NEW
1. Expensive land.	1. Less expensive land.
2. Excessive costly and useless cubic contents of structure.	2. Minimum useful cubic contents of structure, also reducing amount of mechanical heat and ventilation.
3. Costly special structural framing due to excessive spans and large balcony overhangs.	3. Simplified and economical structural framing, using standard structural shapes.
4. Costly overornamentation, affording poor aesthetic environment, besides being disturbing to restful screen exhibition.	4. Simplicity in decoration, accented by effective lighting complementing the screen performance.
5. Poor vision of screen due to seating arrangement inherited from the stage theatre form. (Seats placed too much to one side of or too high above screen and full view of screen prevented by preceding heads.)	5. Full vision of screen highly improved by placing seats within physical areas best adapted for screen vision. (The valuable area charts and the Parabolic Reversed
6. Lack of bodily and ocular comfort due to seating positions in poor relation to position of screen and inadequate study of physical comfort in chair design.	6. Scientifically fixed angles and placing of seats, as provided for in Parabolic Reverse Floor design, as well as scientifically designed chair.
7. Different admission prices for different portions of theatre (necessary only because of inferior seat locations common in most existing theatres).	7. Single admission price possible, all seats having practically the same degree of desirability in well designed structural form.
8. High admission prices.	8. Reduced admission prices.
9. Excessive walking and stair climbing to seats.	9. Minimum of effort expended in reaching seats.
10. Costly stage construction and rigging (in most cases never made use of).	10. Complete elimination of all traces and influences of a stage.
11. Elaborate equipment, costly draperies and other furnishings.	11. Simplified equipment and elimination of dust-collecting draperies.
12. Ornamental proscenium frame, hangover from stage theatre. (Poor transition from audience to screen.)	12. Elimination of obvious proscenium frame. Side walls of auditorium made to blend towards screen.
13. Faulty screen masking and poor screen lighting.	13. Recessed screen masking, eliminating fuzzy and moving edges of picture. More scientific study of screen lighting.
14. Poor shape and size of present screen.	14. Much study is yet needed along these lines. (This is the producer's problem.)
15. Excessive projection angles, causing distorted images on screen. This is due to poor locations of booth caused by unadaptable form of stage theatre.	15. Diminished projection angles, made possible by scientific study of motion picture theatre form.
16. Poor acoustical quality due to makeshift acoustical correction and unscientific study of theatre form.	16. Exacting acoustical quality. Obtaining proper response to broad range of frequencies.
17. Costly film booking.	17. Greater film buying power for small exhibitor.
18. Theatre construction by speculative builder insufficiently interested in functioning of theatre.	18. Low construction costs, enabling exhibitor to build for himself, assuring proper function of theatre.
19. Maximum expenditure for advertising exploitation and house staff.	19. Minimum advertising for neighborhood house and minimum staff required.

FIG. 7. Ben Schlanger's chart comparing the principles of palatial theatre of the "jazz age" to the modern, streamlined theatre of the thirties. Compare the two sides to measure the change in values embodied in the theatre palace and the new small, modern theatre of the Depression years. (*Motion Picture Herald*, November 19, 1932, p. 9)

Designing Multi-Cultural America

FIG. 8. Lobby of the Lake Theatre in Oak Park, Illinois, Thomas Lamb architect, 1935. As one of the major designers of the theatre palace, Thomas Lamb converted to the new style theatres like the Lake which projected all the principles popularized by Ben Schlanger. Observe the geometric floor design, the matching of rails and ceiling motifs and the streamlining stripped of excess. (Courtesy Theatre Historical Society, Chicago, Illinois)

FIG. 9. Auditorium of the Lake Theatre. Inside the architect eliminated the proscenium arch, the screen merges into the world of the audience and the seating is on one "classless" level. (Courtesy of the Theatre Historical Society, Chicago, Illinois)

Designing Multi-Cultural America

FIG. 10. Exterior of the Will Rogers Theatre, Chicago, Illinois. Rapp and Rapp, architects, 1936. Geared to the world of "today," the Will Rogers, named after the current film star, is constructed in the machine style, while its asymmetrical parts provide a look of dynamic movement that echoes the busy street corner. Located in a working- and lower middle-class, ethnic neighborhood, the Will Rogers demonstrated both the penetration of luxury styles into local neighborhoods and the conversion of another set of noted architects to the modern style. Compare Rapp and Rapp's Brooklyn Paramount, Figures 2 and 3 with new mode. (Theatre Historical Society, Chicago, Illinois)

FIG. 11. Mural in the lobby of the Will Rogers Theatre in Chicago, Illinois. Utilizing the regionalist style of the period, this mural narrates the many facets of Will Rogers' life, a star who as an outsider and Indian appealed too the tastes and values of an American working class of immigrant background. Notice the inscriptions saying "My ancestors didn't come over on the Mayflower, they Met the Boat" and those condemning selfishness and Puritan values. The implicit condemnation of the elites—the "Mayflower" crowd and the celebration of an American folk hero serves to link the modern movie theatre with popular values antithetical to those of elite tastemakers. (Courtesy Chicago Historical Society, Russell Philips, Photographer)

Designing Multi-Cultural America 223

FIG. 12. The concept of engaging the screen fare with public events and the world of the street receives its classic expression in this photo of a newsreel theatre in New York's Times Square in 1940. (Courtesy Museum of Modern Art/Film Stills Archive)

NOTES

**Research for this article was completed with the aid of the Graduate School of the University of Minnesota. I wish to thank the research assistants who assisted me in this project: Minda Novek, Steven Lassonde, Chris Lewis and Collette Hyman. Several scholars also provided critical reading of the article: Jeffrey Brooks, John Wright, David Noble, Lewis Erenberg, Elaine Tyler May, Riv-Ellen Prell, Harry Boyte, and Philip Faria.

1. Ralph Ellison, *Going to the Territory* (New York: Random House, 1986), p. 141. George Schutz, "Modernistic Art: Its Significance to America and the Photoplay," *Exhibitor's Herald* (October 27, 1928): 38. For contemporary descriptions of the Music Hall complete with pictures, see "The Radio City Theaters," *Motion Picture Herald* (hereafter cited as *MPH*) (January 14, 1933): 8-37. The Hays quote is from Thomas and Virginia Aylesworth, *New York: The Glamour Years, 1919-1945* (New York: Gallery Books, 1987), p. 102.

2. Raymond B. Fosdick, *John D. Rockefeller, Jr.: A Portrait* (New York: Harper Brothers, 1956). For Hartely Alexander, see *The National Cyclopaedia of American Biography*, 46 (New York: James T. White Co., 1963), pp. 174-175 and Harry Eames, "A Tribute to the Memory of H.B. Alexander," UCLA Special Collections, Los Angeles, California. For Alexander's view of America's world destiny, coupled with fears of immigration and the machine age, see H.B. Alexander, *Liberty and Democracy* (Boston: Marshall Jones Company, 1920), pp. 124-175. The quotes come from "Rockefeller City: Thematic Symposis" (Business Interests, Rockefeller Center, Inc., Theme and Decoration, Box 94), Rockefeller Archive Center, North Tarrytown, New York. I wish to thank Harold Oakhill, archivist, for making this material available to me. See also Merle Crowell, Director of Public Relations Rockefeller Center, New York, "The Story of Rockefeller Center," *The Architectural Forum*, 56 (May 1932): 428-430, and Eugene Clute, "The Story of Rockefeller Center, The Allied Arts," *The Architectural Forum*, (February 1933): 128-132

and Louise Cross, "The Sculpture for Rockefeller Center," *Parnassus* 5 (October, 1932): 1-3.

3. For Raymond Hood see Robert A.M. Stern, Gregory Gilmartin and Thomas Mellins, *New York 1930: Architecture and Urbanism Between Two World Wars*, (New York: Rizzoli, 1987), pp. 575-581. Walter H. Kilham, Jr., *Raymond Hood, Architect* (New York: Architectural Book Publishing Co., 1950). For the collaboration of Hood and Stone, see Edward Durell Stone, *The Evolution of an Architect* (New York: Horizon Press, 1962). For the Beaux Arts tradition, see Michele H. Bogart, *Public Sculpture and the Civic Ideal in New York City, 1890-1930* (Chicago: University of Chicago Press). For Hood's reformist vision of modernism, see S.J. Woolf, "An Architect Hails the Rule of Reason," *The New York Times Magazine* (November 1, 1931): 6; Raymond M. Hood, "The Spirit of Modern Art," *Architectural Form* 51 (November, 1929): 445-449. Though none of the major examinations of the Center emphasize the central ideology of corporate renewal, it can be gleaned from the material presented in Alan Balfour, *24 Rockefeller Center, Architecture as Theatre* (New York: McGraw Hill, 1978) and Carol H. Krinksy, *Rockefeller Center* (New York: Oxford University Press, 1970), pp. 81-82. For contemporary accounts, see *Rockefeller Center* (New York: Rockefeller Center, Inc., 1932), p. 38, and the address by Rockefeller Jr. in John Crowell, *The Last Rivet*, (New York: Columbia University Press, 1939), pp. 38-39. A shrewd contemporary account can be found in Frederick Lewis Allen, "Radio City: Cultural Center?" *Harpers* (April 2, 1932): 535-445.

4. For the initial hopes of trade journalists see "Observations," *MPH*, (December 17, 1932): 7. For a description of opening night, see "Gorgeous Theatrics Mark Roxy's Radio City Debut," *MPH* (December 31, 1932): 10-11, 36. For the description of the failure, see Terry Ramsaye, "Static in Radio City," *MPH* (January 14, 1933): 11, and "$100,000 Cut Off Radio City's Overheads, May be Chance Now for Profits," *Variety* (hereafter cited as *V*) (January 24, 1933): 23, 54.

5. Terry Ramsaye, "New Deal-Superman and Today," *MPH* (March 18, 1933): 9-10; Anita Brenner, "Art and Big Business," *The Nation*, 136 (January 4, 1933): 12; Cross, "The Sculpture for Rockefeller Center." Ben Schlanger, "Two Late Theatre Forms: A Criticism," *MPH* (February 11, 1933): 8. Within days, the prices were lowered, see *New York Times* (November 23, 1932). "Roxy Lets Fly at the 'Wolves' on Broadway," *New York Herald Tribune*, (February 15, 1932).

6. "Rockefeller Center Now Threatens to Climb Out of the Red," *Fortune*, (December 1936): 139-148. For the revival, see "Radio City Music Hall, World's Largest Theatre is Mecca for Tourists from All Over the World," *Life* (April 26, 1943): 40-49. "33 Million Dollars in Government Loans Now Obtainable to Repair and Modernize Theatres," *MPH* (September 22, 1934): 29; "Observations," *MPH* (April 7, 1934): 7.

7. "Ben Schlanger," *Journal of the Society of Motion Picture and Television Engineers* (November, 1970): 1030, and "Ben Schlanger," *The Biographical Encyclopedia of Who's Who of the American Theatre*, ed. Walter Rigdon (New York: James Mememan, Inc., 1966), p. 806. For Schlanger's association with Hood, and his promotion of a new theatre style, see *The Bulletin of the Beaux Arts Institute of Design* (December, 1924, October, 1925, and December 1925). R.W. Sexton, "Changing Values in Theatre Design," *MPH*, (March 14, 1931): 25, 68. For a representative example of the equation between the new style and Americanism, see "Modernism in American Theatre Styling," *MPH* (March 14, 1931): 25, 68. For a representative example of the equation between the new style and Americanism, see "Modernism in American Theatre Styling," *MPH* (September 17, 1938): 13-15, and Ben Schlanger, "Motion Picture Theatres of Tomorrow," *MPH*, (February 14, 1931): 12-15. John W. Root and Wallace Rice, "Design and the Motion Picture," *Exhibitor's Herald* (November 24, 1928): 7-9.

8. For an excellent summary of the scholarly literature on nineteenth century politics, republicanism, and the class oriented voting of the New Deal era, see Richard Oestreicher, "Urban Working-Class

Political Behavior and Theories of American Electoral Politics, 1870-1940," *Journal of American History* (March 1988): 1257-1286. The classic statement of 1930s culture as backward-looking can be found in Warren Susman's *Culture as History: The Transformation of American Society in the Twentieth Century* (New York: Pantheon, 1985), pp. 156-157. For the continuing influence of the paradigm, see Alan Trachtenberg, *Reading American Photographs: Images as History, Mathew Brady to Walker Evans* (New York: Hill and Wang, 1989), p. 247. Jeffrey Meikle, *Twentieth Century Limited: Industrial Design in America 1925-1939* (Philadelphia: Temple University Press, 1979) and James Sloane Allen, *The Romance of Commerce and Culture: Capitalism, Modernism and the Chicago-Aspen Crusade for Cultural Reform* (Chicago: The University of Chicago Press, 1983), p. xiv.

9. For the typical separation of modernism from political ideology, see Balfour, *Architecture as Theatre* and Stern, *New York, 1930*, p. 580. For a survey of the literature on hegemony and popular culture, see Jackson Lears, "The Concept of Cultural Hegemony: Problems and Possibilities," *American Historical Review* 90 (June 1985): 567-593, and for a view of popular culture as resistance, see George Lipsitz, *Time Passages: Collective Memory and American Popular Culture* (Minneapolis: University of Minnesota Press, 1990), pp. 99-163, 233-257. For an overview of the historical literature pertaining to republicanism, see Gordon Wood, "Hellfire Politics," *New York Review of Books* (February 28, 1985). On the lack of continuity between nineteenth century republicanism and the twentieth century, see John Diggens, "Republicanism and Progressivism," *American Quarterly* 37 (Fall, 1985): 572-98. For a different view, see David Noble, *The End of American History: Democracy, Capitalism and the Metaphor of the Two Worlds in Anglo-American Historical Writing* (Minneapolis: University of Minnesota Press).

10. On the distinction between Victorian life and vernacular or popular culture, see John A. Kouwenhoven, *Made in America: The Arts in Modern Civilization* (New York: Doubleday and Company, Inc., 1948); David Grimsted, *Melodrama Unveiled: American Theatre and Culture* (Berkeley, California: University of California Press, 1987), p. 110 and Lawrence Levine, *High Brow, Low Brow: The Emergence*

of Cultural Hierarchy in America, (Cambridge: Harvard University Press, 1988). On the rise of an American mass culture see Lary May, *Screening Out the Past: The Birth of Mass Culture and the Motion Picture Industry* (New York: Oxford University Press, 1980) and Lewis Erenberg, *Stepping Out: New York Nightlife and the Transformation of American Culture, 1890-1930* (Chicago: University of Chicago Press, 1983), pp. 3-60.

11. For the historical canon, see Donald M. Lowe, *History of Bourgeois Perception* (Chicago: University of Chicago Press, 1982), pp. 59-83; Donald J. Olsen, *The City as a Work of Art: London, Paris, Vienna* (New Haven and London: Yale University Press, 1986) and Carl E. Schorsek, *Fin-de-Siecle Vienna: Politics and Culture* (New York: Knopf, 1980), pp. 24-116. Cort Theatre, Scrapbooks and Clippings File, Billy Rose Theatre Collection, Lincoln Center Branch, New York Public Library. On uplift and refinement of the American movie house and the Capitol theatre, see the special issue of *Architectural Forum*, 42 (June, 1925): 360-390, and *American Architect*, 131 (May 20, 1927): 681-90. For a first hand account of uplifting the movie house, see Carrie Balaban, *Continuous Performance, The Story of AJ Balaban as Told to His Wife* (New York, G.P. Putnam and Sons, 1950). On placement of the box office see Emil Milnar, "Motion Picture Theatre Data," *Pencil Points*, 3 (July, 1922): 11-13. The quote is from Harold Rambusch, "Decorations," in R.W. Sexton, *American Movie Theatres of Today* (New York: Architectural Book Publishing, 1930), pp. I, 24.

12. For the national trend, see Charlotte K. Herzog, "The Motion Picture Theatre and Film Exhibition, 1896-1930," (Ph.D. dissertation, Northwestern University, 1980); David Naylor, *American Picture Palaces: The Architecture of Fantasy* (New York: Van Nostrand and Reinhold, 1981). R.W. Sexton, *American Theatres of Today* (New York: Architectural Book Publishing, 1927), p. 14. On the advent of Times Square and the movies, see William Lass, *Crossroads of the World* (New York: Popular Library, 1950). For the Broadway movie houses, see Stern, *New York, 1930*, pp. 229-271, and Ben Hall, *The Best Remaining Seats* (New York: Clarkson N. Potter, Inc., 1961). Lewis Mumford, "The City," in *Civilization in the*

United States: An Inquiry by Thirty Americans, ed. Harold E. Stearns (New York: Harcourt, Brace and Company, 1922), p. 9.

13. See S.L. Rothafel obituaries in *The New York Sun*, (January 13, 1936); *New York Herald Tribune* (January 14, 1936). For his formula, see S.L. Rothafel, "What the Public Wants in the Picture Theatre," *Architectural Forum* (June 1925): 362-365. Arthur Snyder, Jr. "Paramount Stage Shows," *Times Square Paramount Annual* No. 3 (Alameda, California: Theatre Historical Society), pp. 25-39. Fred Niblo, "Americanizing the American Pictures," *Theatre Magazine* (May 1928): 14.

14. For the rise of constant innovations that included the atmospheric theatre, see John Eberson, "A Description of the Capitol Theater, Chicago," *Architectural Forum* (June, 1925): 373-374. Lamb quoted in Stern, Meyer and Holler, "The Chinese Theatre, at Hollywood, California," *The American Architect*, 132 (August 20, 1927): 251-267. Grauman's Chinese Clipping File, Academy of Motion Picture Arts and Sciences Library, Los Angeles, California.

15. Thomas E. Talmadge, "The Screen, a New Art, Should Pave Road to a New Architecture, and R.E. Hall, "Today's Jazzy Interiors of Theatres Short-Lived, Declare American Architects," *Exhibitor's Herald* (March 17, 1928): 9-10.

16. Samuel Katz, President, Publix Theatres Corporation, "Theatre Management," in *The Story of the Films*, ed. Joseph P. Kennedy (Chicago: A.W. Shaw Co., 1927), p. 273. John F. Berry, "Development of Theatre as Taught to Publix Managers," *Exhibitor's Herald* (May 10, 1926): 15-17, 37-39. John F. Barry, Director Publix Theatre Manager's Training School, "The Times Square Paramount," *Theatre Historical Society Annual* 3 (1976): 3.

17. *Film Daily Yearbook*, 1930, pp. 997-1003 (hereafter cited as *FDY*); *FDY*, 1931, p. 39; *FDY*, 1932, pp. 963-65, and FDY 1933, p.957.

18. *V* (January 8, 1930): 78, 80-8; *V* (January 7, 1931); *V* (January 5, 1932): 3; *V* (January 7, 1931): 5; *Film Daily Yearbook, 1932*: 1-7; R.W. Sexton, "Changing Values in Theatre Design," 25, 68; Tom

Waller, "The Year in Pictures," *V* (December 29, 1931); 4; Martin Quigley, "Less Heat and More Light from Hollywood," *MPH* (December 5, 1931): 9-12.

19. Jurgen Habermas, *Legitimation Crisis* (Boston: Beacon Press, 1975), pp. 71-75. For an earlier criticism of the period style as escapist and inappropriate for the modern age, see "Deluxe Picture Palace," *The New Republic* (March 27, 1929): 176. On the push for modernism, see "Better Theatres" section of the *MPH*. See, "Why Remodel?" *MPH* (April 11, 1931): 5. John Eberson, "Theatre Trends," *FDY* (1932): 1019-29. For an earlier version of similar views, see John Eberson, "Theatre Trends," *FDY* (1930): 943.

20. Paul T. Frankl, *Machine Made Leisure* (New York: Harper and Bros., 1932), pp. 5, 13, 136, 173-180.

21. A brilliant outline of the distinct national trends of European modernism can be found in Carl Schorske, "An International Style," *The New York Times Book Review* (March 25, 1979): 13, 36. A discussion of the wider context for this style in Germany, France and Russia can be found in John Willett, *Art and Politics in the Weimar Period: The New Sobriety, 1917-1933* (New York: Pantheon Books, 1979). For examples of the art deco and consumer styled restaurants, shops and exhibitions in the 1920s, see Stern, *New York 1930*, pp. 290-368. For the film theatre variant of these trends, see Georges Clarriere, "Three Smart Cinema Styles from Paris," *MPH* (March 14, 1931): 12-17. David Atwell, *Cathedrals of the Movies: A History of British Cinemas and their Audiences* (London: The Architectural Press, 1980), pp. 139-159. Morton Shand, *Modern Picture Houses and Theatres* (Philadelphia: Lippincott, 1930), and Anonymous, *Modern Cinemas* (London: The Architectural Press, 1936).

22. O.A. Shvidkkovsky, ed., *Buildings in the USSR, 1917-1932* (New York: Praeger Publishers, 1971); Shand, *Modern Picture Houses*, pp. 20-25; Atwell, *Cathedrals of the Movies*, pp. 139-159. Robert O. Boller, "Modernism: Its Meaning in Practical Remodeling," *MPH* (March 9, 1935): 14, 35-37.

23. For the overall context of modernism in the 1930s, see Meikle, *Twentieth Century Limited*. Robert Boller, "What Style of Theatre Design Fits the Variety of the American Scene?" *MPH* (July 25, 1936): 8-9. The essays which link together Wright's aesthetics with reform can be seen in Frank Lloyd Wright, "In the Cause of Architecture," *Essays by Frank Lloyd Wright for the Architectural Record* (New York: Architectural Record Books, 1927, 1975), pp. 131-151. Joseph Urban, *Theatres* (New York: Theatre Arts, Inc., 1930), pp. 15-16.

24. Ben Schlanger, "Theatres of Tomorrow," in *American Theatres of Today* (1930), II, pp. 3-9 and 51-59; "Looking Toward a Better Theatre," *MPH* (November 19, 1932): 8-9; "Planning Today's Simplified Cinema, A Practical Consideration of a New Theatre Design," *MPH* (September 21, 1935): 8-7, 30, 35. For the success of his ideas, see "Trend to Smaller Capacity Continues," *MPH* (February 6, 1937): 5. "The New Rialto at Forty-Second 'n' Broadway," *MPH* (February 8, 1936): 5, 10-12.

25. Ben Schlanger, "Planning Low Cost Theatres," *MPH* (April 7, 1934): 14-16; "Motion Picture Theatres of Tomorrow," *MPH* (February 14, 1932): 12-14, 56-7; "Motion Picture Theatres," *Architectural Record*, 81, (February 1937): 17-24. Schlanger, "Planning Today's Simplified Cinema."

26. Ibid. Also see "Editorial," *MPH* (April 8, 1933): 17; Boller, "Modernism," 14. On the expert, see Ben Schlanger, "The Architect and the Engineer," *MPH* 20-21; "Observations," *MPH* (June 3, 1933): 5; Irving Bowman, "Modern Theatre Construction," *MPH* (August 1, 1931): 19, 82.

27. Frankl, *Machine Made Leisure*, pp. 136-140; Boller, "Modernism: Its Meaning in Practical Remodeling," *MPH* (March 9, 1935): 14, 34 and "What Style Fits."

28. Ben Schlanger, "Remodeling to Welcome Today's Patrons," *MPH* (October 20, 1934): 24, 62. "Tomorrow," "Planning Low Cost," "Planning Today's Simplified Cinema." Susman, *Culture as History*. Eugene Clute, "New Schemes in Modern Remodeling," *MPH*

(October 20, 1934): 11-14; "The Studio Theatre: A Machine Age Cinema," *MPH* (September 26, 1931): 14-18. Boller, "Modernism," pp. 14-15.

29. Ben Schlanger, "New Theatres for the Cinema," *Architectural Forum*, 57 (September 1932): 253-260; "Vision in the Motion Picture Theatre," *MPH* (July 30, 1932): 8-12; Douglas Fox, "The Film Guild Cinema, An Experiment in Theatre Design," *MPH* (March 16, 1929): 15-19. For a similar precursor, see, "Carnegie Theatre: The Spirit of Today in Cinema Designing," *MPH* (November 24, 1928).

30. Anonymous, "The Thalia Theatre," The Architectural Forum (September, 1932): 201-202; "St. George Playhouse," *The American Architect* (April 5, 1928): 454-458; Ben Schlanger, "The Screen: A Problem in Exhibition," *MPH* (October 24, 1931): 14-15; "Production Methods and the Theatre," *MPH* (April 8, 1933): 8-10.

31. Ben Schlanger, "Use of the Full Screen Area Today," *MPH* (June 3, 1933): 11-13. "New Theatres for the Cinema." "Applying the 'Continental Plan' to American Theatre Seating," *MPH* (May 30, 1936): 8-12. "Two Versions of the Reversed Floor," *MPH* (October 22, 1932): 12-14. A survey of the films of the 1930s, emphasizing their backward-looking qualities can be found in Andrew Bergman, *We're in the Money: Depression America and Its Films* (New York: New York University Press, 1971); Robert Sklar, *Movie Made America: A Cultural History of American Movies* (New York: Random House, 1975), pp. 175-214; Susman, *Culture as History*, pp. 150-210; Lawrence Levine, "Hollywood's Washington: Film Images of National Politics During the Great Depression," *Prospects*, 10 (1985): 169-96. The interpretation closest to that presented here can be found in Robert S. McElvaine, *The Great Depression: America, 1929-1941* (New York: Times Books, 1984), pp. 196-224. The quote is from John Clellon Holmes, "15c Before 6:00 PM: The Wonderful Movies of the Thirties," *Harpers* (December, 1965): 51-55.

32. See for example Robert Boller, "Designing to Fit the Local Scene," *MPH* (April 3, 1937): 8-10. "The Community Theatre Idea," *MPH* (February 5, 1938): 9-10; Schlanger, "Planning Low Cost." "Kirkendale Urges Cooperation with Community," *MPH* (June 10,

1933): 22. The name comparison was derived from the titles listed in the theatre directory of *Film Daily Yearbook* of 1930 and 1940. Obviously romantic names remained on the older theatres, but the trend in the trade journals is towards communal and patriotic names by the late 1930s.

33. See Boller, "Designing to Fit the Local Scene." For Duluth and Minneapolis, see Herbert Scherer, *Marquee on Main Street: Jack Liebenberg's Movie Theatres, 1928-1941* (Minneapolis: University Art Gallery, University of Minnesota, 1982); Robert Boller, "The Ute: A Design Exploiting Native Western Culture," *MPH* (April 4, 1936): 9-12. Stern, *New York 1930*, pp. 260-261. The murals, of course, draw on the same regionalist styles that filled post offices and public buildings in the era. See Marlene Park and Gerald E. Markowitz, *Democratic Vistas: Post Offices and Public Art in the New Deal* (Philadelphia: Temple University Press, 1984).

34. Interview with Larry Storch, July 6, 1988. For the orientation to civic groups, see "Kirkendale Urges Cooperation with Community," *Exhibitor's Herald* (February 1, 1930): 20, "100% Representation Needed for Success of Theatre," *MPH* (March 28, 1931): 19, 95; "The Little Fellow," *MPH* (July 4, 1931): 8. "A Typical Theatre in an Average Town," *MPH* (January 8, 1938): 7. Press books for all the cited premiers are in Warner Brothers Collection, University of Southern California Film Archives Library. Also see FDY, 1940, pp. 802-9.

35. For the difference in quality between first run and second run houses, see *Better Movie Movement* (Minneapolis: The Women's Cooperative Alliance, 1921), pp. 42-44, 54-56, as in Gilman Papers, Box 34, Minnesota Historical Society. For the increase of movie going among ethnic groups in the Northeast and the spread of first class theatres into working class areas, see W. Lloyd Warner, *The Social Life of a Modern Community* (New Haven: Yale University Press, 1941), pp. 412-419, and Caroline Ware, *Greenwich Village 1920-1930* (Boston: Houghton Mifflin, 1935), pp. 330-38, 350-51, 366-369. For the amount of modern theatres built after 1933, see Ben Schlanger, "Cinemas," *Architectural Record*, 84 (July 1938): 113-115. African-Americans were, however, unlike Latinos, a major market for

films of the 1930s. See "800 Negro Theatres in 32 States Point to Growing Demand," *MPH* (August 14, 1936): 27, and *FDY, 1940*, pp. 45-47.

36. Scholars have typically assumed that compared to the 1920s attendance declined in the depression. Yet they based these assumptions on the inflated statistics released by the movie industry in the 1920s. For a more accurate assessment, showing that attendance rose in the depression, see Lary May with the assistance of Steve Lasonde, "Making the American Way: Modern Theatres, Audiences and the Film Industry, 1929-1945," *Prospects*, Vol. 12 (1988): 107-116. On the South, see "Redesigned in the Newer Materials," *MPH* (October 15, 1938): 63-65. On blue laws and limited showings in the rural areas, see *FDY, 1928*, p. 7. For the contrast in the thirties, see *FDY, 1938*, pp. 56-103 and 1032-1033. The quote is from *MPH* (November 16, 1935): 23.

37. For the United States and Europe, see Paul Monaco, *Cinema and Society: France and Germany During the Twenties* (New York: Elsevier, 1976), pp. 18-31; for a comparison with the United States in 1930, see *FDY* (New York, Quigley Publishing, 1929), p. 304, and Lary May, *Screening Out the Past*, pp. 165-166.

38. George Mosse, *The Nationalization of the Masses* (New York, 1985); Habermas, *Legitimation Crisis*; Carl Schorske, *Fin-de Siecle Vienna;* and Jeffrey Brooks, *When Russia Learned to Read: Literacy and Popular Literature, 1861-1917* (Princeton: Princeton University Press, 1985), especially pp. 295-396. For the continuing popularity of the cathedral style in Europe, see Dennis Sharp, *The Picture Palace* (New York: Frederick Praeger, 1969); David Atwell, *Cathedrals of the Movies: A History of British Cinemas and their Audiences* (London: The Architectural Press, 1980). Given the paucity of research on European audiences and markets, the argument about the different nature of the two mass cultures can only be stated in tentative outline. However, the fact that Europeans saw the American film industry and its product as radically different can be seen in Victoria De Grazia, "Mass Culture and Sovereignty: The American Challenge to European Cinemas, 1920-1960," *Journal of Modern History*, 61 (March, 1989): 53-87. For studies that suggest

that the audience was divided by classes, see Bruce Arthur Murray, "Film and the German Left in the Weimar Republic" (unpublished Ph.D. dissertation, University of Minnesota, 1985); Anton Kaes, "Mass Culture and Modernity: Notes Towards a Social History of Early American and German Cinemas," *America and the Germans*, vol. II, ed. Frank Trommlerr and Joseph McVeigh (Philadelphia: University of Pennsylvania Press, 1985), pp. 317-332. The class stratification of taste in France is argued in Pierre Bourdieu, *Distinction: A Social Critique of the Judgment of Taste*, trans. Richard Nice (London and New York, 1986). On Russia, see Richard Taylor, "The Birth of Soviet Cinema," in *Bolshevik Culture*, eds. Abbott Gleason and Richard Stites (Bloomington: Indiana University Press, 1985), pp. 190-205, and George Huaco, *The Sociology of Film Art* (New York: Basic Books, 1965), pp. 146-151.

39. The backward use of modernist design and popular culture to satisfy backward looking myths, corporate power, and an homogenous Americanism is the theme of Meikle, *Twentieth Century Limited*; Allen, The Romance of Commerce and Culture; Susman, *Culture as History*. And of course, the classic Frankfurt School statement by Theodore W. Adorno and Max Horkheimer, "The Culture Industry: Enlightenment as Mass Deception," in *The Dialectic of Enlightenment* (New York: Herber and Herber, 1972), pp. 120-167. The classic post-modern statement is in Jean Francois Lyotard, *The Postmodern Condition* (Minneapolis: University of Minnesota Press), pp. 71-82, and Walter Benjamin, *Illuminations* (New York: Harcourt, Brace and World, 1968), p. 255.

40. William Fox, "Possibilities of the Motion Picture Unlimited," *Fox Exhibitors' Bulletin* (June 1914): 31, as in Fox File, Museum of Modern Art Film Library, New York City.

PART IV

Political Communication and the Movies

For the final section of this volume, the editor has selected two inquiries that amply illustrate the uses of political communication as an approach to the movies. For here we are given to understand that the movies are in fact forms of communication which can be used by the "author" or creator of that form to communicate a widespread message, and that that message may be one that involves the representation of persuasion, and more specifically, propaganda. This leads us to the idea that to understand the politics of the movies, one might focus either on the messenger or the message. In the former instance, this suggests understanding the politics of the communicator, or delving into the nature of the movie communication itself. We here suggest the expansion of the familiar *auteur* theory to include in what sense was the creative talent political. The great "pantheon" of directors who did have some financial and artistic control over their movies might be usefully studied as to what kind of political vision seems inherent in their work. Here again they might disavow any political vision and certainly intentions, and indeed they may well be right; but the fact that they did communicate a coherent and identifiable way of seeing the world has political implications. Too, when certain kinds of communication are utilized by a medium like the movies, this has implications as to what kinds of messages are being communicated, for what purpose, and with what effect. If movies use erotic communication, it may be the case that this is done in order to attract audiences who desire to see erotic depictions, but with social effects far beyond the intentions of the communicators. If movies use political communication, this may be done because the communicator wishes to say something of political importance, or calculates that audiences might be receptive to a certain kind of political message. Given the right circumstances, forms of political communication may appear in movies as a legitimate and expected part of film experience. The inclusion of political propaganda in movies seemed "natural" during World Wars One and Two, but did not during the Vietnam War (with the exception of *The Green Berets*). What is excluded from communication is as important to understand as what is included. The communication approach attempts to understand the circumstances and reasons political communication is or is not included in movies, the forms it takes when it is included, and the reception it has when audiences see it and use it.

Charles Maland traces the history and contentions of the *auteur* theory, noting that it had certain appeals, including the fact that we were used to the idea of the author in literature, so it seemed "compelling and logical" that we approach film the same way. What was immediately controversial was the problem of identifying the dominant person who was the creative force in the making of the film. This downplayed the collaborative nature of filmmaking and the influence of studio organizational authority or financiers, but it did recognize that film is an art that involves creativity and even genius. It did flirt with a kind of "great man" theory of the movies, seeking and finding a "pantheon" of great directors who were elevated to genius status. This would also involve the controversy not only over who were and were not the truly great directors, but also whether people who were the directors of a popular art form should be thought of as great artists ranked with the giants of literature or painting. And, as Maland points out, early auteurism was "anti-sociological," in that it disdained directors who made films with social and political themes, and "ahistorical," in that it ignored the history of film, the career changes and moves of the directors, and even the larger political history. Maland offers instead a "reformed" auteurist approach, studying the director or creative team as one involved in making a "public form of communication," with narrative conventions, organizational and financial constraints, the particular "mix" of people making a particular movie, historical context, and so on. He suggests incorporating the communicative approach of Kenneth Burke into a mature auteurism, seeing moviemaking as indeed having a creative talent, but one that recognizes that successfully making films requires a "rhetorical strategy." Examining filmmakers and films as rhetoric then grounds the inquirer in a communications theory, and allows for the development of strategic communication in a situational field to observe how the creative process in fact does operate. With that in mind, how political communication enters the field becomes observable as a part of that creativity.

Dan Nimmo discusses the ways in which political propaganda appears in films, developing a typology of this major form of political communication. But he warns that propaganda is a "slippery concept" that must be approached with the process of communication in mind. In particular, we must be cautious about the attribution of intent, since intention is difficult to pin down and is "easily confounded." Looking for intentions in communication is like describing causality in nature: it can become an infinite regress, ignores all kinds of cross-pressures, "feedback," and unintended consequences, and begs the real question about propaganda, which is, what kind of political messages come across, and what kind of political learning is going on? Nimmo is thus led to a typology based on the work of philosopher Charles Sanders Peirce and communications theorist William Stephenson. In this way, one avoids not only the intention trap but also the equally misleading trap of saying that all films are propaganda, without specifying in what ways propaganda may become incorporated into the filmmaking process and what ways it may be taken and used by audiences. Clearly not all films are propaganda any more than they are all political; so it is to ask of the student of political communication to observe the process of propagandizing as it occurs in various patterns. The universe of propagandizing is a plural universe, to the extent that something not even intended as propaganda can become propaganda if it is taken as such. What is important here again is understanding that as a form of communication, propaganda will display certain characteristics. A filmmaker may see propaganda as part of a larger rhetorical strategy; propaganda may be covert or unrecognized as such; audiences may see persuasive messages in a film when there was no, or at least ambiguous, intention to include such; or there may be conscious symmetry between the persuader and the persuadable (as may have happened with the wartime films mentioned above). When the movie message in effect is interpreted as politically relevant, then we are likely seeing the process of propagandizing in action. If communication is a process of propagating messages, then political communication is a process of propagating political messages; when those messages have a discernible impact, then we are seeing political propaganda operate, in movies or any other medium.

POLITICS AND AUTEURS
From Chaplin to Wajda

Charles Maland
University of Tennessee

How do movies and politics relate? What can we learn about politics from movies—or about movies from politics? We can search for answers to these questions in many ways, and the appropriateness of any one method depends on such factors as the kind of film under study, the era in which it was made, the extent to which it draws on conventions of genre, the availability of archival material related to its production, and so on. One method of exploring the relationship between movies and politics limits itself to the examination of films made by a particularly talented filmmaker—what Francois Truffaut called an "auteur." This essay will explore the question of what the auteur approach to film study can contribute to an examination of the relationship between politics and movies.

I

The auteur approach to the study of films, which holds that the director is or should be the central creative force in making a film, was a dominant if not *the* dominant critical approach to the study of films in the United States from the middle 1960s to the middle 1970s. Highlighting the work of an individual director did not, of course, originate in the 1960s: filmmakers like George Melies and D.W. Griffith received widespread acclaim in the early decades of the movies.

Taken as a systematic approach, however, auteurism is rooted in France in the 1950s. There a group of young critics and aspiring filmmakers, including Francois Truffaut, Jean-Luc Godard, Jacques Rivette, Claude Chabrol, and Eric Rohmer, developed an attitude toward the cinema while writing for *Cahiers du Cinema*. Rivette's "The Genius of Howard Hawks" (1953) and Truffaut's "A Certain Tendency in the French Cinema" (1954) are key documents in the development of "la politique des auteurs." Rivette's essay implied auteurism in the way it analyzed films as an expression of the director's world vision. Truffaut's piece, on the other hand, both assumed the importance of the director and built a ranking system when it attacked the then-popular literary adaptations by directors like Delannoy and Autant-Lara and celebrated the genuinely personal and original work of directors like Renoir, Bresson, and Tati. As it developed in the pages of *Cahiers* and later in other French journals, "la politique des auteurs" became a polemical battleground in which directors were ranked and celebrated as true "auteurs" or downgraded as mere "metteurs en scene." Never an articulated theory, it rather proposed that we organize our attentions by considering films as the work of particular directors.

The approach became popular in the United States in the 1960s for several reasons. First, the approach had a gifted proselytizer, Andrew Sarris, whose "Notes on the Auteur Theory in 1962" was an early articulation and defense of the "auteur theory." The article generated a critical debate and was sharply attacked by Pauline Kael, among others, but the publication of Sarris's *The American Cinema* in 1968 helped legitimize and popularize the approach. A second reason for the popularity of auteurism was that the films of a number of gifted film directors—Bergman, Fellini, Truffaut, Godard, and Antonioni, among others—began to obtain relatively widespread release at art houses and college film societies through the 1960s. The distinctive and often complex work of these directors helped convince many that film, before then scorned by much of the American intelligentsia as simple-minded entertainment, was an important narrative art form. Finally, the growth of college courses in film studies added to the popularity of the auteur approach. Many former teachers of literature, long familiar with studying Chaucer and Shakespeare, Austen and Dickens, Faulkner and Hemingway, found auteurism a compelling and logical way to approach the movies.

This early auteurism contained clear limitations, particularly to those interested in considering the relations between politics and movies. One drawback is its unabashedly polemical grounding. Some early auteurists were engaged in a ranking system, a game of inclusion and exclusion, that allowed them to defend their favorites and damn the rest. Little careful analysis of films and still less serious reflection on their cultural significance emerged from this battleground of favorites.

Another limitation was its anti-sociological bias. In the United States at least, auteurism emerged in part as an alternative to the kind of liberal, socially concerned reviewing and criticism which had been popular in the 1930s and, to some extent, in the 1940s, but which came under attack during the Cold War. Sarris himself, in his introduction to *The American Cinema*, attacks "politically oriented" critics who would judge art by social or political standards, and specifically sets up auteurism as an antidote: "*Auteur* criticism is a reaction against the sociological criticism that enthroned the *what* against the *how*" (36). Starting with an aversion to "socially significant" films, Sarris understandably gave low rankings to directors who regularly made politically significant or social problem films, filmmakers like Sidney Lumet or Stanley Kramer or Elia Kazan.

Allied with this anti-sociological bias is the ahistorical character of auteurism. Early auteurism celebrated the director's personal stamp on his films, and it was zealous in pursuing even the most detailed of repetitions from one film of a director to the next. Given that zealotry, however, it is remarkable how uninterested early auteurism was about history. Sam Rohdie put it well when he complained that for much of this early auteurism, "*auteurs* are out of time. The theory which makes them sacred makes no inroad on vulgar history, has no concepts for the social or the collective, or the national" (10). This Romantic conception of the artist, which made creative genius the center of critical focus, plucked the director from the economic and industrial imperatives of filmmaking and placed him on a pedestal, as if the director did not work within an industry and a culture at a particular historical moment.

From the mid-1970s on, auteurism was challenged for all these limitations, and more (Caughie, Buscombe). Attention in film studies began to move toward questions of how films generate meaning through the interplay of narrative and cinematic style, which semiology and neo-formalism sought to address. Genre theories and discussions of intertextuality sought to identify how films gain meaning within the context of other films which came before (or after) it. In the past decade further questions about the relationship between the audience (rather than the creator), the text, and the broader culture have generated more interest in psychoanalytic, historicist, and ideological approaches to the study of film. Auteurism today is much more likely to be synthesized with some of these other approaches (Kolker, 1-3). Because of this, it is also better equipped to approach the question of the relationship between auteurs and politics.

How, then, can the auteur approach be connected to politics, broadly conceived, in a useful way? From my perspective, several assumptions are important if we are to answer this question. First, we must take account of the production history of particular films (and particular directorial careers), and be selective about deciding who is an auteur. If the director of a film had little or nothing to do with the screenplay of a movie or little control over which projects to work on, we had better look to an approach other than auteurism to learn more about the relationship between politics and movies. This is not to say that the director must be a Costa-Gavras, always concerned with making overtly political films. Rather, it is to say that we ought to learn something about the director's position within the film industry and his involvements during production before we select him or her as the subject of an auteurist analysis.

Second, auteurist criticism must also admit from the start the tension between a director's personal preoccupations and the aesthetic and economic demands of the medium. No filmmaker working at the center (or even the periphery) of mainstream narrative filmmaking can be concerned only with private, personal obsessions or preoccupations. Narrative film is of necessity a public form of communication, and as such the auteur must be concerned with the question of how he or she can treat significant subject matter, political or otherwise, using conventions of narrative film in a way that others (not necessarily a mass audience) will want to see it. While the pressures on a filmmaker may be more commercial in some film industries (like the American) and more political in others (like a number of Eastern European countries), an auteurist critic must be sensitive to the ways that these pressures encourage, if not force, the filmmaker to work within certain conventions or forms. If we are sensitive to these pressures, the question of how some auteurs treat political concerns through film narrative and style becomes a fascinating one.

Finally, the auteur approach can be made more vital if we attend to the broader historical-ideological context within which the director worked. The ahistorical flavor of early auteurism was perhaps its most significant weakness, and a dynamic auteurism in search of political significance must attend to two questions: 1) how can the historical context out of which an auteur's films arose illuminate those films; and 2) how does the interplay of narrative and cinematic style in a particular film generate an ideological perspective (which in turn might shape the historical context)? Kenneth Burke once suggested that literature could be looked at as a rhetorical strategy for dealing with or responding to a particular historical situation. Such works, Burke writes, may be considered "as strategies for selecting enemies and allies, for socializing losses, for warding off an evil eye, for purification, propitiation, and desanctification, consolation and vengeance, admonition and exhortation, implicit commands or instructions of one sort or another" (304). This situation/strategy approach could be usefully grafted onto auteurism, grounding it in history and ideology.

If I could chart such an approach, it would look something like this:

Historical context
/
AUTEUR - FILM(S) - IDEOLOGY
/
Industrial context

At the start of the approach is the selection of the auteur. To select an auteur, the critic searches for evidence from the industrial structure within which the director (or other potential auteur candidate) worked and from the production history of the particular film over which the auteur did have (or came to achieve) considerable creative control and broad involvement. Once that is established, the critic may examine biographical evidence from the auteur's life that may help one understand the ideological perspective that the auteur came to develop. From there we move to the center of the approach—the films themselves. Close formalist attention to the narrative and stylistic qualities of individual films, and to the formal similarities and differences among the director's films—both close analysis and careful comparisons—is essential, but that analysis should be directed toward identifying the ideological perspective presented in a particular film, and how the director's ideological perspective continues (or evolves) over a career. In attempting to plumb the film's ideological perspective, the critic will also attend to the context, within both the film industry and the broader culture, seeking to understand how those contextual factors may have helped shape the film.

Applying this approach to a particular auteur is no easy task, and each director would pose different problems. Studying the films of a political filmmaker like Costa-Gavras, for example, would be convenient because of his overtly political subject matter but would be complicated by the fact that he has worked within a number of different film industries. Fritz Lang, whose films might be less overtly political than Costa-Gavras', worked for the first third of his career in Germany and the last two-thirds in the United States. The auteur critic would be able to consider the German films like *Metropolis* and *M*, connecting them to the late Weimar years, but would also have to take into account how living in another culture and within the very different American film industry shaped his films. Studying the films of an American director like Martin Ritt (*The Front, Norma Rae*) or Sidney Lumet (*Daniel, Running on Empty*), both of whom have been drawn to political issues in many films, would be complicated by the fact that both directors have been involved (whether by choice or economic necessity) in projects that seem little related to the dominant concerns of their other, more political, films. Similarly, some filmmakers are more drawn to political issues in their films early in their careers (Kazan), while others become so later (Chaplin). This approach to auteurism would even recognize that certain actors who have become powerful in the American film industry following the breakdown of the studio system, even if they don't direct a film, could be subjects of auteur studies: Jane Fonda, Clint Eastwood, Warren Beatty, and Sylvester Stallone all would seem to be interesting possible subjects for studies of the relationship between auteurs and movies. Regardless of the figure chosen, this brand of auteurism—a political auteurism, if you will—would firmly ground the filmmaker in an industrial and historical context, exploring the ideological implications of the auteur's films.

II

To demonstrate briefly how this political auteurism might illuminate the relationship between movies and politics, I would like to contrast two filmmakers, Charlie Chaplin and Andrezej Wajda, and two of their films, Chaplin's *The Great Dictator* (1940) and Wajda's *Man of Marble* (1976). I have chosen these two filmmakers and two films in part because they contrast in many ways. The British-born Chaplin worked within the American film industry from 1913 to 1952; Wajda has worked within the Polish film industry since the early 1950s, with some involvement in various international productions at various points in his career. Chaplin acted in his films; Wajda did not. Chaplin owned his own production facilities; Wajda headed a film production unit that was a part of the nationalized Polish film industry. Chaplin's film is a comic satire. Wajda's is a complex, *Citizen Kane*-like biography of the fictional hero's rise and fall that tends more toward tragedy. Chaplin's is a carefully balanced, linear narrative. Wajda's is a modernist, disjunctive narrative. Despite these and other differences, however, both films are historically rooted and present clear ideological perspectives by engaged directors. As we shall see below, the central ideological thrust of *The Great Dictator* is a Popular Front anti-fascism, while *Man of Marble* combines a distinct Polish nationalism and a democratic socialism which is critical of the Communist Party bureaucracy. For each film, beginning with *The Great Dictator*, we will look briefly at the details of the auteur's biography, the industrial structures within which the director worked, the films themselves, and the response elicited by the film within its culture.

In the case of many auteurs, biographical factors may help illuminate the ideological perspectives that emerge from their films. Chaplin, born in London to two music hall singers, lived in uncertainty and considerable poverty after his parents separated and his mother at times found it financially and psychologically difficult to care for her children (Chaplin, chs. 1-3; Robinson, ch. 1). As is unsurprising for one who experienced such a Dickensian childhood, Chaplin long held a sympathy for the oppressed and dispossessed. In addition, from early on he demonstrated a talent at acting, particularly pantomime, and as an adolescent and young adult he worked in the theater and English music halls, honing his timing and comic skills. This genius at pantomime combined with Chaplin's constitutional sympathy for the underdog when he created Charlie, the familiar Little Tramp, less than a year after he entered the movie industry at Mack Sennett's Keystone Studios in 1913.

Within a year and a half, Chaplin had been vaulted to national and even international fame (Maland, ch. 1). Chaplin owed much of his success to this comic persona and his pantomime, and he retained his sympathy for the dispossessed even after he became independently wealthy. Both of these factors are important in an auteurist reading of *Great Dictator*, for Chaplin's reliance on pantomime was challenged after the introduction of sound films (*The Great Dictator* is the first film in which he used dialogue extensively), and his sympathy for the dispossessed contributed both to his decision to make the film and to the ideological perspective it developed.

Any viable auteurism must attend to the industrial structure within which the auteur worked. Chaplin himself quickly achieved a position of renown and considerable power in Hollywood thanks to his enormous success at making comic short films in the 1910s, which enabled him to amass a fortune in a few short years. (His third contract, signed with Mutual Film Corporation in 1916, earned him $10,000 per week for a year plus a bonus of $50,000 for signing. His next contract nearly doubled that amount.) That fortune enabled Chaplin to attain an independence in Hollywood just as the film industry was consolidating into the studio system: in 1918 he began building his own production facilities on the corner of La Brea Avenue and Sunset Boulevard. The following year he became a founding member of United Artists with stars Mary Pickford and Douglas Fairbanks, and director D.W. Griffith. To protect themselves from the growing power of studios like Paramount and to retain rights to their own films, these four people set up United Artists as a company which would distribute the films that each produced independently. All of Chaplin's films from *A Woman of Paris* (1923) through *Limelight* (1952) were distributed through United Artists. As producer, director, writer, and star of his films, Chaplin possessed by Hollywood standards a remarkable creative control of his films.

It would be misleading, however, to say that Chaplin could make films however he wanted: even the relatively independent auteur works within an industrial and aesthetic context, and if the auteur's films vary too significantly from what audiences have come to expect, they may either alienate the audience or even fail to find one at all. Chaplin worked within an industry that had developed an ethos of movies as "entertainment." Movies were supposed to provide audiences with a pleasurable narrative experience in exchange for the price of a ticket.

Within this context the pressures on filmmakers were primarily commercial: those who learned to make consistently profitable films could thrive in the system. Chaplin, developing a distinctive blend of comedy, romance, and pathos in his films, did just that in movies like *The Kid*, *The Gold Rush*, and *City Lights*.

In *The Great Dictator*, however, Chaplin had to respond to two challenges—one from within the film industry, one external to the industry—to the "personal genre" he had fashioned. The internal factor was the introduction of sound, which transformed the silent film industry between 1927 and 1929. Since much of Chaplin's popularity relied on the comedy generated by the Tramp's pantomime (and since Chaplin felt that his British accent would be inappropriate for his down-and-out persona), this was a significant challenge. Chaplin's response to this dilemma has been well treated by Ira Jaffe and Garrett Stewart, among others. Suffice it to say here that following the introduction of sound, Chaplin made two films that had recorded sound tracks which made ample use of music and sound effects but included little (*Modern Times*) or no (*City Lights*) spoken language. As he was contemplating a new film project in 1937, Chaplin felt considerable pressure to conform to what had become standard in the industry nearly a decade earlier.

More significant given our purposes here was an external factor: the pressure on artists during the Depression to respond to or depict significant social issues in their art (Susman, Pells). Following the Stock Market Crash in 1929 and subsequent world economic depression by 1931 and 1932, artists began to find themselves encouraged by leftist critics to create works of social significance. Partly because of his constitutional sympathy for the underdog and partly because his economic independence permitted him to do so, Chaplin found himself responding to this new climate of opinion. He first did so in *Modern Times*. Although the familiar Tramp figure is at the center of the film, it also includes a number of optical references to unemployment, hunger, strikes, and police violence against strikers. Partly because the Charlie persona doesn't speak in the film (except for singing a gibberish song), the political perspective seems muted and ambiguous in *Modern Times*.

Ultimately Chaplin decided to respond to both challenges—sound films and leftist pressures on artists—by making a dialogue film which would tackle what was fast becoming in the late 1930s the most significant social issue of the day: the growing power and aggression of Hitler and the Nazis. This was unsurprising in one way: acquaintances had as early as 1933 commented on the physical resemblance of Chaplin and Hitler and encouraged Chaplin to make a film about the Fuhrer (Maland, 165-166). In addition, Chaplin was increasingly persuaded, in part because of his sympathy for the dispossessed Jews, by the Popular Front call for leftists to cooperate in opposition to the growing power of Hitler and the Nazis. By 1938 Chaplin had committed himself to making a dialogue film in which he would play two roles and satirize Hitler.

Here it might be appropriate to say a word about the Popular Front. Proposed and supported by the Soviet Union in 1935 as a response to the growing militarization of Nazi Germany, the Popular Front encouraged those opposed to fascism to set aside ideological differences and cooperate to challenge the growing power of Hitler. It was a kind of ecumenical grouping of the political left and center that flourished between 1936 and 1939. The Nazi-Soviet Non-aggression Pact of August, 1939, threw the Popular Front into disarray, particularly Communist Party members, but a strong anti-fascism survived in the United States after the war broke out in Europe. When the Nazis broke the pact and attacked the Soviet Union in 1941, the Popular Front revived and sustained itself through the war years. Ceplair and Englund (chs. 4-6) treat the impact of the Popular Front and Soviet-German relations on Hollywood. Suffice it to say here that Chaplin, who was never a Communist, was influenced by the climate of Popular Front anti-fascism when he was conceiving the film and writing the screenplay and that his hatred of fascism remained unwavering throughout the Depression and World War Two.

Because Chaplin was working within the entertainment ethos of the Hollywood film industry, however, the film posed special challenges. How could he retain that part of his audience that associated Chaplin almost solely with Charlie's pantomime and pathos? How could he make his political points through dialogue and action without violating the prevailing tenets of "entertainment" in Hollywood? And since World War Two broke out just as shooting was to begin, what position would the film take concerning fighting the Nazis? This last question posed a particularly touchy issue, since the United States government was officially neutral toward the European war while the film was being shot, edited, and released, and the country was torn over the isolationist/interventionist controversy.

Within this political and historical context, Chaplin and his collaborators fashioned his film and expressed an ideological perspective. Chaplin's *The Great Dictator* develops its Popular Front anti-fascism through topical satire with Chaplin himself playing two parts: a Jewish barber similar to the Charlie persona he had played in earlier films and a Hitler-like dictator named Adenoid Hynkel. Unlike most of Chaplin's earlier films, *The Great Dictator* is filled with satirical names which refer to real people, places, and events. Hynkel, the Phooey (Der Fuhrer), leads the Sons and Daughters of the Double Cross (the swastika) and is assisted by Minister of War Herring (Goering) and Minister of the Interior Garbitsch (Goebbels). Benzino Napoloni (Mussolini), who comes to visit Hynkel, is referred to as "Il Digaditch" (Il Duce). Germany is called Tomania, a blend of the word for food poisoning and the suffix "mania"—madness. Italy is Bacteria— another poison infecting the world's body politic. In the military review scene, Napoloni mentions the name of his capitol city: "Aroma." Austria is called Osterlich.

Chaplin also clearly defines the historical setting of the film—from near the end of World War One to the Nazis' invasion of Austria in 1938—in two ways. The first way is through the use of several documentary montages. These include headlines with specific historical references, as well as documentary newsreel footage, some of Nazi Party rallies. Early in the film, headlines move the film from the Armistice to the rise of Hitler by referring to details like Lindberg's trans-Atlantic flight, the onset of the Depression, and persecution of Jews. The film also alludes to specific historical events: the Nuremburg Nazi Party Rallies of 1933 and 1938, called to mind during Hynkel's speech at the start of the film and the barber's speech at the end; Mussolini's visit to Germany in September 1937, during which time he affirmed his alliance with Hitler; and Hitler's Anschluss of Austria in 1938. This specificity of historical reference marked a departure for Chaplin; in his earlier films—*City Lights* is a prime example—names, places, and events had no such specific historical referents.

On the other hand, *The Great Dictator* resembles previous Chaplin features in the way it divides characters into two opposing moral universes, one good and one evil (think, for example, of Charlie and the kid versus county authorities in *The Kid* or the flower girl's world versus the millionaire's world in *City Lights*). The credits in *The Great Dictator* group characters into "People of the Ghetto," the most important of which are the barber and Hannah (played by Chaplin's third wife, Paulette Goddard), and "People of the Palace," Hynkel and his followers. In the context of the film, the former are victims, the latter victimizers. And as Julian Smith has noted, the narrative crosscuts between the two groups in an extremely balanced way: forty-seven minutes of the film are devoted to scenes with Hynkel in the palace or with his associates elsewhere, and forty-six minutes present characters in the ghetto (114).

The narrative of the film provides the structure for Chaplin's satire. The opening title sets the film's tone: "This is a story of a period between Two World Wars—an interim in which Insanity cut loose, Liberty took a nose dive, and Humanity was kicked around somewhat." The narrative begins with the barber, a German soldier in World War One, helping to save a fellow soldier, Schultz. As he does so, however, he gets a blow to the head and suffers amnesia for over a decade. Released from the hospital following Hynkel's rise to power, he returns to his barber shop in a Jewish ghetto, unaware of how Hynkel and his followers are mistreating Jews. At one point, attacking a soldier who has painted "Jew" on his shop window, he barely escapes imprisonment when Schultz, now an influential officer, saves him. He quickly learns the situation, however, thanks in part to his neighbors, especially Hannah and her parents, the Jaeckels. As the film progresses, we learn of Hynkel's dictatorial megalomania and of his increasingly cruel policies toward the people of the ghetto. Aided by Schultz, who becomes disillusioned with Hynkel, the people of the ghetto plot an assassination attempt. Schultz and the barber, however, are caught and imprisoned. As the persecution intensifies, Hannah and others remaining in the ghetto are forced to flee to neighboring Osterlich. The barber and Schultz escape from their prison camp wearing storm trooper uniforms. Hynkel, duck shooting in civilian clothes just before the invasion of Osterlich, is mistaken for the escaped barber and arrested. The barber, now posing as the Phooey, makes it to the Osterlich border with Schultz. He is greeted by his troops, and following a montage depicting the successful and nearly bloodless overtaking of the country, is escorted to a huge platform and asked to address his troops and a huge crowd of Osterlich citizens. In the film's most controversial scene, Garbitsch introduces who he thinks is Hynkel, and the barber makes a three-and-a-half minute speech, which Chaplin later included in his autobiography (399-400), criticizing the cruelty and inhumanity of the dictators and their followers and calling for soldiers to throw down their arms.

An auteur must work within the economic and industrial imperatives of a particular film industry, and Chaplin was no exception. Since the central strand of his film was so overtly political in an industry that generally left messages to Western Union, he compensated for that dimension by presenting considerable pantomime. A good example comes in the first scenes when the Jewish barber, a soldier in World War One, fails to operate an artillery gun and later tries to examine an unexploded shell which points, almost like a magnet, toward the barber no matter which way he runs around it. Other examples include the weaving dance the barber does after Hannah mistakenly hits him over the head with a frying pan, his famous shaving sequence (perfectly timed to Brahm's "Hungarian Dance Number 5"), and the pudding sequence, in which the barber and his associates hope to avoid finding a coin in their puddings which would select the prospective assassin of Hynkel. Chaplin also uses mime and slapstick when playing the Hynkel character, as when he delivers a speech in gibberish Teutonic using dictatorial gestures early in the film or later jockeys with Napoloni in his office for a power position. Much of this brand of humor reminds us of Chaplin's earlier work.

Despite the highjinks and slapstick, however, the ideological perspective of the film is clear and decisive, emerging from a sympathetic treatment of the barber and other members of the ghetto and an excoriation of Hynkel and his cohorts. The settings associated with each group suggest the contrast. The barber's shop faces a modest city street. The courtyard between his shop and the Jaeckel's home, as well as the merchants who sell their wares on the sidewalks, give the city a European feeling, but the furnishings in the Jaeckel's home and the costumes and manner of the people in the ghetto give it a folk flavor. These settings all suggest a warmth and simplicity associated with positive (and often threatened) values in Chaplin's films. In contrast, the dictator moves in settings which suggest power, egomania, and splendor. He delivers his speech on a massive platform which prominently displays symbols of propaganda. Hynkel's huge office dwarfs anyone who enters, and his surroundings suggest his egotism: he has a bust of himself on his desk, his file cabinets are false-fronted mirrors in front of which he preens on occasion, and he sometimes goes briefly into a room and poses for a sculptor and painter who work simultaneously on tributes to the Phooey. All in all, Hynkel's settings suggest a callous and egotistic leader who lives in splendor, far removed from the people whom he manipulates and for whom he shows consistent disdain.

The characterizations also develop this contrasting ideological perspective. The barber, Hannah, and the other citizens of the ghetto want only to live and let live. They yearn for a world where they can simply survive and work in peace. Hannah, a victim of modern civilization—she's an orphan whose father was killed in the First World War—enunciates this philosophy to the barber: "Life could be wonderful if people could be left alone."

In contrast, Hynkel and his followers are portrayed as cruel, opportunistic, and egomaniacal. Paul Goodman has convincingly argued that central to the film is its "invective" against Hynkel's qualities: his megalomania, narcissism, compulsion to dominate, and disregard for human life. His behavior is reprehensible, from his gibberish denunciations of liberty and democracy in his opening speech to his comment after a person dies demonstrating a prototype parachute: "far from perfect," is Hynkel's only response to the tragedy. One key scene blending pantomime with the film's ideological thrust is the famous globe ballet scene, in which Hynkel, lost in a revery of world domination, repeatedly tosses a globe balloon into the air and catches it on its fall until it finally explodes in his face. The Phooey's lust for power, Chaplin suggests, will prove his downfall.

The core of Chaplin's ideological perspective attacks fascism from a Popular Front perspective. Both positions are outlined most explicitly at the conclusion of the film. Chaplin's understanding of fascism is best summed up in Garbitsch's brief address just before the barber's final speech:

> Victory shall come to the worthy. Today, democracy, liberty, and equality are words to fool the people. No nation can progress with such ideas. They stand in the way of action. Therefore we frankly abolish them. In the future each man will serve the interests of the state with absolute obedience. Let him who refuses beware. The rights of citizenship will be taken away from all Jews and non-Aryans. They are inferior and

therefore enemies of the state. It is the duty of all true Aryans to hate and despise them.

This speech explicitly expresses Chaplin's understanding of the fascism which his film opposed.

Because Hynkel and the People of the Palace are so strong and the People of the Ghetto so helpless, however, the film seems to lead to a dark conclusion. If the good are weak and the evil powerful, doesn't the world seem doomed? A central aesthetic and political question raised by *The Great Dictator* is this: how ought the good, and the advocates of democracy who empathize with them, respond to the cruelties of the fascists? This was a very real dilemma for Americans when *The Great Dictator* was being shot and released, for in the late 1930s, many antifascists were also pacificists or at least extremely reluctant to support any American involvement in another European war. Like the people of the ghetto (though less directly affected), many Americans were agonizing about how to respond to the threats of the dictators, especially after the war broke out in September 1939.

Several details in *The Great Dictator* suggest an answer. Early in the film, after two storm troopers harass the barber, Hannah smashes them in the head with a frying pan. It gives her a feeling of release and catharsis. As the scene closes, she tells the barber, "That did me a lot of good. You sure got nerve the way you fought back. That's what we should all do: fight back. We can't fight alone, but we can lick 'em together." While an American viewer in October 1940 could take this as an affirmation that the Allies supported by the United States could counter the Fascist threat, in the context of the film itself, active resistance by Jews to Hynkel and his supporters seems futile: those forces of darkness are too organized, too well armed, and too powerful to overcome. What, then, does Chaplin suggest? What perspective and tactics does he defend?

The famous ending—the part of the film which drew the most critical attention when the film was released—suggests an answer. Following Garbitsch's comments, cited above, the disguised barber, at Schultz's urging, walks up to the microphones and delivers a speech of three and one-half uninterrupted minutes that counters Hynkel's speech near the opening of the film. Chaplin, who had resisted dialogue long after the rest of Hollywood had accommodated itself to the new technology, here finally affirmed the power of the word. This was a turnabout, for both *Modern Times* (in the phonograph record sales pitch) and an earlier scene in *The Great Dictator* (when the inventor demonstrates his bullet-proof uniform) use the line, "actions speak louder than words," indicating Chaplin's aesthetic resistance to the domination of language in movies. However, in this final speech, Chaplin broke the irksome bonds of silence imposed on him by Charlie's essential pantomime and in doing so defined his ideological perspective.

Although the speech contains its contradictions and inconsistencies, when examined closely, it defends democratic Popular Front politics in its struggle with fascism. As he concludes, the barber appeals directly to the Tomanian soldiers, imploring them *not* to fight for the dictator but rather to take power from him and return it to "the people." The barber does not specifically beat the drums of war against the fascists—he is, after all, urging the Tomanian soldiers to abandon their dictator, in which case any war would be over. However, he does clearly imply that if the perverted dictators can be stopped in no other way, it may be necessary to fight for the well-being of the world, so that the kindness and decency of the people of the ghetto can survive and thrive.

Ultimately, one word capsulizes Chaplin's strategy for concluding his most overtly political film: "hope." As Garbitsch is introducing him, the barber hears Schultz urging him to speak: "it's our only hope." Pensively, the barber repeats the word, "hope," then makes his way to the microphones. The speech expresses hope in what Chaplin saw as a world gone mad, and the fact that it is followed by the soldiers' cheers and the barber's comments, via radio waves, to Hannah about seeing a better world on the horizon only reinforces the point. Chaplin's political sentiments and message were ringing and clear in the film: anti-fascists must actively oppose and, if necessary, fight against the threat and inhumanity represented by the film's surrogate Hitler. Within the structure of comic pantomime and satire, Chaplin fashioned a clear denunciation of fascism in the midst of a broader controversy in the United States about the country's response to the war in Europe.

The Great Dictator generated a widespread popular and critical response, as one might expect when the world's most famous movie comedian made a film about the world's most feared dictator. Although Chaplin had worried about the box-office prospects of the film while he was making it, *The Great Dictator* was an enormous popular success. Even though it was not released in many European countries until after the end of World War II, it earned over $5 million in rentals world wide, more than any previous (or subsequent) Chaplin film. According to United Artists' records, the film earned Chaplin a $1.5 million profit on an investment of $2 million (Balio, 165). The film was so successful that when Bosley Crowther compiled in 1942 a list of the ten top moneymaking films in the previous five years, *The Great Dictator* ranked third of the roughly 2,400 American films released during the period (12-13).

The film also generated a great deal of critical discussion. Because the film was so topical, it was even reviewed in publications that rarely wrote about movies. In the American press the critical consensus seemed to be that the film was an important one but that the ending was a mistake which just didn't work. A corollary to this consensus is that more conservative newspapers and critics were generally more negative. A characteristic comment from a conservative reviewer was Archer Winston's view, in the *New York Post*, that although he liked much of the comedy, "the speech is so completely out of key with all that has preceded it that it makes you squirm. Even if you understand perfectly the noble motives for it . . . nevertheless, it is an artistic boner of the first water." In the liberal press, the film fared somewhat better. In the *New York Times* Bosley Crowther praised *The Great Dictator* as "a superlative accomplishment by a great and true artist . . . unquestionably the most significant—if not the most entertaining—film that Chaplin has ever made." In even more positive terms, Crowther wrote that Chaplin was "making a most profound and tragic comment upon a truly evil state of affairs" (3).

Crowther's was one of the most positive reviews of the film: not all liberal reviewers were as enthusiastic, particularly about the ending. And most of the more conservative reviewers were uneasy about this overt political address. This must be attributed at least in part to the fact that the film, particularly the barber's speech, constituted a distinct departure from what viewers had come to expect of Chaplin—and what they had come to expect of Hollywood films generally. If we try to summarize what the reviewers felt about the political perspective in the film, however, it is generally accurate to say that interventionists and advocates of the Popular Front praised the film while isolationists disliked it.

From an auteurist perspective, *The Great Dictator* was important for at least two reasons. The first is that it represented the first time in which Chaplin expressed a clear and forceful political position in his films, in large part because he had finally capitulated fully to sound films (it's difficult to express specific ideological positions solely through pantomime). Second, the fame made Chaplin something of a political celebrity, which was not always to his advantage. In 1941 the Senate Subcommittee on War Propaganda announced that it would investigate *The Great Dictator*, along with a number of films to see if their "premature anti-fascist" views improperly endorsed an interventionist position; the committee disbanded after Pearl Harbor without calling witnesses (Ceplair and Englund, 160-161). In a more positive vein Chaplin delivered the final speech of *The Great Dictator* at one of Roosevelt's pre-inaugural balls in 1941, and the following year he became actively involved in the fight against fascism by giving a series of speeches in favor of opening a Second Front in Europe (Maland, 186-194). In a sense, *The Great Dictator* tripped the dam of Chaplin's public political activities. Although his Popular Front anti-fascism contributed to the American war effort, the politicization of Chaplin's image would suffer when the political climate turned cold in the years immediately following World War II.

III

Andrzej Wajda's *Man of Marble* is very different from *The Great Dictator*, just as the two auteurs differ. Like Chaplin, however, Wajda's childhood and young adulthood casts light on his later work in the film industry. The son of a military officer, Wajda was born in a small town in northeast Poland in 1926, eight years after Poland had been reestablished as a country following 150 years of foreign occupation. Because of this fact, Polish patriotism had a special intensity, especially in the army and Wajda's family, where "God and Country" was an important motto (Michalak and Turaj, 129). In his subsequent career, Wajda continually demonstrated his patriotic nationalism and interest in the history of Poland.

Wajda's experiences in World War Two and its aftermath also prepared the way for and shed light on his work as a filmmaker. When his father was killed after the outbreak of World War Two, Wajda's mother moved the family to the city of Radom, south of Warsaw. There Wajda was involved in underground anti-Nazi activities of the Home Army, which gave him the proper anti-fascist political credentials after the war when he desired to continue his schooling and develop his interest in the visual arts. After studying painting at the Academy of Fine Arts in Cracow, he transferred to the newly established film school in Lodz in 1949. The years chronicled in the flashback sequences in *Man of Marble*—the so-called "Stalinist years" of the late 1940s and early 1950s—coincide with the years that Wajda studied film and began to work himself into the film industry. Indeed, Wajda gives the careful viewer an indication of his involvement in the era his film concentrates on by listing himself as assistant director in the credits of the documentary film embedded in *Man of Marble* called *Architects of Our Happiness*.

Wajda made *Man of Marble* in a very different industrial structure and cultural context than Chaplin confronted with *The Great Dictator*. Among the Polish intelligentsia, the cinema is held in higher regard than it is in the United States, and according to Michalek and Turaj, the film director possesses high status in Poland: he is "nothing less than an exponent of universal aspirations and concerns, a creator who has gained the status heretofore reserved for poets, writers, and artists" (xi). Wajda goes even farther, arguing that in Poland, in part because of the instability of its political history, the arts generally have served an especially vital social function: "For various reasons—historical, social, mythological—culture in Poland has always been a meeting-place of social, historical, civic, and moral debate. Art and culture were the forum for ventilation of fundamental issues to do with the model of socialist life, the role of the individual, the meaning of history, the basic hierarchies of collective existence." In fact, Wajda continues, art and culture, including the cinema, took "over themes and messages that in other societies were the proper domain of political institutions and public opinion" (13). Partly because of this emphasis on culture in Poland and partly because of the structure of the film industry, commercial pressures are minimal in the Polish cinema, so much so that, as Michalek and Turaj put it, the "threat of unpopularity is of no concern" to the filmmaker (xii).

Yet if the American film industry places particularly strong *commercial* pressures on the filmmaker, the Polish filmmaker has to learn to function within *political* constraints, as Wajda had to with *Man of Marble*. The Polish film industry has been state owned since the late 1940s, and since 1955 has been organized into a semiautonomous film unit system. This Creative Film Unit system divides film production into a number of separate film units—there have been as many as nine functioning in Poland at any one time. Each unit is headed by an artistic director (usually a prominent director) who in turn is supported by a production manager and a literary director in charge of script development. The political pressures on filmmakers arise from the fact that when a film unit approves a project, it is sent forward to governmental authorities who must give approval before any project can be budgeted and funded (Michalek, xiii).

Wajda and scriptwriter Alekander Scribor-Rylski first submitted to authorities in the early 1960s a script about the rise and fall of a model Polish worker during the early 1950s—the "Stalinist years." The project touched on a number of politically sensitive issues, particularly in its searching criticism of Party policies during the era, and it was rejected by government authorities. Although the project continued to be resubmitted, it was not accepted until the winter of 1975-76 (Michalek 176). At least two reasons contributed to the approval. First, Wajda had personally become more internationally known and more powerful within the industry when in 1972 he became artistic director of the "X" film unit. But Wajda's name alone did not guarantee approval of projects he supported. The idea also seems to have been approved, paradoxically enough, because of political and economic instability in Poland in the middle 1970s. Antonin and Mira Liehm, historians of Eastern European film, have generalized that "in moments of political crisis when centralized power became temporarily weak, film (in Eastern Europe) took advantage of its role and prestige as 'the most popular art'" by engaging itself in controversial political subjects prohibited in more stable times (2). The regime of Edward Gierek, which had shown economic promise when he first took office in 1970, began to founder in 1974 and 1975 because of massive debts to western countries, inflation, and the failure of foreign markets for Polish products to materialize. Rising prices and the shortage of food and other consumer goods created frustrations among workers which not only resulted in the Radom and Ursus riots of June 1976 but also created the temporary weakness in centralized power that contributed a greater openness in the cultural sphere (Ascherson 106-118). Within this context Wajda seized an opening and received permission to make the politically controversial *Man of Marble*.

Wajda's film is very different from Chaplin's satiric allegory. The film borrows its central structural device—a multiple perspective flashback structure—from *Citizen Kane*, a film that Wajda says was the first to "deeply impress" him in film school (Bickley, 6). Both films start with a narrative present, then, as an investigator tries to learn more about the title character, move into flashbacks about that character from the point of view of various people who knew him. *Man of Marble* uses this structure with one key difference. In *Kane* the investigator, Thompson, is not an important character except insofar as he provides a linking device for eliciting the various recollections about Kane. In *Man of Marble* the investigator, a film student named Agnieszka, is much more fully developed and central to the thematic concerns of the film. Struggling to make her diploma film about the rise and fall of a model worker in the early 1950s, Agnieszka is on a quest for truth, not only about Polish society during the Stalinist years but also about the relationship between the past and present.

The focus of Agnieszka's film is Mateusz Birkutl, the man of marble, so called because he served as a model for statues of heroic workers during the years when socialist realist art was the prescribed aesthetic mode in Poland. Birkut is portrayed in the film as a prodigious worker and dedicated socialist but also as a somewhat naive victim of a corrupt Party bureaucracy. We learn that from his peasant roots, Birkut went to the city after World War Two to help in the rebuilding and industrialization of Poland. Trained as a bricklayer, Birkut helps to build the steel works city of Nowa Huta (just outside of Warsaw) and achieves fame and honor when he and a supporting crew set a record for most bricks laid in one shift—over 30,000. The record is captured on film by a young filmmaker named Burski, and Birkut becomes famous around the country thanks to movies, statues and paintings which feature him. On a trip in which he demonstrates his bricklaying methods to local workers, however, Birkut is handed a red-hot brick and severely burns his hands. Unable to continue because of his injury, he becomes a popular committee worker involved with housing assignments. When his fellow worker Witek is falsely accused of plotting against Birkut in the hot brick incident, however, Birkut defends him to Party officials. Despite the warnings of a secret police agent, Michalak, Birkut pursues the case, is relieved of his position and, eventually, is imprisoned for his criticism of Party decisions. All statues and paintings of him are taken down and even his wife, Hanka, renounces him as a traitor to Poland. Though Agnieszka has little information about his whereabouts after the middle 1950s, she does learn that he was released from prison in 1956 following the return of Wladyslaw Gomulka to political prominence, that he had died, and that his son was working in the Lenin Shipyard in Gdansk. When we piece together all the fragments of Birkut's life, we have a portrait of an idealist worker hero who falls from grace after refusing to compromise his principles in the face of a corrupt Party bureaucracy.

Agnieszka is the protagonist of the plot's narrative present, a youthful member of the intelligentsia who aspires through film to tell the truth about the past in hopes of illuminating the present. Clad in blue jeans, filled with nervous energy, almost obsessive in pursuing her politically sensitive topic, the tall and slender Agnieszka seems certain to come into conflict with her own superiors. And she does. Her main antagonist in the film is her producer, the liaison between Agnieszka and officials who decide whether her work will be appropriate for showing on television. Several times complaining about her American-style investigative reporting (the film was made shortly after Bernstein and Woodward's Watergate investigative efforts), the producer urges her to make a documentary about a safer, more acceptable topic, like steel production. After shooting in unauthorized spaces, bothering important officials who knew about Birkut's story, and looking at classified archival footage, Agnieszka has her camera taken from her and loses right to more film stock. Her diploma film stalled, Agnieszka continues to seek out Birkut after encouragement from her father. When she finally does locate Birkut's son, she takes him back to Warsaw to confront the producer about what she has learned. It is no accident that Wajda frequently shoots Agnieszka in low angle, for her persistence and relentless pursuit of the truth is paralleled in the flashbacks only by Birkut.

The plot unfolds in an extremely interesting way through the use of the multiple perspective structure. Even before the credit sequence the film presents some fragments of newsreel footage of Birkut and a scene in which Agnieszka argues with her producer about the film she's making. Thereafter the film intersperses schemes from the narrative present with five more scenes of newsreel footage (some of the footage are finished newsreels from the 1950s, some unfinished and unreleased newsreels, and some outtakes) and flashbacks from the perspectives of four different people: Burski, the man who made the documentary of Birkut, *Architects of Our Happiness* (which is presented early in the film when Agnieszka is looking at footage in the screening room); Michalak, the member of the secret police who warned Birkut against protesting the arrest of his colleague Witek; Witek himself; and Birkut's former wife, Hanka.

The film's ideological perspective, a blend of Polish nationalism and democratic socialism critical of the Party bureaucracy, emerges from several thematic strands. A central strand indicates that the corruption of the system rewards deceit and blind loyalty while punishing honesty and integrity. This is developed largely through Birkut and the four people who tell Agnieszka about their experiences with him. Birkut, who maintains his honesty and sense of justice, is deposed from his position of renown and forgotten (appropriately enough, the working title of Agnieszka's film is *Falling Stars*). Burski, who some critics have suggested constitutes in part Wajda's parody of himself, has become an internationally known film director, living in the suburban luxury and regularly attending film festivals abroad. Michalak, in perhaps the pointed irony of the film, has been rewarded for his loyalty to the secret police with a position as manager of a strip-tease show in the Palace of Culture (Fox, 4). Witek, who recants his forced confession and allows Birkut to go to prison in his stead, has become the director of the Katowice Steel Works. Hanka, a gifted gymnast when Birkut marries her, publically renounces him as a traitor to Poland when he is imprisoned and out of favor. She has moved to the resort city of Zakopane, married an opportunistic cafe owner, and lives in a fashionable house. While the best suffer, the worst prosper.

The deceit of the system is also apparent through the presentation of the newsreel footage. The finished newsreels, ostensibly made to report truthfully on reality, provide Agniezska with less truth about Birkut than the fragments of censored footage. *Architects of Our Happiness*, Birkut's completed social realist documentary, clearly stages its reality (as we learn in some of the flashback sequences) yet presents itself as unstaged. Another finished newsreel, *Traitors in the Dock*, is filled with manipulative stylistic devices. The sound track uses sinister, manipulative non-diegetic music and voiceover narrator whose stern voice indicts Witek and other "traitors." Visually, the judge is shown as vigilant and strong in high key lighting and a slightly low angle, while the accused men look down, away from the camera, and their faces are bathed in shadows. These staged newsreels claim to present truth. Other footage of the same trial, never used for newsreels because it shows Birkut protesting the set-up trial, has no staging and very little editing, and it includes no non-diegetic sounds like the emotive music in *Traitors in the Dock*. Although this rough and unfinished footage presents Agnieszka with an accurate picture of how Birkut tried to defend Witek then came to be imprisoned himself, it is censored by the authorities and never used. The system manipulates and distorts reality to preserve its social control.

In the face of this systemic deceit and corruption is Mateusz Birkut, who is presented as dedicated to the ideals of building a socialist state. Early footage of Birkut shows us he is from a humble peasant background. He is also, we assume when he crosses himself before beginning his bricklaying record, a Catholic. This is a significant detail, for since World War Two the Catholic church has maintained a stronger profile in Poland than in any other Eastern European country and has at times played an important political role in opposing government policies (see, for example, Ascherson, p. 141). Yet Birkut also becomes enthusiastic about helping to build the new socialist state; his efforts both as a bricklayer and later, after his hands are injured, as a popular committee worker involved with housing, underline his contribution to that goal.

When he sees the ideals of socialist equality and justice betrayed, however, he protests vigorously, which eventually leads to his downfall. This is seen most graphically in his attempts to have Witek freed. When his local protests to free Witek fail, he goes to Warsaw against Michalak's advice. There he is forced to wait in a long hall until a chilling Party official tells him in no uncertain terms to drop the case and, in the official's words, "trust the people's justice." Disillusioned, he returns to Nowa Huta, gets drunk, and throws the brick he had saved to commemorate his bricklaying record through the window of the security force offices where Witek had been arrested. After trumped-up charges and Witek's trial send Birkut to prison, he is released during the 1956 political thaw. Arriving home on the train, he is given a hero's welcome, and Witek offers him "rehabilitation" and an elected position on the works committee if he will only give a speech to gathered workers which would publicly recant his "errors and distortions" and affirm worker solidarity. Because he denies these alleged "errors,"

Birkut refuses, but he also loses the chance for his job. Shortly thereafter, after Birkut tracks down Hanka in Zakopane, Hanka's boss (and later her husband), offers Birkut a Courvoisier or Johnny Walker and tempts him with a job at his cafe where his responsibility would be squaring things with the authorities. (Like Birkut, Gomulka had been accused of anti-state activities in the Stalinist years; he was released and returned to power in 1956, the same year as Birkut's release. This made Birkut potentially a politically influential person.) The cafe owner tells Birkut that he would earn much more than a bricklayer's salary; within two years he would own a car and a house. "You were a paragon and you still are," says the cafe owner in key lines, "Everyone else has packed it in. Do you want to be the last to get wise?" Again Birkut refuses to sell out to the corrupt system.

The film remains inconclusive about what happens to Birkut between 1956 and his death. Two details, however, suggest what happened to him and carry considerable weight in defining the film's ideological perspective. The first detail is the final newsreel footage presented in the film; Agnieszka sees it just after her film has been taken from her. This rough footage apparently takes place during the elections early in 1957 which officially brought Gomulka back to power. Birkut has entered the polling place. There a news reporter shoves a microphone in his face and asks him if he plans to forget about the "raw deal" he received and cast his vote. Birkut looks directly into the camera and affirms his Polish nationalism: "We've had our ups and downs but this is our country." With that he turns, moves toward the ballot box, and casts his vote. Despite the system's corruption, Birkut retains his love of country and his hope that it can be made to live up to its socialist ideals.

A second detail, originally shot to be included in *Man of Marble* but not actually presented until its sequel, *Man of Iron* (1981), also links Birkut more firmly to an ideological position critical of the system. In the scene, which would have appeared near the end of the film, Agnieszka searches for the grave of Birkut in a Gdansk cemetery. Unable to find it, she leaves a bouquet of flowers at the cemetery gate. As Wajda explains, "During the revolt at the shipyards in Gdansk (in 1970), Birkut lost his life. There no longer remains a trace of him. The man of marble has become a phantom" (Crowdus, 9). By linking Birkut to this protest from recent Polish history, in which Polish police and military troops shot at and killed protesting workers in Gdansk and other cities, Wajda suggests that Birkut remained committed to the ideals of creating a just and decent society. Although he had fallen from the limelight, no longer a man of marble, this "casualty of the Stalinist years" had remained a paragon in his commitment to Poland and a just, equalitarian society (Ungar, 7).

The scene at the Gdansk cemetery, however, never appeared in the film. Working within an industry in which political rather than commercial pressures are paramount, Wajda decided to cut the scene (it later appeared in *Man of Iron* during the heady days of Solidarity). As we have seen, screenwriter Scribor-Rylski and Wajda had for years been denied the right to make *Man of Marble* because of its critical treatment of Poland in the 1950s. The scene at the Gdansk cemetery in 1970 constituted a similar and even more sensitive topic because it was more recent. As Michalek and Turaj note, it was hard to include the scene in 1976 because "by then the riots of 1970 were being subjected to the same kind of silence the film is about" (157). Instead, the film concludes with Agnieska and Birkut's son Maciek—representatives of the intelligentsia and the working class—striding assertively down the long corridor toward the producer's office.

Even without the cemetery scene and despite this relatively open ending, *Man of Marble* presents a clear ideological perspective. In Mateus Birkut, the man of marble who falls from grace because of his uncompromising vision of a human socialism, and Agnieszka, the persistent investigator whose dogged pursuit of the truth leads to a similar fall, *Man of Marble* affirms Polish nationalism and criticizes the corrupt realities of Polish socialist bureaucracy. Simultaneously it affirms the ideals of honesty, justice, human dignity, and socialist equality, and—in its final shot of Agnieszka and Maciek—the necessity of cooperation between the working class and their intelligentsia in effecting social change.

The reception of *Man of Marble* suggests that the film contributed to the political climate in Poland which led to the consolidation of the Solidarity movement in the late 1970s. Completed in the fall of 1976, the film generated consternation and opposition when it was screened for the authorities. Because it was attracting attention both in Poland and abroad, however, authorities decided not to risk the embarrassment of withholding it but instead to release it in only one theater, the Wars Theater in the New Town section of Warsaw. When the film opened on February 25, 1977, crowds gathered outside the theater. Scalpers sold tickets at up to fifteen times the ticket price, and those who managed to get into the premier rose and sang the Polish national anthem after the performance (Fox, 3). Fearing that the crowds outside would start a demonstration, authorities dispersed it by announcing that the film would be shown at a number of other theaters. After this decision *Man of Marble* subsequently received a regular and widespread release (Michalek and Turaj, 158).

The film's searing critique of the Party bureaucracy led to discussion and condemnation by Party officials. At a plenary meeting of the country's highest political body, the Communist Party Central Committee, *Man of Marble* was openly condemned. Censorship forbade positive reviews of the film in the Polish press and limited negative comments to try to minimize the film's importance. As a result of the political implications of *Man of Marble* and Krzysztof Zanussi's *Camouflage*, the Vice-Minister of Culture and some of his subordinates were fired; the replacement, Janusz Silhelmi, stopped production in 1977 on some controversial films and threatened the film unit system itself. (Were it not for Wilhelmi's death in a plane crash in 1978 the system may have been tampered with earlier than after martial law was declared in 1981.) At the Gdansk Film Festival in September, authorities arranged that neither *Man of Marble* nor any other film made by Wajda's "X" unit would win any award. If this official response to the film was clear, so was the position of the opposition. When *Man of Marble* was ignored at the awards ceremony in Gdansk, film journalists decided to give *Man of Marble* an unofficial award. After the official ceremony, a huge group of spectators and journalists met on the stairs to see Andrzej Ochalski, the leader of the ad hoc awards committee, present Wajda with the award: a brick tied with a red ribbon, the same object that Mateusz Birkut threw through the police station window to register his protest against Witek's unjust arrest. Audiences generally responded to the film as well: it was a huge success at the box office and became "the center of political discussion in Poland" in 1977 (Michalek and Turaj, 64-65, 158). Eventually, after martial law was declared in Poland in December 1981, Wajda's "X" film unit was abolished, and Wajda withdrew from Poland, involving himself in such international productions as *Danton* and *Love in Germany*. The film's ringing enunciation of opposition to Party corruption and deception, and call for cooperative resistance to that corruption, helped to solidify the political polarization occurring in Poland in the late 1970s; moreover, the intense and divergent response the film elicited suggests how deeply divided the Polish political structure was becoming.

In 1980, speaking on the responsibilities of artists in the contemporary world, Wajda told the Polish Filmmakers Association in Gdansk that "the fundamental obligation of the artist towards the contemporary Polish experience . . . is to tell the truth." Telling the truth, he continued, would involve "in the first place a jettisoning of the orthodoxies that have distorted our way of looking at Polish society" (Wajda, 294-95). *Man of Marble* could easily be considered Wajda's artistic manifestation of this truth-telling goal. In production history, the film itself, and the reception it generated all cast light on the relationship between auteurs and politics.

These readings of Chaplin's *The Great Dictator* and Wajda's *Man of Marble* are by no means exhaustive. They do, however, suggest something of the similarities and differences between the two auteurs. Both had worked themselves into powerful positions within their respective film industries. Both consciously set out in their films to develop a forceful political perspective. (This is by no means universal for auteurs. Though all films have ideological implications, other auteurs—Carl Dreyer or Robert Bresson are two who come to mind—are much less specifically interested in politics than Chaplin or Wajda were in these films.) Both found ways to express their ideological perspective in such a way that large audiences saw the films and vigorously debated their merits. Both subsequently ran into difficulties with government officials in part because the political perspectives expressed in the films were associated with the directors themselves.

On the other hand, because the cinema as an institution and as an industry functions differently in each society, Chaplin and Wajda had to function amidst different pressures. Chaplin had to struggle with the aesthetic challenge of sound films and the commercial pressures on American filmmakers to make films that would entertain audiences. Wajda had to contend with the political uncertainty of what the government authorities would accept, balancing gingerly on the tightrope between the "permissible and the impermissible" (Bickley, 4). Ultimately, Wajda chose to cut the politically sensitive Gdansk cemetery scene in hopes that the film would be acceptable enough to the authorities that it would be released. And it was.

Amidst these similarities and differences, I hope to have suggested the shape a political auteurism might take. In the United States at least, much early auteurist criticism emerged in part as a reaction against liberal social criticism of movies. As such, it tended to minimize consideration of historical or sociological issues. At the same time, it at times displayed a misunderstanding of the collaborative nature of filmmaking and a naivete about how the industrial structure of a film industry provides boundaries around and limitations on the auteur. Political auteurism, by limiting the number of filmmakers who can legitimately be called auteurs, by acknowledging the importance of the industry and era in which the auteur works, and by being sensitive to the ideological implications of the auteur's films, can be extremely useful in helping us come to terms with the dynamic and elusive relationship between movies and politics.

Works Cited

Ascherson, Neal. *The Polish August*. New York: Viking, 1981.

Balio, Tino. *United Artists*. Madison: Wisconsin, 1976.

Bickley, Daniel, and Lenny Rubenstein. "Between the Permissible and the Impermissible: An Interview with Andrzej Wajda." *Cineaste* 11 (Winter 1980-81): 4-8, 49.

Buscombe, Ed. "Ideas of Authorship." In Caughie, 22-34.

Burke, Kenneth. "Literature as Equipment for Living." *The Philosophy of Literary Form*. 2nd ed. Baton Rouge: LSU, 1967: 293-304.

Caughie, John, ed. *Theories of Authorship*. London: Routledge and Kegan Paul, 1981.

Ceplair, Larry, and Steven Englund. *Inquisition in Hollywood: Politics in the Film Community, 1930-1960*. New York: Doubleday, 1980.

Chaplin, Charles. *My Autobiography.* New York: Simon and Schuster, 1964.

Crowdus, Gary. "*Man of Marble*: A Missing Scene and a Sequel." *Cineaste* 11 (Winter 1980-81): 9.

Crowther, Bosley. *New York Times*, 22 March 1942, sec. 6, pp. 12-13.

Crowther, Bosley. "Review of *The Great Dictator.*" *New York Times*, 20 October 1940, sec. 9, p. 3.

Fox, Geoffrey. "Men of Wajda." *Film Criticism* 6:1 (1981): 3-9.

Goodman, Paul. "Chaplin Again, Again, and Again." *Partisan Review*, 7 (Nov./Dec. 1940): 58-64.

Jaffe, Ira S. "Fighting Words: *City Lights* (1931), *Modern Times* (1936), and *The Great Dictator* (1940)." *Hollywood as Historian.* Ed. Peter Rollins. Lexington: Kentucky, 1983: 49-67.

Kolker, Robert. *Bernardo Bertolucci.* New York: Oxford, 1985.

Lehman, Peter and William Luhr. *Authorship and Narrative in the Cinema.* New York: Putnam, 1977.

Liehm, Antonin and Mira. *The Most Important Art.* Berkeley: U of California P, 1977.

Maland, Charles. *Chaplin and American Culture: The Evolution of a Star Image.* Princeton: Princeton, 1989.

Michalek, Boleslaw, and Frank Turaj. *The Modern Cinema of Poland.* Bloomington: Indiana, 1989.

Pells, Richard. *Radical Visions and American Dreams.* New York: Harper and Row, 1973.

Rivette, Jacques. "The Genius of Howard Hawks." *"Cahiers du Cinema" in the 1950s*. Ed. Jim Hillier. Cambridge: Harvard, 1985: 126-31.

Robinson, Davis. *Chaplin: His Life and Art*. New York: McGraw-Hill, 1985.

Rohdie, Sam. "Education and Criticism." *Screen* 12:1 (1972): 10.

Sarris, Andrew. *The American Cinema*. New York: Dutton, 1968.

Smith, Julian. *Chaplin*. Boston: Twayne, 1984.

Stewart, Garrett. "Modern Hard Times: Chaplin and the Cinema of Self-Reflection." *Critical Inquiry* 3 (Winter 1976): 295-314.

Susman, Warren. "The Thirties." *The Development of an American Culture*, ed. Stanley Coben and Larman Ratner. Englewood Cliffs, N.J.: Prentice-Hall, 1970: 179-218.

Truffaut, Francois. "A Certain Tendency in the French Cinema." *Movies and Methods*. Ed. Bill Nichols. Berkeley: U of California P, 1976: 224-237.

Ungar, Malgorzata. "Interview with Aleksander Scribor-Rylski." *Kino*, special issue on Polish film (1983): 6-9.

Wakeman, John, ed. *World Film Directors, Volume 2: 1945-1980*. New York: Henry Wilson, 1988.

Wajda, Andrzej. "The Artist's Responsibility." *Politics, Art and Commitment in the Eastern European Cinema*. Edited by David W. Paul. London: Macmillan, 1983: 293-297.

Wajda, Andrzej. "Wajda's Censored Speech." *Cineaste* 13, 3 (1984): 13.

Winston, Archer. "Review of The Great Dictator." *New York Post*, 18 October 1940, Chaplin clippings file, Billy Rose Collection, New York Public Library.

POLITICAL PROPAGANDA IN THE MOVIES
A Typology

Dan Nimmo
University of Oklahoma

Consider the synopsis/scenario of each of four films. The first depicts the scenery and lifestyles in Wales in World War II—industrious, thriving people; steel furnaces ablaze; factories producing war material; prosperous communities; bucolic countrysides. But wait. The narration reminds viewers that in the past the "wealth of the world was rocking." Suddenly, after World War I, "days came when the pits stopped, the factories closed their Gates, the furnaces died out, and the Great sheet of smoke that floated over industrial Wales came down like blinds over the blind windows of the mean streets." Now there were but "houses without hope, the locked shop and the leaking roofs." The towns were now filled with "old young men" lined up in the dole queue, "dragging through the squalor with their hearts like lead" with "nothing in their pockets, nothing home to eat." So, "remember the procession of the old young men. It shall never happen again. IT MUST NOT HAPPEN AGAIN." The movie returns to wartime Wales, Wales in World War II: "Britain at war asked these once denied, helpless and hopeless men, for all their strength and skill at the coal face and the dock side, at the foundry." Over the crescendo of a Welsh choir the film ends: "So the world shall know their answer and the world shall never deny them again."

The second film portrays the agonies and indignities suffered by a Communist official in Czechoslovakia. All goes well; his is a promising career, his future is assured. That is, until a power struggle erupts in the Communist party and the once upwardly mobile functionary finds himself ousted from his party position. That, however, is not enough. He is tortured, threatened, interrogated to the point of desperation, dehumanized. He meekly confesses to crimes he did not commit.

In the third film we encounter a tall, gaunt, drawn, and grim-faced sheriff of a small town somewhere in the western United States. He is a troubled man. He has long since decided to put away his badge for the woman he loves, his bride. But, arriving on the noon train will be a bandit and his three sidekicks sworn to kill the sheriff and all who defend him. Duty comes first so he decides to face up to the threat and protect the community. Suddenly the sheriff finds himself alone, not only against the four desperados but alone in the town itself. For the townspeople have deserted him. A former mistress is loyal, but only for a brief moment. Even his wife turns her back on him, ignoring the plea of the film's theme song, "Do Not Forsake Me . . . . " The train arrives, the Sheriff faces down the bandit-terrorists in a final shootout, and vindicates his courage against the cowardice of the townspeople.

Finally, we have a film set in a large city in Germany. Small girls are being lured off by an unknown, sadistic murderer. His methods are cunning. For example, he gently offers a balloon to a little girl who will obviously become his next victim. The police search for the criminal, but to no avail. Where the police fail, however, the underworld element of the town succeed. In a chilling scene the whimpering sadist finds himself trapped in a darkened warehouse. Hauled before a jury of criminals, he shrieks and sobs as he confesses a compulsion to kill young girls: "Who knows what is like to be me . . . How I must, don't want to but must . . . Must . . . Don't want to . . . Must . . . ." The police appear in time to prevent his execution.

On the surface these four films have markedly different aims, motives, intents. The first is a documentary produced in Great Britain during World War II (1943) entitled *Wales—Green Mountain, Black Mountain*. A product of the Films Division of the Ministry of Information, the intent was to influence British perceptions of the war effort and the future that would unfold once the war ended. *The Confession*, the second movie, was French produced and appeared in 1970. As an entertainment film it was certainly intended by its director, Constantin Costa-Gavras, to turn a profit; but its political subject matter and the manner of its treatment—like other of his movies such as *Z* (1968) and *Missing* (1982)—hint that more than entertainment is at issue. The third movie represents the film genre of the Hollywood western, *High Noon* (1952). Entertainment, not influence, was its aim, at least so one would assume. The film won a Best Actor Academy Award for its star, Gary Cooper. Finally, the classic fourth film, *M* (1931), came from Weimar Germany and purports to entertain, presumably with no other motives in the mind of director Fritz Lang.

Thus, we have a documentary, a tale of personal tragedy, a western, and one of lurid suspense. Each derives from a different nation's film industry, and the reasons for the production of each film differ. Yet even the casual reader will note, and perhaps wonder at, the guarded phrasing in the above paragraph: "on the surface," "one would assume," "hint," and "presumably." Why such caution? The answer lies in the topic which this chapter endeavors to address, namely, the manner and ways that political propaganda enters into the fabric of movies. Propaganda is a slippery concept that indeed must be approached with caution. Definitions abound but they offer no consensus on the precise character of propaganda as a phenomenon and few guides as to how one might determine when a particular movie does or does not contain political propaganda. The pages that follow endeavor to do four things: (1) elaborate the problem of specifying the propagandistic content in movies, (2) offer a typology as a guide to approaching movie propaganda, (3) discuss representative films in categories suggested by the typology, and (4) ponder the politicization of popular film.

The Problematic Character of Propaganda

Central to the problem of characterizing what propaganda is all about is the notion of intentionality. Here there are two schools of thought. One consists of all those analysts of propaganda who put intention uppermost in their definitions of propaganda. Here, for example, are a few of the many definitions that emphasize the role intentionality plays in propagandizing: propaganda is the attempt to form, alter, or control attitudes "with the intention that in any given situation the reaction of those so influenced will be that desired by the propagandist";[1] "the attempt to affect the personalities and control the behavior of individuals towards ends considered unscientific or of doubtful value in a society at a given time";[2] "any attempt to persuade anyone to a belief or to a form of action";[3] "the typical propaganda situation is that A by one method or another communicates with B so as to tend to affect B's behavior";[4] "propaganda is an attempt to influence opinion and conduct. . . ";[5] "propaganda is the deliberate and systematic attempt. . . to achieve a response that furthers the desired intent of the propagandist";[6] etc. Over and over again in the writings of scholars, be they notables—such as H.L. Childs, Leonard Doob, Harold Lasswell, the Institute for Propaganda Analysis, Edward Bernays, or Jacques Ellul—or young analysts just beginning their careers, the notion of propaganda as deliberate intent repeats itself.

But there is an alternate theme. It is voiced in the writings of French political scientist J. Driencourt: "propaganda is everything."[7] Communication scholar Hugh Rank does not go so far as to include "everything" in propaganda's purview, but comes close when speaking of "organized persuasion" that extends to all means of commercial advertising, public relations, corporate publicity, promotions of "good causes," efforts of special interest groups, religious organizations, political parties, and governments.[8] Even one of the leading scholars of the intentionality school, Leonard Doob, qualifies his own view when he speaks of the use of "suggestion" in messages: the process of suggestion, he says, "may be called propaganda, regardless of whether or not the propagandist intends to exercise control."[9]

Clearly, depending upon where one comes down on this "propaganda is intentional vs. everything" distinction has a bearing upon any discussion of political propaganda in the movies. Reconsider, for example, each of the four films described in the opening of this chapter. *Wales* had propagandistic intent. In fact, it had two propagandistic intents, one not necessarily consistent with the other. During World War II the War Cabinet led by Prime Minister Winston Churchill had as its chief, almost sole, aim that of winning the war. As Nicholas Pronay has noted in his study of propaganda in British films during World War II, Churchill never deviated from a single war aim: "You ask what is our aim?," asked Churchill. "I can answer in one word—victory." The Churchill government left unanswered the question of what shape the peace to come would take, preferring not to detract from the war effort and to avoid creating unreasonable expectations about the future. There were war aims, but no peace aims.[10]

Thus, from government's point of view the content of British film propaganda was intended to extol the war effort, not to address postwar concerns. To that end the Films Division of the Ministry of Information produced or bought a series of documentaries during the period

1940-1945 that ostensibly depicted how Britain was coping on a wartime footing. For the most part these were screened in working-class movie houses and factory canteens, not in the upscale theaters frequented by cabinet members and high government officials. What the Churchill government did not realize was that these documentaries, although focusing in part on the war effort, spoke more directly to what the peace *should* be like once victory was achieved. This is because MOI's production and acquisition of films was strongly influenced—directly or indirectly—by members of the Documentary Film Movement. The "Documentary Boys" (as they were called) did not always agree on specific policy aims, but they did lean toward the view that among the many things Britain was fighting for in World War II was social reform, even social revolution. Given the bureaucratic setup of the MOI and its Films Divisions, the general ignorance of high government officials (and of journalists as well) regarding the propaganda potential of film, and the lack of exposure of government policy makers to the documentaries themselves, the "Documentary Boys" were able to make films with a cohesive and integrated propagandistic message.

The documentaries, of which *Wales* was typical, had a formula. Each opened with depiction of a wartime activity—shipbuilding, coal mining, social life under war conditions in various regions, the doings of young people, the programs of wartime social agencies, or the wartime contributions of specific groups. Such content spoke to the war aims which the upper-echelon of the MOI took for granted the films were about in the first place. But after the opening each film would then review the hard social and economic times of the prewar years—unemployment, poor housing, hospitals, schools, etc. In some films there were specific references to such conditions arising out of promises made in World War I, but broken. Then would come the message that now, in World War II, the dreadful conditions had disappeared. Why? Because government, not private industry and enterprise, was mobilizing resources for social betterment—something government leaders had denied was possible prior to the war effort. What was the lesson to be learned? People must not let everything gained during the war effort be taken away with the peace. They must be active and militant in preserving what had been achieved: through the vote (films did not spell out specifics of how to vote), organization, and demands for a planned economy.

Through approximately three dozen films employing this formula in a five-year period people in factories, working-men's organizations, adult-education classes, church halls, schools, and elsewhere underwent repeated exposure to a single formula reiterating common sets of stereotypes and arguments. Wrote one member of the Documentary Movement involved in MOI film production:

> Whether you like it or not we are undergoing a world revolution here and now, and it is a revolution which must continue with increasing strength. For that is the only thing the people of Britain are fighting for. It is today the job of the documentary to integrate the immediate war effort with the facts and implications of radical social and economic changes that are part and parcel of it . . . . Our films must be the shock-troops of propaganda.[11]

The MOI documentaries raise no problems to those who define propaganda as involving intentional efforts to persuade, control, activate, etc., but they do suggest the difficulties of gauging just whose intentions are actually served in such propaganda. The intent in propaganda is easily confounded, depending on who intends to do what and who responds to that intent. To those charged with administering the Ministry of Information and its Films Division the documentaries served their propaganda aims admirably, or at least the content that rallied people behind the war effort appeared to do so. But certainly it was not the intention of these officials to launch a longterm propaganda program advocating social revolution and planned economy. They were as astonished as anyone when, with the war winding down, voters rejected the Churchill government in favor of Laborite Clement Atlee and his party (a rejection in keeping with the message reiterated in the MOI documentaries). In the end Churchill's wartime propagandistic intent (i.e., win the war now, plan for peace later), was undermined by a much different propagandistic intent from the "Documentary Boys" (i.e., this war is being fought for social and economic revolution).

Constantin Costa-Gavras' *The Confession* is an entertainment film about a distinctly political topic. It is about political events that are matters of record. There is little question that in its denunciation of communist totalitarianism there was every effort to communicate precisely the kind of message suggested by the definitions of propaganda cited as representing the intentionality school. In similar ways much the same can said of other Costa-Gavras political movies: *Z* (1968), which is a political thriller denouncing dictatorship on the right; *State of Siege* (1972) that provides a balancing of views of both ends of the political spectrum in telling the story of a CIA agent captured by guerrillas in South America; and *Missing* (1982), which questions U.S. aims and actions in Chile, not only with respect to the overthrow of a foreign government but also toward its own Anerican citizens. Are such movies any less propagandistic than the MOI films, or the *Why We Fight* series produced in World War II by the U.S. War Department's Documentary Film Unit, because they were intended to *entertain* (one hesitates to say primarily entertain) as well as influence views? The intentionality school offers no useful guidance in answering that question. Nor does it offer clear guidance in answering a similar question when dealing with the third of our movies, *High Noon*.

High Noon raises the difficulties of gauging intent in political propaganda in a different way. On one level the movie is only about politics in the most peripheral way. To be sure there is a public official, Sheriff Will Kane, going about his sworn and legally authorized political duties of applying the law and protecting the community. As so often happens in the political realm Kane is torn between his obligations as a public servant and as a private individual. He administers his staff (deputy), manages government property (his office and weapons), and employs political rhetoric—terse though it is—in pleading with the townspeople. But all these political matters are largely incidental to the thrust of the film, i.e., one man alone standing against the odds. Instead of political propaganda *High Noon* is a classic fable, morality play, or enduring myth retold in the western genre.[12]

Yet, according to those acquainted with the intent of the movie, the manifest content of *High Noon* masked a distinctly political message. The film's scriptwriter, Carl Foreman, had been cited by the U.S. House of Representatives Un-American Activities Committee (HUAC) in 1951 for alleged communist connections. According to Foreman, "What *High Noon* was about at the time, was Hollywood and no other place but Hollywood."[13] Many people in the movie industry when called before HUAC had informed on their colleagues. An industry "blacklist" denied employment to filmmakers with alleged past associations with communism. The Screen Actors Guild condemned members that allegedly traveled the Communist Party line. *High Noon* depicted the abandonment of filmmakers by their colleagues: the lone sheriff, left to his own resources by townspeople and wife, must deal with a spiteful and vengeful gang of cutthroats without aid, support, or even understanding of others of the true stakes involved. Thus did *High Noon* intend and accomplish what HUAC critics of the movies feared most, i.e., the blending into an entertainment film about a largely non-political subject, without detection, a leftist political message.

Fritz Lang's *M* deals with a manifest content that is even more distantly removed from politics than the overt subject of *High Noon*. There is, of course, the role of the police, a governmental agency, unable to track down the child murderer, Franz Becker (played by Peter Lorre). And, if Lang intended politics, there is certainly in *M* a prominent role for "private government," i.e., "bands, and gangs, and groups private in form but public in function, outlaws administering law beyond the law, with private armies, courts, and sanctions even to the use of the extreme penalty"[14] in the capture, trial, and sentencing of Becker by the city's criminal element. On the whole, however, *M* is an entertaining movie about a largely non-political topic that suggests very little intent to influence views or actions.

Yet, as in the cases of the other three films discussed here intent is not always in the eye of the beholder of manifest content, nor even in the eye of the intender. When Lang announced he would make the picture, then to be titled *Murder Among Us*, he received threatening letters not to do so. He was also denied access to one of Berlin's largest movie studios. In a contentious meeting with the studio's manager, whom he seized by the coat lapels, Lang asked why there was so much opposition to making a movie about a real-life child murderer. The manager relaxed and acknowledged that he now understood. But Lang too had understood, for in seizing the manager he had noticed the half-hidden swastika pin that indicated membership in the Nazi party. Lang later said, "On that day I came of age politically."[15]

What Lang realized was that his intentions were not his intentions as perceived by the Nazi. What was non-politics to Lang, was, in the absence of explanation, politics and propaganda to the Nazi officials. The depiction of a small, effeminate, neat, respectable man as being at heart a murderer driven by uncontrollable urges, carried with it associations that were not complimentary to Nazi politics, even though not intended by Lang and, perhaps, not easily recognizable to audiences. But as with HUAC's investigations of pro-communist themes and sympathizers in postwar America, what is propagandistic intent depends on who is defining intent and the political climate surrounding those definitions.

A Typology of Movies as Political Propaganda

When, then, is a movie one of political propaganda? The intentionality school would have analysts look to the motives and aims of the films' makers. But, the ends of one set of interests involved in producing a movie may not be those of another (*Wales*); the entertainment and political motives of a single producer may not be clear in their priority (*The Confession*); the manifest content of a film may mask passionate intentions (*High Noon*); and, the intent of a producer may be perceived in a vastly different light by those who have supervisory control (*M*). But, does the problematic quality of intentions make it necessary to grasp an alternative view, i.e., "propaganda is everything," and assume that the content of all movies is political propaganda, thus aligning analysts with the Nazi studio manager or the most vociferous of HUAC's members?

Many scholars, James Combs[16] and Terry Christensen[17] to name but two, have demonstrated that movies, whether their manifest content is political or not, send messages *that are political*. And movies of all genres—be they screwball comedies, musicals, westerns, science fiction, historical sagas, gangster, private eye, romance, war, religious, or what have you—touch directly or indirectly on matters that go to the heart of politics: conflict and consensus, power and authority, order and disorder, etc.[18] Thus, we encounter sagacious Judge Hardy giving his son, Andy, sound fatherly—and political—advice in man-to-man talks about school, girls, siblings, cars, and more—in the *Andy Hardy* series. We get cynical commentary from Rick Blaine (Humphrey Bogart) in *Casablanca* (1942): "If it's December 1941, in Casablanca, what time is it in New York? I bet they're asleep all over America." Or, more blatantly, private investigator Sherlock Holmes (Basil Rathbone) in World War II surroundings prophesies the coming war:

> There's an East wind coming all the same. Such a wind as never blew on England yet. It will be cold and bitter, Watson, and a good many of us may wither before its blast. But it's

God's own wind none the less. And a greener, better, stronger land will be in the sunshine when the storm is clear. (*Sherlock Holmes and the Voice of Terror*, 1942)

Then, he prophesies Anglo-American unity:

Holmes: This is a great country, Watson. Look up there ahead—the Capitol: the very heart of this democracy. It's not given to us to peer into the mysteries of the future, but in the days to come, the British and American people will, for their own safety and good of all, walk together in majesty, justice and in peace.

Watson: That's magnificent, I quite agree with you.

Holmes: Not with me, with Mr. Winston Churchill. I was quoting from a speech he made not so very long ago in that very building. (*Sherlock Holmes in Washington*, 1943)

The question, however, is when do Judge Hardy's homilies, Rick Blaine's cynicism, and Sherlock Holmes' prescience convey not simply political messages, but propaganda as well? Perhaps one way to deal with that question is to move away from intentionality and all-or-nothing alternatives to consequences. That is, adopt Charles S. Peirce's dictum: "Consider what effects, that might conceivably have practical bearings, we conceive the object of our conception to have. Then, our conception of these effects is the whole of our conception of the object."[19] To conceive of the effects that movies might have we can employ William Stephenson's continuum based upon his ludenic theory.[20] For Stephenson "communication-pain" involves any form of discourse that achieves some other end; thus, like work, communication-pain is a means and not an end in itself. "Communication-pleasure" is discourse of any kind for the pleasure to be derived solely from the experience itself, not as a means to something else; it is thereby aligned with play rather than pain. Viewed from the perspective of the filmmaker a movie may be intended to provide pleasure (entertainment for its own sake, as with *M*) but may have painful intent as well (to influence views, as in *The Confession*). But, if "we consider what effects, that might conceivably have practical bearings" a film may produce (and "conceivably" is crucial), then a film with or without painful, propagandistic intent (i.e., seeking an end beyond the experience) could be propaganda in content even if designed for communication-pleasure, i.e., purely as entertainment.

Building upon Stephenson's distinction and Peirce's focus on effects, not intent, we can conceive of a continuum of films shading from those that goad people to action of some sort to those that are enjoyed for their own sake (and may move people to inaction, or acquiescence). And, in similar fashion we can conceive of a continuum shading from films with minimal political content, to those that feature politics as backdrop for other ends, to those distinctly political in content. For purpose of convenience, however, let us treat the two dimensions as dichotomies: films affecting communication-pain versus those producing communication-pleasure; films with political content versus those not political. The result is a fourfold typology that, although highly simplified, provides an opportunity to speak of effects that movies might *conceivably* have that are propagandistic: pain/political (overt propaganda), pleasure/political (partially veiled propaganda); pain/non-political (covert propaganda); pleasure/non-political (potential propaganda).

Representative Categories of Political Propaganda in Movies

To illustrate how this typology might be of utility in describing the political propaganda in popular movies, we turn to each of the four categories. It will be apparent that the four categories are not neatly discrete, but shade into one another on category boundaries. Obviously it is not possible to consider all manner of movies; a few representative films will suffice.

Overt Propaganda in Movies

Documentaries, such as the British MOI or the U.S. *Why We Fight* series exemplify movies about political topics that do more than entertain. What makes both series particularly interesting as overt propaganda is that what they did made each controversial as persuasive documents. As already noted, the MOI films had two overt messages, namely, rally around Britain during time of war and demand social reform in the peace to follow. With the Laborite victory that placed Conservatives in opposition, it finally became clear to one and all what the "Documentary Boys" had accomplished. Lord Boothby remarked that the MOI may not have won the war for Britain but it certainly won the election for Labor. Needless to say, when the Labor government sought to continue the Films Divisions's operations on its own behalf after the war, the opposition resolved to abolish the unit should they return to power.[21] Thus did an overt propaganda operation become a continuing source of partisan conflict in British politics.

The overt propaganda in the *Why We Fight* series came in for its own share of postwar controversy. The seven films in the series were designed for viewing by members of the armed forces before going overseas. However, the films were also shown to civilian audiences in the U.S. and abroad. Two of the films produced conflict because of mixed propaganda messages they conveyed. *The Battle of China* was not given public release. Its presentation of political conditions in China, which from the perspective of "why *we* fight" appeared satisfactory, was by 1944 clearly unbalanced—with no mention of the Communist forces in China and relatively little of Chiang Kai-Shek. *The Battle of Russia* (1944) was withdrawn from general circulation during the Red Scare of the McCarthy era; its warm, sympathetic portrayal of Soviet valor scarcely coincided with Cold War policies of the times.

Documentaries of overt propaganda are certainly not limited to wartime. Just as the Laborites attempted to continue the Films Division on its behalf after World War II, so too did the U.S. government continue to churn out propagandistic documentaries in the postwar world. Typical products included: *Your Job in Germany* (1945), produced for U.S. occupation forces, blamed World War II on the "inherent belligerence" of the German people and was released by Warner Brothers to civilian audiences as *Hitler Lives?*; John Huston's *Let There Be Light* (1946), which dealt with what is now labeled post traumatic stress syndrome of returning World War II soldiers—a film classified and banned from screening for a long period; such Cold War films as *Communist Blueprint for Conquest* (1956), *The Communist Weapon of Allure* (1956), *Communist Target: Youth* (1962). Not to be ignored in any such representative listing is the 1971 film painting a most unflattering portrait of President Richard Nixon, *Milhouse: A White Comedy*. And, long before *The Day After* (1983) stirred controversy over the depiction of a nuclear holocaust, an early docudrama related the nightmare suffered by a typical American family (the Mitchells) after a nuclear bomb falls on New York City—*Atomic Attack* (1950).

As the early docudramas illustrate, overt propaganda films are not limited to documentaries. Feature films, combining elements of communication-pleasure and communication-pain, of a propaganda nature abound. Although without the carefully plotted dramatic storyline expected of purely entertaining movies, the films of Leni Riefenstahl such as *Triumph of the Will* (1936) and *Olympiad* (1936) are classics in this category. So also is Fritz Hippler's *The Eternal Jew* (1940), that contrasts the "self-serving" Jew with the Nazi ideal of sacrifice for fatherland, depicts the Jewish "love for money," and claims the Jew is a parasite without a soul. Compare the 1940 film *Jud Süss* that contrasts Aryan-Jewish stereotypes using a pseudohistorical dramatization featuring many of Germany's film celebrities. The plotline involves a Jew who swindles, cheats, and defiles the ideal Aryan—a beautiful blond maiden. The close shows the defiler twisting from the hangman's rope. Heinrich Himmler ordered every SS troop to view the film; the German actors playing Jews in the movie requested that Joseph Goebbels announce publicly that they were not Jews but dedicated Aryans serving the state.[22]

Partially Veiled Propaganda in Movies

Although an entertainment film loosely based on an actual political figure—a financial adviser to an eighteenth century Duke of Wurttemberg—*Jud Süss* leaves no doubt that it is overt propaganda. *The Confession* too is entertainment about a politically charged topic, but the communication-pleasure emphasis partially veils Costa-Gavras's politically charged message. Just as Miklos Jancso's earlier film, *The Round Up* (1965)—with its depiction of chained and hooded prisoners, naked women beaten by uniformed men, the wife of a guerrilla leader used to force him to give himself away—*The Confession* is *about* politics not just *related* to politics as a backdrop. *The Round Up* "is a far more searching attack on the horrors of oppression than more overt forms of propaganda," for, "by choosing a place in the past, it has the virtue of protesting against *all* oppression, whether Fascist or Communist, even though made in Hungary under Russian control."[23]

As Christensen spells out, there are scores of entertainment movies which utilize political topics as backdrops.[24] The propagandistic intent and consequences of these films vary widely. Contrast, for example, a few such movies wherein the propaganda is partially veiled in varying degrees. *Mission to Moscow* (1943), based upon the real-life experiences of U.S. Ambassador to the Soviet Union Joseph E. Davies, paints a flattering portrait of the Russians. Indeed, the film was made at the request of President Franklin D. Roosevelt by Warner Brothers precisely to flatter Joseph Stalin. Called out of retirement by Roosevelt, Davies (portrayed by Walter Huston) travels to Moscow. On his way he stops off in Nazi Germany. There he witnesses evidence of the dehumanizing effects of the Nazi regime—marching Jews identified only by numbered tags. But at the Russian border Davies finds a more cheerful atmosphere as he is greeted with food, drink, and laughter. Russian leaders are wise, Russian soldiers brave, Russian women dedicated to work and family. The film dismisses Soviet purges, aggression against Finland, and non-aggression pact with Nazi Germany as necessary means to more altruistic ends. Here is a "glowing portrait of Russia that is strictly party-line propaganda."[25] Just how glowing is typified in an exchange between two Soviet commissars in the movie:

1st Commissar: "We are entering a new era, don't you think so?"

2nd Commissar: "I think we have done remarkably well!"

By contrast *The Seduction of Joe Tynan* (1979) veils its message so heavily that it seems to have no propaganda at all. Yet, it is there. Not "strictly party-line propaganda" as in *Mission* but, instead, propaganda about party politics. Handsome, appealing, warm, humorous, family man and dedicated husband, liberal Senator Joseph Tynan (played by Alan Alda) confronts pressures surrounding his vote on confirmation of a racist appointee to the Supreme Court. Through it all Tynan willingly accepts sexual seduction by a counsel for a black group (played by Meryl Streep) opposing the nominee, seduction of his ego by those holding out promises of a presidential nomination, and seduction of his principles as he breaks his word, acts hypocritically toward allies and constituents, and alienates his wife. The message is clear: political ambition is its own seduction, the honorable need not apply.

Lying between the politically oriented entertainment film that wears its propaganda message on its sleeve, i.e., *Mission*, and the film that veils its message in sex, ambition, and cynicism, i.e., *Joe Tynan*, are numerous movies that have become classics, both for their stories and for their messages. *Mr. Smith Goes to Washington* (1939) and proves, after a valiant fight against all odds, that the people can and do speak, democracy works. *Citizen Kane* (1941) runs for governor as a populist-progressive against the "machine" and, in the process, teaches audiences that politics is a cynical business. In *State of the Union* (1948) Grant Matthews seeks the presidency only to learn that "the difference between Democrats and Republicans is that they're in and we're out"; disgusted with the rottenness of it all, he withdraws to find happiness in a repaired domestic home life. With the help of *All the King's Men* (1949), Willie Stark grows from humble man of the people to petty gubernatorial tyrant, proving again the message that power corrupts. *My Son John*, (1952), communist sympathizer and spy, awakens to his sin when his mother turns him in to the FBI, and becomes an informer, only to be killed by the communists who shoot up his taxi—which crashes on the steps of the Lincoln Memorial. U.S. Senator Brig Anderson commits suicide in *Advise and Consent* (1962) after being blackmailed by a fellow senator, who hears the senate majority leader say in disgust, "Fortunately this country is able to survive patriots like you"—a not-so-veiled message in the post-McCarthy era. As *The Candidate* (1972) Bill McKay learns that the excitement, cynicism, and glamour of campaigning does not prepare one for office; "What do we do now?," he asks of his campaign manager following his victory. And, political media consultant Pete St. John teaches what winning *Power* (1986) is all about in the television age: "My job is to get you in. Then you do whatever your conscience tells you to do."

Covert Propaganda in the Movies

It is a far distance from *Jud Süss* to *High Noon*, at least as viewed from the perspective of a half century since the former film appeared. As already noted, few viewers today watching the 1940 Nazi-backed entertainment film would question its overt message. Viewers of the plight of Sheriff Will Kane, however, without knowledge of the blacklisting practices of Hollywood during the Cold War would not recognize the film's veiled message.

One area that illustrates the use of feature films about ostensibly non-political subjects to do more than provide entertainment and pleasure to audiences lies in movies with implicit themes about racial tolerance and/or intolerance. Thomas Cripps[26] provides a convincing argument that during World War II there was a dual stream of propaganda in popular films regarding relations between races in the U.S. On the one hand, there were government films—documentaries, features, and featurettes—that presented a portrait of harmony between blacks and whites joined in the common effort for victory over aggressive intolerance; such films made no suggestion that traditional patterns of racial segregation would vanish once the war ended. On the other hand, there was a genre of Hollywood-based movies whose "non-political" messages held out the promise to blacks of improved economic, social, and political conditions in postwar America.

Representative of the propaganda films of official Washington was *Henry Browne, Farmer*, such black contributions to the war effort as growing oil-bearing peanut crops, or by volunteering for training at the all-black Tuskegee Air Force Base. *The Negro Soldier* heaped praise on a separate but equal U.S. Army in which blacks would be recognized for their separate, but segregated, contributions. Underlying these and other government films was the theme that racial discrimination was not native to America but was the product of foreign intrigue and agitation. *Don't Be a Sucker* and fall for any other explanation was the theme of one such film. In this movie, produced by the U.S. Signal Corps and released through Paramount to civilian audiences without profit, "Mike" leads a contented life. But a voice-over warns that there are forces plotting to "take it away from him." Those forces are foreign, not American. "I saw it in Berlin," says a Hungarian-American professor to his class, just before storm troopers break in and drag him away.

In contrast with the "racial harmony through segregation" theme of official film, Hollywood productions developed a different set of propagandistic messages. Racial integration rather than segregation came to dominate these movies. It began with the depiction in war movies of ethnically representative fighting units—squads, platoons, etc. But the theme appeared in other than war films. For example, in Alfred Hitchcock's *Lifeboat* (1944) black stoker Joe Spencer is among the ethnically diverse group that finds itself struggling for survival—a portrayal of promised equality that allegedly raised the morale of black members of the armed forces when they viewed it.[27]

Perhaps the most apt example of such covert propaganda in movies comes not out of a documentary or a feature film but what was a forerunner of today's music videos. This consisted of a movie short, a one-reeler, that made a plea for brotherhood. *The House I Live In* was originally a radio drama, a fictional account of a man who had lost his son in the war and wanders through the streets of a mythical, but typical, American small town searching for a meaning to what has happened. Writer Albert Maltz, producer Frank Ross, and singer Frank Sinatra decided to turn it into a brief film on racial tolerance. Although in its final production religious rather than racial bigotry became the target, the basic message about the promised future of America remained. The film opens with Sinatra leaving a recording session to take a cigarette break. In the alley as he is smoking he finds a gang of boys bullying one kid because "We don't like his religion." Sinatra lectures them on the virtues of religious and ethnic diversity. The—by this time—not so covert propaganda is summarized in Sinatra's singing:

> The house I live in,
> A plot of earth, a street
> The grocer and the butcher
> And the people that I meet;
> The children in the playground,
> The faces that I see;
> All races, all religions,
> That's America to me.[28]

Other types of movies about non-political topics clearly do more than merely entertain for pleasure's sake. Many of the commercial films produced in Vichy France, for example, were far more than they appeared at first glance. Thus, *Jardin sans fleurs* (1942) promoted the cause of family and *patrie* by telling the story of unhappiness that surrounds childless couples and the barrenness of villages depopulated by lowered rates of child bearing. Elizabeth Strebel points out that a large number of such Vichy films implicitly deal with a problem with political overtones. That problem was the disintegration of the family; a movie focus on the disaster surrounding the dissolution of families would, presumably, instill a desire to strengthen family ties, a fundamental of Vichy political culture. Repeated throughout films of the period were themes dealing with family disintegration: the absence of small children in many films; when children are present they appear as detestable, monstrous, unloved, or unwanted—in *L'Assassin a Peur la Nuit* a father rescues his young son about to fall off a cliff only to box his ears; teenagers plea for the love of alcohol-soaked fathers; many couples are unable to have children; when children are born they are illegitimate; and abortions are frequent, but treated as absolutely taboo.[29]

Similarly, although dealing with subject matter not often regarded as political, the cinemas of other nations have contained covert political propaganda. Among the many examples we find *The Strike* (Soviet, 1925), a message about the insensitivity of luxury—represented by a pet monkey, meerschaum pipe, and rimless glasses; in *The General Line* (Soviet, 1928) the total grossness of privilege is the theme; in *The Cabinet of Dr. Caligari* (German, 1920) evil appears foreign, purity German; and in *Ichiban Utsukushiku—The Most Beautiful* (Japanese, 1944) audiences learned that mere personal problems, no matter how serious, should ever get in the way of the productive, efficient working group.

Potential Propaganda in the Movies

Of the vast numbers of movies produced worldwide, relatively few deal with political matters. And, since most exist to attract audiences, and thus reap profits, entertainment for its own sake, i.e., communication-pleasure, rather than message transmission is uppermost in the minds of producers and directors. "Messages are for Western Union," Hollywood potentate Samuel Goldwyn allegedly said. However, this certainly does not mean that entertainment movies about non-political subjects carry no propagandistic content, intended or not. To deny that *Little Big Man* (1970), *Rocky* (1976), or *Being There* (1979) are not political propaganda because each does not deal with politics per se is to say that Fritz Lang's *M* carried no political message simply because he was able to convince the Nazi studio manager that it did not.

Christensen's *Reel Politics* demonstrates persuasively that all movie genre's—comedies, musicals, gangster, science fiction, etc.—and not just war, historical, or political films contain the potential to propagandize.[30] His account is sufficiently comprehensive on the matter that no purpose would be served here in undertaking a genre by genre inventory of potential propaganda in past films. Instead, both to illustrate the point and close this discussion of political propaganda in movies we turn to a genre which he curiously does not consider (aside from the intended political message contained in *High Noon*), i.e., the western.

The western was a staple of the American film industry for decades. Moreover, as an exported art form—such as the Italian spaghetti westerns that made Clint Eastwood into celebrity and cult hero—the western has provided a formula for imbedding politically relevant messages in films produced elsewhere. Yet, aside from obvious recognition of the mythical political qualities in westerns—law and order, new frontiers, conflicts of interests between sodbusters and cattlemen, and so on—one is hard put to find acceptance of the political propaganda potential in the western. Indeed, some critics claim that the western is a retreat from things political, a refuge away from political controversy. Robert Sklar quotes one movie reviewer: "When things get tough in Hollywood they start the horses galloping. Nobody can yell 'propaganda' at a motion picture full of cows, horses, gun play, brave women, and daring men."[31]

The movie reviewer mentioned by Sklar was speaking of *Red River* (1948), Howard Hawks' sweeping western filled with standard western fare—ranching, a cattle drive, rivalry between gunfighters, brawling, a stampede, attacks by Indians, and the love of a beautiful woman with a tainted background in the brothels of New Orleans. No message, no ideology, no causes, no politics. Simply an old-fashioned shoot-'em-up. Here was communication-pleasure without political claptrap. But was it? Sklar thought not. To round out this consideration of movie propaganda let us recount his argument.

The plotline of *Red River* can be summarized briefly: Thomas Dunson (John Wayne) departs a wagon train and a woman who loves him to begin a life in Texas. Miles away from the train he turns to see smoke rising from the direction he came. He and his sidekick suspect an Indian attack, prepare for it, and defeat the attackers. A small boy wandering with a cow appears; he too was with the wagon train and confirms it lost to Indians. Dunson, his sidekick, and the boy continue to the banks of the Rio Grande, settle on land seized from a Mexican rancher, and begin to build a cattle herd. The scene shifts to immediately after the Civil War. Dunson now owns a cattle empire. The boy now grown, Matthew Garth (Montgomery Clift), has returned from the Civil War. In the face of an impoverished South there is no market for Dunson's cattle. He and Garth lead the first cattle drive over the Chisholm Trail. Conflicts arise between Dunson and his drovers, eventually between Dunson and Garth. Garth seizes control of the drive leaving Dunson behind. Garth changes direction and heads the herd toward Abilene, Kansas, where there is a rumored new railhead. Along the way the drovers encounter a wagon train under Indian siege. They drive off the Indians, after which Garth falls in love with one of the women of the train (Joanne Dru). In Abilene Dunson catches up and they brawl. In the end Dunson and Garth reconcile and Dunson makes him a full partner in the ranch.

What is there about this to make the movie political propaganda, not merely horse opera? For Sklar "it is a film about the issues of empire." There is "territorial expansion of one society by the usurpation of land from others," and there are "consequences arising therefrom—in the relations between men and women, in the relations between men and other men, in the social compact that binds people together for a common purpose." And these human themes, "important as they are, are subordinate to even more fundamental issues of economic survival, of commodity production, above all the need to find a market for one's goods." It is for Sklar a film about "capitalism."[32]

And, he might have added, a movie about the politics of capitalism. Political themes run through the film. Usurpation of land occurs when Dunson seizes from the Mexican rancher what Dunson can take and defend, but to which he has no legal right. Speaking of the beef herd he hopes to build, he says, "Wherever they go, they'll be on my land. My land!" The social compact between Dunson and Garth comes with the former's agreement to put Garth's brand on the cattle when Garth has earned it; between Dunson and his drovers contract is apparent when three drovers attempt to leave the drive. He orders them found, returned, and hanged for failure to live up to their bargain. And, there is also a theme of the positive side of capital development. When Garth rides into Abilene with the herd, townspeople welcome him with open arms; he is free to let the cattle roam through the center of town. Such a welcome would make warm the heart of a Donald Trump. Not only town development is at issue. So too is development of the nation. As Sklar notes, "Texas beef will make Americans strong in body; sold to the world it will make America strong in balance of payments." But there is also tyranny—Dunson's steadfast refusal to engage in any type of liberal reform, i.e., avoid the danger of going through Missouri by heading the herd toward the rumored railhead. And, there is mutiny as Garth seizes control of the trail drive. But it is mutiny justified in the name of individual accountability, of setting capitalism free from the bondage of shortsighted tyrants.

Red River is hardly apolitical or apropagandistic. Regardless of Howard Hawks' intent, the movie propagates deeply held values of a political economy—not only to Americans but to the whole world as well.

Politicization of the Movies

During World War II the Bureau of Motion Pictures in the U.S. Office of War Information circulated suggestions to filmmakers regarding their conduct during the war. They urged that each filmmaker before undertaking a movie ask a series of questions. The most crucial of those questions: "Will this picture help win the war?" The bureau was simply echoing what master propagandists had always said since the arrival of filmed techniques. For Lenin the cinema was the most important of all the arts for disseminating messages; for Stalin it was the "greatest means of mass agitation"; Trotsky found it the "best instrument of propaganda"; Goebbels found it the most "far-reaching media that there is for influencing the masses."[33] The very earliest of films, regardless of design, carried directly or indirectly, manifestly or latently, political messages. Witness *Birth of a Nation* (1915). And where politics is involved, where political content appears, there is the potential for propagandistic impact, no matter what the intent. "On that day I came of age politically," reported Fritz Lang of glimpsing the small swastika inside the studio manager's lapel. No matter what the genre or content, all movies can—and many frequently do—come of age politically. It is the task of the filmgoer to recognize this and pay heed. "That's entertainment" is indeed far more than that; it is politics.

NOTES

1. Terence H. Qualter, *Propaganda and Psychological Warfare* (New York: Random House, 1962), p. 27.

2. Leonard W. Doob, *Public Opinion and Propaganda* (Hamden, Conn.: Archon Books, 1966), p. 240.

3. William Hummell and Keith Huntress, *The Analysis of Propaganda* (New York: Holt, Rinehart & Winston, 1949), p. 2.

4. Malcolm G. Mitchell, *Propaganda, Polls, and Public Opinion* (Englewood Cliffs: Prentice-Hall, 1970), p. 23.

5. F.C. Bartlett, "The Aims of Political Propaganda." In Daniel Katz, Dorwin Cartwright, Samuel Eldersveld, and Alfred McClung Lee, eds., *Public Opinion and Propaganda* (New York: Henry Holt and Co., 1954), p. 464.

6. Garth S. Jowett and Victoria O'Donnell, *Propaganda and Persuasion* (Beverly Hills: Sage, 1986), p. 16.

7. Quoted in Robert Taylor, *Film Propaganda* (New York: Barnes and Noble, 1979), p. 20.

8. Hugh Rank, *The Pitch* (Park Forest, Ill.: The Counter-Propaganda Press, 1982), p. 9.

9. Doob, quoted in Taylor, *Film Propaganda*, op. cit., p. 20.

10. Nicholas Pronay, " 'The Land of Promise:' The Projection of Peace Aims in Britain." In K.R.M. Short, *Film and Radio Propaganda in World War II* (Knoxville, Tenn.: University of Tennessee Press, 1983), pp. 51-77.

11. Quoted in Pronay, ibid., p. 63.

12. Frank McConnell, *Storytelling and Mythmaking: Images from Film and Literature* (New York: Oxford University Press, 1979).

13. Quoted in Terry Christensen, *Reel Politics* (New York: Basil Blackwell, 1987), p. 93.

14. Charles E. Merriam, *Political Power* (New York: Collier-Macmillan, 1934), p. 60; see also his *Public and Private Government* (New Haven: Yale University Press, 1944).

15. Quoted in Otto Friedrich, *Before the Deluge* (New York: Avon Books, 1972), p. 376.

16. James E. Combs, *Polpop: Politics and Popular Culture in America* (Bowling Green: Bowling Green University Popular Press, 1984); Dan Nimmo and James E. Combs, *Mediated Political Realities* (White Plains, N.J.: Longman, Inc., 2nd ed., 1989).

17. Christensen, *Reel Politics*, op. cit.

18. See, for example, Edward D.C. Campbell, Jr., *The Celluloid South* (Knoxville, Tenn.: University of Tennessee Press, 1981); Michael T. Isenberg, *War on Film* (East Brunswick, N.J.: Associated University Press, 1981); John E. O'Connor and Martin A. Jackson, eds., *American History/American Film* (New York: Frederick Ungar, 1980); Baxter Phillips, *Swastika: Cinema of Oppression* (New York: Warner Books, 1976); John R. May and Michael Bird, *Religion on Film* (Knoxville, Tenn.: University of Tennessee Press, 1982).

19. Charles S. Peirce, *Values in a Universe of Chance: Selected Writings of Charles S. Peirce* (New York: Doubleday, 1958), p. 181.

20. William Stephenson, *The Play Theory of Mass Communication* (Chicago: University of Chicago Press, 1967).

21. Pronay, " 'The Land of Promise'," op. cit.

22. Jay W. Baird, *The Mythical World of Nazi War Propaganda, 1939-1945* (Minneapolis: University of Minnesota Press, 1974).

23. Phillips, *Swastika*, op. cit., p. 103; emphasis in original.

24. Christensen, *Reel Politics*, op. cit.

25. Ibid., p. 68.

26. Thomas Cripps, "Racial Ambiguities in American Propaganda Movies." In Short, ed., *Film and Radio Propaganda*, op. cit., pp. 125-145.

27. Ibid.

28. Richard R. Lingeman, *Don't You Know There's A War On?* (New York: Perigee Books, 1970), p. 229.

29. Elizabeth Strebel, "Vichy Cinema and Propaganda." In Short, ed., *Film and Radio Propaganda*, op. cit., 271-291.

30. Christensen, *Reel Politics*, op. cit.

31. Richard Sklar, "Empire to the West: *Red River*." In O'Connor and Jackson, eds., *American History/American Film*, op. cit., p. 168.

32. Ibid., p. 169.

33. Quoted in Taylor, *Film Propaganda*, op. cit., p. 28.

AFTERWORD

Taken together, the work gathered in this volume gives the reader a general idea of current inquiry by adventurous scholars in the field of movies and politics. They represent different approaches and foci, but they all share in common the conviction that something politically important goes on with and in the movies, and that these important processes can be understood. This collection demonstrates that able people are working on the question of what about the movies is political, but also suggests that scholars to come should pursue this field of inquiry further. For example, much of this volume has concerned itself with movies and politics with emphasis on the impact of politics on the movies. But equally valid is the question, what about politics is movie-made? Since Reagan, this latter question has become more urgent, since many of us suspect that our political expectations and images may derive from media experience such as the movies.

In any case, we want to end this work with a suggestion. This volume has included a wide array of perspectives on the relationship between movies and politics, but they all seem to have in common the unspoken assumption that the movies are a social habit that involves political learning. Perhaps future scholars can pursue that idea. Conceiving the politics of moviemaking and moviewatching as a process of political learning might let us see more clearly the commonalities of the different approaches included here. Political learning may well be going on at each stage of the movie process, even if it is unrecognized as such. But aesthetic experience, for movie creators, movie benefactors, and movie consumers, is a major means of learning, some of which can become politically relevant. We may therefore need to construct a *political aesthetic*, a conceptual inventory that helps us understand the process of political learning in and through the movies. This might be part of a larger "science of eiconics" through which we understand learning through the signs and meanings of the movies, but also as a project of understanding the aesthetic dimension of politics and the political dimension of aesthetics. In any case, if we keep in mind the fact that all parties to the movie transaction are engaged in the process of learning, we might become better able to understand what is going on politically with the movies. For learning is never apolitical: all forms of creative expression, and attendance to those creative expressions, involves the introduction of new "mazeways" of ideas and images into the ongoing process of social life. Coping with the political is part of that process, so creative expression such as the movies becomes a medium for changes in those ideas and images about politics. Aesthetic expression such as the popular feature film then becomes a powerful way of seeing the world for large numbers of people exposed to the medium, and potentially becomes a way of political seeing. It is that potential that has been the subject of this book, and the matter that interests students in the many fascinating ways that movies and politics intersect. If this collection has demonstrated that movies are not only an integral part of our lives but also our political lives, then it has succeeded. In that case, the work gathered in this volume should challenge us to build upon the foundation offered here, to boldly construct another tier of political knowledge about the magic lantern that has enthralled and educated us from its inception a century ago.

CONTRIBUTORS

John G. Cawelti is Professor of English at the University of Kentucky. He is the author of numerous works, including the landmark *Adventure, Mystery, and Romance*, and most recently (with Bruce A. Rosenberg), *The Spy Story*. He is active in several academic associations, and is on the editorial board of the *Journal of Popular Film and Television*.

Douglas Kellner is in the Department of Philosophy at the University of Texas at Austin. He is the author of much work on the movies, television, and contemporary criticism, most recently his *Camera Politica* (with Michael Ryan) and *Critical Theory, Marxism, and Modernity*. He is active in such academic associations as the Popular Culture Association.

Charles Maland is Professor of English at the University of Tennessee. He is the author of *American Visions*, *Frank Capra*, and *Chaplin and American Culture: The Evolution of a Star Image*.

Richard Maltby is the Chair of American and Commonwealth Arts at the University of Exeter in England. He is the author of various works, including *Harmless Entertainment: Hollywood and the Ideology of Consensus* and *Reforming the Movies: Hollywood, the Hays Office and the Campaign for Censorship, 1922-1929*.

Lary May is in the Program in American Studies at the University of Minnesota. He is the author of *Screening Out the Past: The Birth of Mass Culture and the Motion Picture Industry*, edited *Recasting America*, and has written many articles. He is active in several academic associations that deal with questions of American studies.

Dan Nimmo is Professor of Communication at the University of Oklahoma. He is the author of a wide variety of works in the field of political communication, including *The Political Persuaders*, *Popular Images of Politics*, *Political Communication and Public Opinion in America*, *Nightly Horrors: Crisis Coverage in Television Network News*, and *Mediated Political Realities*. He is active in academic organizations such as the International Communication Association.

Harold Schechter is Professor of English at Queens College of the City University of New York. He is the author of such diverse books as *The Bosom Serpent*, *The New Gods: Psyche and Symbol in Popular Art*, *Deviant*, a book on legendary Midwestern maniac Ed Gein, and *Deranged*.

Jonna G. Semeiks is a teacher and writer, and co-editor of *Patterns in Popular Culture*. She is an advisory editor for the *Journal of Popular Culture*.

June Sochen is Professor of History at Northeastern Illinois University in Chicago, where she teaches American cultural history and Women's history. She has written or edited ten books, written articles on such films as *Way Down East* and *Mildred Pierce*, and is most recently the author of *Enduring Values: Women in Popular Culture*.

INDEX

All in the Family, 34, 37
Ambler, Eric, 39
anti-feminist films, 71
anti-sociological bias, 241
archetypes, 33, 34, 38, 122; auteur theory, 239-241, 245, 267; biographical background and, 245
Bara, Theda, 94
Bellah, Robert, 43
Bond, James, 40
Buchan, John, 40, 36, 39
Burke, Kenneth, 243
Cagney, James, 139, 145
Capone, Al, 133, 140-144
Catholic Church: film censorship and, 137-138, 160-162, 167-170
Chaplin, Charles, 244-266
Cold War, 6, 7, 37, 54, 62, 226, 263, 264, 267
Conservative ideology: family and, 63; gender and, 57
Costa-Gavras, Constantin, 242, 244, 272
Davis, Bette, 98, 101
Engels, Friedrich, 56
Fleming, Ian, 36
Fonda, Jane, 5, 105, 106, 244
formulas, 35, 37, 38; ideological content and, 36, 38, 40; social problems and, 43; audience response to, 35, 43, 46-47
Gish, Lillian, 94
Gitlin, Todd, 37-38, 41
Gomery, Douglas, 133
Gramsci, Antonio, 33
Greene, Graham, 39
Haskell, Molly, 101, 111-112
Hays, Will, 138, 148, 165, 170
Hepburn, Katherine, 101-102, 106
hero-myth, 123
Heston, Charlton, 5
Hitchcock, Alfred, 39
Hollywood films: U.S. foreign policy and, 291
Hood, Raymond, 186, 188, 190
House Un-American Activities Committee, 277
ideological analysis, 32-33, 55; ideological

content 35, 39; audience response and, 36-37, 41-42; creators' intent and, 36
ideology critique: race, gender, class and, 31, 36, 39, 45, 56, 57, 61, 64, 69, 71;
ideology and hegemony: hegemonic purpose, 33
individualism, 32, 38, 43-44, 47-48, 58, 144
Lamb, Thomas, 192-193, 195, 219
Lang, Fritz, 244, 291
Legion of Decency, 137, 154, 169-170
LeQueux, William, 39
Liberal ideology: U.S. interventionism and, 71, 255
Ministry of Information, 272, 277
Motion Pictures Producers and Distributors Association (MPPDA), 133, 136, 138, 147, 149, 150, 156-159, 161-162, 165, 167-170
Oppenheim, E. Phillips, 39
Peirce, Charles Sanders, 280
Persian Gulf War, 61, 66
political ideology as mode of inquiry, 23
political communication 20, 23; as an approach to movies, 235
political propaganda, 289; intentionality theories and, 277, 280
Popular Front, 248, 255
Prohibition, 140, 146, 162, 167
Reagan, Ronald, 5
Reaganism, 59, 65, 71
Reaganite, 58, 60
Red Scare, 5,
Redford, Robert, 5, 105
Rohmer, Sax, 36, 39
Rothafel, S.L., 186-188
Schlanger, Ben, 188, 205, 213, 218
See It Now, 45
Sinclair, Upton, 5
Stewart, James, 5
theatre architecture: communal values and, 189, 193, 196, 211; machine style 199, 203; social, cultural change and, 189, 198, 199, 208;
Vietnam War, 115-117, 121
Wajda, Andresz, 245, 256-260
War films ; as military propaganda, 71, 60, 62; American fables and, 108; gender and, 86; propaganda and, 71; race and 67, 71;
Wayne, John 5
Weaver, Sigourney, 110
World War I, 5, 203

World War II, 5, 105, 111,
  248, 255-256, 291
Wright, Will, 32
Yates, Dornford, 39

FILM INDEX

84 Charlie Mopic, 125
Adam's Rib, 103
Advise and Consent, 31
Aliens, 110-111
An Officer and a Gentleman, 71
Apocalypse Now, 115
Birth of a Nation, 291
Blue Thunder, 78
Born on the Fourth of July, 125
Casablanca, 31
Casualties of War, 125
Citizen Kane, 245, 259
City Lights, 247, 249
City Streets, 148 165
Corner in Wheat, 5
Death Wish, 35, 43
Desert Hearts, 71
Desperately Seeking Susan, 71
Dirty Harry, 35, 79
Dispatches, 117
Fatal Attraction, 31
Full Metal Jacket, 71, 125
Girlfriends, 71
Guess Who's Coming to Dinner, 31
Heartbreak Ridge, 65
Hearts and Minds, 117

High Noon, 32, 272, 277, 289
In the Heat of the Night, 31
Iron Eagle, 58, 66-67, 79
Iron Eagle II, 67-68
Julia, 106
Klute, 106
Kramer v. Kramer, 71, 111
Latino, 71
Little Caesar, 139, 144-145, 149
M, 280
M*A*S*H*, 40-41, 71
Man of Iron, 263-264
Man of Marble, 245, 258
Marked Woman, 99
Metropolis, 244
Missing in Action, 43, 71
Modern Times, 247, 254
Murphy's Romance, 31
Navy Seals, 68
Ordinary People, 71
Pinky, 45
Platoon, 65, 71, 79, 115-119, 126
Public Enemy, 139, 146-148

Quick Millions, 148
Rambo, 43, 47, 57, 64, 115, 122-124, 125
Red Dawn, 58, 71
Red River, 289
Rio Bravo, 32
Rocky, 43
Running on Empty, 229
Salvador, 71
Scarface, 139, 149, 151-153, 154-155
Sherlock Holmes and the Voice of Terror, 280
Sherlock Holmes in Washington, 280
Singin' in the Rain, 133-134
State of Siege, 277
Take a Letter, Darling, 104-105
Terms of Endearment, 71
The Boys in Company C, 65
The Candidate, 5
The Deer Hunter, 115
The Delta Force, 68
The Doorway to Hell, 139, 144-146, 149
The Finger Points, 139, 148
The Great Dictator, 245-250, 253, 256-257, 266
The Lady Vanishes, 39
The Last Parade, 139, 148
The Philadelphia Story, 103
The Searchers, 124
The Secret Six, 139, 148, 151
The Thirty-Nine Steps, 39
The Voice of the Violin, 5
The Way We Were, 107, 108
The Widow from Chicago, 145

Top Gun, 58-61, 65-67, 71
Triumph of the Will, 59
Wales—Green Mountain, Black Mountain, 272
Woman of the Year, 101-105
Young Mr. Lincoln, 135 156
Z, 31, 272, 277